Stand As a Witness

P9-CBY-118

Stand As a Witness

THE BIOGRAPHY OF ARDETH GREENE KAPP

ANITA THOMPSON

DESERET BOOK

SALT LAKE CITY, UTAH

© 2005 Anita Thompson, except for selected material on pages 49–50, 131, 160, 166, 214, 220–21, 230–31, 249–54, 276–78, 286–87, 294–95, 297, 316–17, 319, 323–25 © Carolyn Rasmus

All rights reserved. No part of this book may be reproduced in any form or by any means without permission in writing from the publisher, Deseret Book Company, P. O. Box 30178, Salt Lake City, Utah 84130. This work is not an official publication of The Church of Jesus Christ of Latter-day Saints. The views expressed herein are the responsibility of the author and do not necessarily represent the position of the Church or of Deseret Book Company.

DESERET BOOK is a registered trademark of Deseret Book Company.

Visit us at deseretbook.com

Library of Congress Cataloging-in-Publication Data

Thompson, Anita.
Stand as a witness : the biography of Ardeth Greene Kapp / Anita Thompson.
p. cm.
ISBN 1–59038–488–1 (hardbound : alk. paper)
1. Kapp, Ardeth Greene, 1931– 2. Mormon women—Biography.
3. Mormons—Utah—Biography. I. Title.
BX8695.K35T46 2005
289.3'092—dc22 2005016060

Printed in the United States of America 72076
Publishers Printing, Salt Lake City, UT

10 9 8 7 6 5 4 3 2 1

For Diana, Alison, and April
my own young women

Contents

Foreword

by Sheri Dew

I can still remember the first time I met Ardeth Kapp. I was young and the most junior of junior editors at Bookcraft Publishers, where her latest book—*Echoes from My Prairie*—was being published. She had come into our offices to visit with George Bickerstaff and Hap Green, the two senior executives of the operation, and while she was there I was introduced to her.

As I went back to my office, I couldn't get our brief interchange out of my mind. It wasn't as though either of us had said anything particularly memorable; it was the impact she had on me almost instantly. The impression she left. The way I felt as I walked back to my office. I remember sitting at my desk afterward and thinking, "Wow! What a woman!"

During the intervening years, it has been my privilege to become much better acquainted with Ardeth Greene Kapp, both by observation from a distance, and up close and personal as over the years we have engaged in numerous projects and pursuits together. When I contemplate all she has accomplished, all she has overcome, all the wisdom she has shared, all the lives she has influenced, and her relentless pursuit of truth and righteousness, perhaps the word that describes her best is simply, "Wow!"

With all she has accomplished and contributed, it is increasingly difficult to appreciate the challenges she has overcome and the distance she has come in the process. When this young, shy, insecure girl left Glenwood, Alberta, Canada, at the tender age of seventeen to attend B. Y. High in Provo, Utah, she felt unprepared to face the world. Her husband, Heber Kapp, who has been the joy of her life, tells about the time early in their marriage when, because children had not yet come, she decided she ought to get a job. She paced for several hours up and down the sidewalk outside a dress shop where there was an opening, just to build up the courage to go inside. For those of us who have hung on her every word for decades now, it's difficult to imagine there was a time when she felt her own share of insecurities. But she did.

She has spoken openly about dealing with her perception that she wasn't very smart; about dealing with the unexpected pain of not being able to have children, when she had hoped for a house full; of being thrust again and again into situations for which she felt unprepared and lacking in skills. None of these insecurities or personal hesitations, of course, match the poised, gracious, bright woman I met that day long ago or the woman I have come to know since. None of them is indicative of the dynamic and dramatic contributions she has made through a life of devoted and rigorous service to the Church, and particularly to the youth of the Church. And further, none of them reveals the extent of her influence on both the young women and the women of the Church.

I for one was long past Young Women age when Ardeth was called to serve as the Young Women general president. Nevertheless, during her service in that capacity I hung on every word that dropped from her lips at general conference and read every book she wrote. She taught in a way that I could truly "hear." She expressed her faith and testimony in a way that moved and motivated me. She shared her belief in the divinity of our purpose and potential in a way that reached me, all while demonstrating what a strong, dedicated, faithful, and ever-gracious woman of God looks like, sounds like, and acts like.

She is a master teacher, an avid student of the gospel, and a woman who faithfully responds to whatever task or assignment she is asked to complete. Although she has not had the privilege of bearing children in this life, she has influenced and mentored and taught and encouraged at least two generations of youth—youth on every continent, youth with every kind of imaginable challenge, youth with the struggles of life ahead of them. And in the process, she has taught again and again that they truly are youth of the noble birthright, and that there is nothing they can't do if they have the Lord with them.

It is never fair or right to compare one person's service with that of another. And it's always a bit unnerving (particularly for the subject) to use superlatives when describing someone's contributions. But in my estimation, one would have to look far and wide to find a woman who has left a more indelible mark on a generation, who has strengthened and inspired more people, or whose impact has been more far-reaching than has Ardeth

Kapp's. Such a statement will make her uncomfortable, but it is true. Very simply, her life has been a Wow!

I will be grateful all of my life for the privilege of knowing and learning from this magnificent woman.

Acknowledgments

I have long been fascinated by reading accounts of well-lived lives that may serve as a roadmap for those who follow. The life story of Ardeth Kapp furnishes such a guide. I express my deepest gratitude for her willingness to share details from her life to provide such a roadmap. The quotations in this biography were drawn largely from numerous interviews with Ardeth, as well as from her family and friends. Other source material include her published writings, as well as the many journals she has kept from an early age. With Ardeth's permission, we have not used ellipses to indicate omissions from journal quotations. Only when quotations are taken from published sources do we include the source documentation.

Additional thanks go to Carolyn Rasmus who generously provided access to her previously written stories and anecdotes gained during her service as administrative assistant to Ardeth during the Young Women years. I also express gratitude to those General Authorities and former general auxiliary leaders who graciously granted interviews; they give valuable insights into some of Ardeth's remarkable leadership skills and the contributions she has made to young women throughout the Church around the world.

Appreciation is also extended to Don LeFevre and Jeanne Burgon, who each read early chapters and provided helpful comments and suggestions. In addition, I express special thanks to Curtis Parker, who gave essential technical assistance, along with unfailing good humor, to magnify the computer skills of his less-than-able mother-in-law.

Sharon G. Larsen, a special friend of many years standing, has been my constant support. She always knew I could do it. To her, I express my sincere gratitude.

I also express grateful appreciation to my husband and our children and grandchildren for their constant love, support, and encouragement. My son, Dwight A. Thompson, in particular, has spent countless hours in a careful reading of each word in the manuscript, to which he has brought his considerable editing skills. In addition, he has provided thoughtful suggestions which have helped to clarify the material. To him and to his wife, Elizabeth, I express my love and gratitude for the generous use of his time and talents.

Deseret Book editor Jay Parry has applied his skills toward the overall improvement of the manuscript. I express my thanks to him for his careful review, helpful comments and suggestions, and the editing which have made it a better product. Thanks also to Shauna Gibby, who provided the graphic design, furnishing the overall look to the finished product. In addition, thanks is expressed to others on the Deseret Book staff who have provided assistance in any way. I appreciate the skills of all who have helped to bring this book to fruition.

INTRODUCTION

All Eternity Will Know You Were Here

From her seat in one of the red chairs facing the congregation, President Ardeth Greene Kapp looked out over the crowd of expectant faces assembled in the Tabernacle on Temple Square in Salt Lake City. She was also keenly aware of vast numbers of faces that she could not see, assembled simultaneously in similar congregations throughout many parts of the world. As the strains of the organ crescendoed, then diminished to a whisper before silencing completely, the chatter of those assembled likewise stilled.

With anticipation, the audience turned their eyes toward the pulpit where President Kapp and her counselors, Patricia Holland and Maureen Turley, were poised to issue both counsel and a challenge in this, the first-ever satellite broadcast especially for the Young Women of The Church of Jesus Christ of

Latter-day Saints.[1] The youthful faces before them glowed with expectation. They would not be disappointed.

On this day, November 10, 1985, she arose early, reached for her journal, and recorded: "This is an historic day! I feel like it is the most significant day of my life since my marriage." Now as she looked into the faces of the young sisters, Ardeth felt an overwhelming sense of love, fulfilling a blessing given by her husband, Heber, shortly after her calling as Young Women general president. He blessed her with a gift of love for the young women of the Church and the ability, through the Spirit, to touch their hearts, touch their lives, and give them confidence, peace, and guidance.

President Kapp, her counselors, general board members, and others had made careful preparation for presentation of the new Young Women motto, theme, and values, which would serve as a guide for young women throughout the Church for years to come.

After the opening song, prayer, and an address by Elder Russell M. Nelson, it was her turn. As she looked at the upturned young faces before her, she felt a great love flowing through her body. How generous was her Father in Heaven! Although denied the blessing of motherhood in mortality, she had now been given the opportunity to love and help guide the 450,000 young women of the Church throughout the world. She began:

"To every young woman throughout the entire Church . . . I see the crest of a great wave forming. . . . I see a wave forming that will move across the earth, reaching every continent and every shore. I call upon you to stand with me to prepare to take

President Ezra Taft Benson receives a copy of the Young Women logo, "Stand for Truth and Righteousness," from Ardeth

your place in a great forward movement among the young women of the Church—a movement of renewed commitment—a movement in which you are destined to shape history and participate in the fulfilment of prophecy. . . .

"Prophets and Apostles are giving a clear signal for you to move forward and to assume your responsibility. . . . You have been given a calling, an especially noble calling, 'to be a righteous [young] woman'—to wield your strength and influence 'during the winding up scenes . . . before the second coming of our Savior' (Spencer W. Kimball, *Ensign,* Nov. 1978, p. 103). . . .

"We call upon the young women of the Church to awake, arise, and go forth! We call upon you to take your place as modern prophets and Apostles have foreseen, to 'rise in power and glory and stand as lights and guides to the people of [your] own nations' (Bruce R. McConkie, *Ensign,* May 1980, p. 72). . . .

"These are your days in the history of the kingdom. Together we can make of them days never to be forgotten. Together we can pledge to listen for the call and then answer, 'I will. Send me,' to stand up and lead out.

"The call is issued. With faith in God and in you and your parents and leaders, I can hear a growing chorus of young women's voices reaching across the land and across the water and heavenward, responding to the call for righteous young women.

"Who will stand up and lead out in defense of the gospel of Jesus Christ and stand as a witness for Christ at all times and in all places? We invite you to add your commitment to thousands of others in the united chorus. 'I will. Send me.'"

Before retiring that night, Ardeth again reached for her journal: "It is 10:37 P.M. The Young Women's fireside was glorious! Beyond all description. A new beginning for Young Women. Everything went superbly well. Angels attended our efforts. We were blessed beyond measure. I promised the Young Women I would write in my journal tonight about my personal commitment to stand for truth and righteousness."

The next day, Heber expressed his thoughts in a letter to his wife: "Priesthood and Young Women leaders will make a turn because of what they were taught last night. I sensed that young women at the Tabernacle were in anticipation of something special. It seemed that they came expecting to be given leadership which would give them direction, guidance, challenge, specific goals to achieve, and a sense of power to accomplish that righteous challenge. They got it all! . . . Leaders will feel to lead and youth will walk forward in the ranks as they lead and follow. The Lord has blessed you. He will continue."

In the weeks following the Young Women satellite broadcast,

letters and telephone calls flooded into Church headquarters. Comments from all over the Church indicated that for many it was one of the most impactful Young Women meetings ever held. Such responses, Ardeth wrote, were "evidence of the answer to our fervent prayers and fasting that attending angels might assist us in the work. . . . That the powers of heaven might distill upon the hearts and minds of those who would listen and observe, and that the message would be communicated by way of the Spirit bearing witness to their hearts. The evidence of answer to that prayer has been overwhelming. We have received many, many letters from . . . people all over in various areas. . . . A seminary group of thirty-five signed their names and said that they wanted to accept the commitment to respond and stand for truth and righteousness. It is a time of great rejoicing."

Excerpts from a letter received at Church headquarters is representative:

"My wife and I and our family watched your recent conference for the young women of the world. Words cannot express the depth of feeling we shared through the conference. We loved all of the proceedings but were especially touched by your message. . . . It was unmistakably the clarion call to be and to act. Your message would have to rank as one of the most profound messages ever given to the young women of the world in our day and probably in any age. It was one of those special sacred messages in which everyone's heart beat as one, when people communicated spirit to spirit. Your words are written upon our hearts, never to be erased. . . .

"God bless you for your sensitivity, insight and courage. You are leaving your mark upon this earth. All eternity will know you were here" (Lyle Cooper, December 10, 1985).

NOTE

1. There had been previous satellite broadcasts for combined organizations, but this was the first one exclusively for young women.

CHAPTER ONE

What Is Out There?

Young Ardeth Greene stood daydreaming at the kitchen window that looked out on the graveled road, the main thoroughfare through town. She gazed past the window shelf with its pots of dusty red geraniums, from which she absentmindedly plucked the dead leaves. The area from one end of town to the other covered only a few blocks. At the north end was the railroad station, with the large grain elevators just beyond. The post office was directly across the street from her home, and the cheese factory was to the south. From there, it was just wide open prairie, with the gravel road stretching east until it melted into the horizon.

"I remember standing there at the kitchen window, looking out over those red geraniums and the road beyond, thinking, 'I wonder what is out there for me, or will I just always be here?' My dream at that time was to have a little house in Glenwood, a white picket fence with hollyhocks all the way around it, and eight or nine children running in and out the door.

Ardeth, 1950, age 19

"A line from my patriarchal blessing, which I received when I was rather young, said, 'You will be surprised in the days to come at the blessings the Lord has in store for you.' I hadn't done very well in school. I didn't play the piano like my brother and sisters. I didn't sing. I would be willing to sing, but I don't have a good singing voice. And yet I think I always had faith that things would be good in spite of all that."

Ardeth's faith and optimism served her well through the years. She looked for the positive in every experience. As the Young Women general president, each day she would say to the Young Women board and staff, "This is an historic day!" She countered any expression of discouragement with the words, "You just wait! This will turn to our good." That was always her feeling. When she was released the staff gave her a wooden plaque with the inscription *"An Historic Day!"*

Dawn

On May 1, 1931, the Empire State Building, the tallest structure in the world at the time, formally opened in the large, bustling city of Manhattan, New York, on the east coast of the United States. The 1,245-foot structure, whose planning began in the 1920s, was hailed as a symbol of American confidence despite the difficulties of the Great Depression. Commentators said that the building would likely stand, along with the pyramids of Egypt, as a testimony to the building skills of the human race (*America's Century,* ed. Clifton Daniel [New York: Dorling Kindersley, 2000], 131).

As magnificent a structure as that building is, no earthly construction, no matter how dazzling the design, can compare with a human tabernacle designed by God and destined to live for eternity. Six weeks earlier, on March 19, 1931, a baby daughter was born to Edwin Kent (Ted) and Julia (June) Leavitt Greene in the western Canadian prairie town of Cardston, Alberta. Ardeth Greene, born in the covenant into the House of Israel, had almost certainly been tutored in the premortal world to prepare her for the role she would assume on a world stage in mortality.

Roots

June Leavitt and Ted Greene, both from Glenwood, Alberta, were married on March 14, 1924, in the Cardston Temple, which had been dedicated just six months earlier. Immediately following their marriage, they moved to an outlying farm about three miles from town. Although Glenwood was a village of only 250 residents at the time, it seemed large in comparison to the isolation of the farm that was their first home.

Ardeth's mother, Julia (June) Greene, and father, Edwin (Ted) Greene

They were elated when, in 1926, their first child was born. However, the baby girl, named Uvada, lived for only two days. In addition to this heartache, June was hospitalized in Cardston for six months with blood poisoning and other serious complications resulting from the pregnancy.

Two years later, on December 28, 1928, June gave birth to a son, Gordon Kay, who was frail but alive. Although she tried to nurse him, June didn't have enough milk for him to thrive. Unable to digest milk supplied through bottle feedings, the baby was gradually starving to death. Eventually, a neighbor who had also recently given birth agreed to nurse Kay as well as her own child.

June's recovery from this childbirth was easier than the previous one, but varicose veins and an open sore on her ankle refused to heal. She was forced to wear heavy elastic stockings for the rest of her life, but that did not deter her from spending long hours on her feet some years later, operating *Greene's General Store.*

Kay still needed an extraordinary amount of care when Ardeth was born three years later. "The report they gave me," Ardeth recalled, "is that I was such a good baby I would just lie in my crib hour after hour while they were taking care of my brother, who really needed the help. My mom told me that there was a lady in our town who would stand over my crib and say, 'There's something wrong with this baby! A normal baby just does not lie there that still, that quiet, that long! There is something seriously wrong with this baby!'" In the meantime, Ardeth continued to grow steadily, oblivious to the fuss over her unusual behavior.

Ted later recorded his thoughts about his new daughter: "In the heart of a deep depression, Ardeth took her first small view of the world of men. She must have liked what she saw, for her attitude from the start was a happy spirit, with a pleasant smile. She seemed to have no concern about the Depression. Apparently, she was interested in shedding some happiness in a depressed world."

As the Great Depression of the 1930s deepened, eking out a living became extremely difficult, and Ardeth's dad lost part of his farm. "It had nothing to do with management, but rather with circumstances," Ardeth said. "These were hard times and money was scarce. One of my early memories is of a pig that we were to take to the train station in Glenwood to be shipped to market. My parents were excited about this, so I was excited as well. I knew that this pig was very important to us. The pig was tied down in the bottom of the wagon, and we got in and put our feet on top of it. When we got to the place where we were supposed to unload it, the pig was dead. I remember Mom weeping, and saying, 'What will we do?' and my wondering how a pig could be that important. But I remember realizing that something terrible had happened besides losing a pig. It's a part of me even now."

When Ardeth was three, her parents were forced to sell their car and every other possession they could do without, pack up their belongings, and move into Glenwood. The small town, whose residents were nearly all members of the Church, was named for Glen Wood, son of Edward J. Wood. Edward Wood was very prominent in the area as president of the Cardston Temple; he also served as the Alberta Stake president for many years.

Ardeth's mother, June, one of the competent and outgoing Leavitts, was a popular young woman. Musically gifted, she sang in a quartet and played the piano in a dance band. She could play anything she heard and was much in demand for her abilities. She later helped to start the Glenwood Band. Always optimistic and energetic, she never sat still. She served on the school board and was active in community affairs. To her way of thinking, whatever one desired was possible if one was willing to work hard enough to obtain it.

On the other hand, Ted Greene did not emerge with the same degree of confidence as that enjoyed by his wife. Too shy to speak in public, he even lacked the courage to give his children a name and a blessing in Church, deferring instead to his more outgoing father-in-law. "By the time Shirley, my youngest sister, was born," Ardeth recalled, "Dad got up the courage to give the blessing. But Papa Leavitt, who was so used to doing it, was in the circle and he just started before Dad had a chance. Her name was going to be Shirley Mae, and he didn't say the Mae part!"

When they began their marriage, June was more social and Ted more reserved, but they each had qualities that strengthened the other. Together they became a great team, dedicated to rearing their children with hope, optimism, and faith in the future. Ardeth later reflected, "From Dad we got our roots and from Mom we got our wings. Both were essential to our progress."

As the years passed, Ted's confidence in his own abilities grew, due in large part to June's behind-the-scenes support and encouragement. He later gained the confidence to give father's blessings to his children; fill a full-time, six-month mission away from home; and serve as a bishop and later as a counselor to the stake president.

Beginnings

Many of the people in Glenwood were related by birth or marriage, and Ardeth grew up with one set of grandparents across the street; a grandmother three blocks away; and aunts, uncles, and cousins within a stone's throw. The family home, the grade school, high school, church, store, and the homes of both grandparents were all within three blocks. Aunt Ione taught Ardeth music, she took tap-dancing lessons from Aunt Wanda, and Aunt Rosanna was her first-grade teacher. Her best friend was a cousin, Colleen, whose home was just through the field. "Colleen's mother and my mother were sisters," Ardeth says. "We were very close. My best friends were my cousins, both boys and girls."

Ardeth, age 6, in front of the kitchen window wearing a bright yellow oilcloth dance costume

Ardeth's first public appearance came at a dance recital not long after their move to town. From the time of her birth, her ankles were weak, and her dad made braces for her shoes which helped her learn to walk. This weakness gave her a somewhat clumsy appearance, and her parents thought that perhaps tap-dancing lessons would help to strengthen the muscles. "I had a little yellow oil cloth tap-dance costume and came out on stage for my debut, made a wrong turn and danced the whole dance with my back to the audience!"

Her father continued working their eighty-acre farm, driving his old truck back and forth from town. He raised cows and sold their calves. He also raised turkeys, pigs, and sheep. A hard-working man, always trying to find a profitable market without much success, he planted alfalfa, barley, and wheat with the hope of a fruitful harvest and a ready market. Ardeth remembered the time her father bought a flock of young turkeys to raise to supplement the family income. Hail falling from huge black clouds killed all of the turkeys. Family members and townspeople met at a local business to pick the turkeys and salvage what they could, but the investment itself was a disaster.

LESSONS AND LEARNING

As occasion required, Ardeth helped on the farm—plowing, planting, cultivating, weeding, and harvesting. She learned some of life's lessons from the never-ending work and the cycle of the seasons. "We had limited resources. We couldn't do it all or have it all. We lived in anticipation and became goal-oriented—next time, next crop, next season. Planning was continuous, and there was no instant gratification. What we planted was what we harvested. Faith in a good harvest was always essential before the seeds could be planted. We learned to pray for direction in making decisions. We prayed for the weather and leaned on the Lord.

Ardeth's father on their 80-acre farm, three miles from town

We learned patience and obedience. You can't control the weather, and you can't rush the seasons." Ardeth later came to learn that these principles often apply to people as well.

"We learned to work together. Everyone had a part to play, and others were depending on you to do your part. Even making ice cream required advance planning and was a team effort. Mom made the caramel filling, then Dad would go to the ice house where we had stored ice from the river, covered with sawdust. The ice had to be broken up, then added to the ice cream freezer. I remember standing on top of the freezer with my hand on Dad's shoulder as he cranked the handle, anticipating that when the work was done, what we wanted to have happen would happen and that the reward would be worth the effort."

"As children, my brother and sisters and I had fun studying the mail-order catalogs dreaming of what we might order. Mom taught us by example that if one has a goal and really works

Ardeth, age 7, and her brother, Kay, age 11. Animals were almost part of the family.

toward it, and doesn't give up, it can be reached. A new pair of shoes, for example, became a reality only after careful preparation. I remember a pair of brown shoes I really wanted. The order was finally sent off and I waited impatiently for about three weeks before they finally arrived. Excitedly, I ripped off the paper, lifted the shoes out of the box, and put them on my feet—only to find they were slightly too small. Because I wanted to wear them immediately and not have to wait the three weeks it would take to return them, plus another three weeks for a new pair to be sent, I said they were fine and wore them anyway. I still remember how they hurt!

"Shortly before Christmastime, the year that the hail killed all of our turkeys, I really wanted a chenille bedspread. I didn't actually expect anything under the Christmas tree, and I understood why, but I couldn't help mentioning it anyway. At that time, a chenille bedspread was something really special. My dad said, 'My dear, if we could get one for you, my concern is that if you get used to luxuries like this you might expect them and it would be hard for you when things get tough.' That was a great lesson, and I was surprised and excited when the longed-for bedspread was under the tree on Christmas morning."

Not long after the family's move to Glenwood, the general store in town burned down and its owner moved to the United States. In her journal June recorded, "I will never know what possessed me to suggest that we might set up shop, but I did so. As we talked about it, the idea gained momentum. We had little in the way of cash, but we had heard of others who had started on a shoestring. So the decision was made to sell what cattle we had and invest in a shop which would carry the name *Greene's Variety Store.*"

For a time, an old granary attached to their home served as the store. June recorded: "November 10, 1934: We opened up the store for business. The building in which we started was 20 x 20 but we still had to spread the boxes of cornflakes, etc., wide on the shelves to make it look like we did have a business."

Ardeth started to work in the store when she was eight or nine. "Although I was not old enough to wait on customers, I helped unpack the transport truck that brought boxes of cereal, bread, and other items. Since it was a general store, we had a shelf of drug store items—not prescription drugs but carbolic salves and other pharmaceutical supplies. The thing I hated most was to unpack the boxes and put all of those little things on the shelves. In that store I learned a lot of lessons. Even as a child, when I could hardly see over the counter, I was serving the public, and Mom made me feel needed and important. She treated me like I was essential to the success of our little country store."

In time, that first little store evolved into a separate, somewhat larger building that was constructed next to the house and named *Greene's General Store.* The new store, which boasted hardwood floors, was completed about the time of Ardeth's twelfth birthday. Before the shelves were put in, her mom decided to celebrate Ardeth's birthday with a party in the new structure. "This was a milestone for us. All the kids from the neighboring communities came to Glenwood. My uncle, aunt, two cousins, and my brother, Kay, had a family band called *The Blue Bombers,* and they played at this incredible dance that we had. Everybody wore stocking feet to dance on the hardwood floors. I remember that all of the girls liked this one particular boy. He gave me a bottle of lilac perfume for my birthday. To think that at twelve years of age I would have a present from a boy! Lilac perfume brings back a host of memories."

SHARON AND SHIRLEY

The opening of the new store brought increased responsibility for Ardeth. By that time, two younger sisters had joined the family. Sharon's birth, one month prior to Ardeth's eighth birthday, came as a complete surprise to her. "Mom went to Cardston every Thursday to go to the bank and to get her hair done. One day when I came home from school, Grandma Greene, who was living with us, told me that my mom had gone to town and that she was going to be there a few days because she was going to come home with a baby sister. I was so excited, and I had not had one clue about it! It was never ever mentioned. Mom always wore a loose store uniform, and I had no idea that she was expecting!" Shirley, the youngest of the Greene siblings, arrived one year after Sharon.

Ardeth was always protective of her younger sisters. She often cared for them while their mother worked in the store, and she loved the sense that they were part of her personal responsibility. She never thought of them as a burden. Sharon remembered feeling that the reason their big sister was always with them was because she wanted to be. "It never occurred to me until years later that she was babysitting us. I thought she took us with her everywhere she went just because she wanted us to be with her. I don't ever remember hearing her say, 'Do I have to take them with me?' We felt wanted and loved by our big sister."

Writing a remembrance of his daughters, Ardeth's dad said:

Ardeth and her brother, Kay, and sisters Sharon (standing) and Shirley (in Kay's arms)

"Her little sisters were Ardeth's constant companions. Even when they wore her clothes and messed up her room, they were still sweet to her. She watched over them like a mother hen. Even in their dating days they were her special charges. She defended them against all comers—especially unworthy boyfriends."

She was not only her little sisters' guardian, but she was their advocate. When they wanted to do something before their assigned chores were finished, their mother would tell them they must complete their work first. Many times Ardeth would intervene, saying, "Oh, Mom, let them go. I'll do it for them."

Ardeth was also their first time-management instructor. On Saturday mornings the three girls sat at the kitchen table while Ardeth made a list of everything that needed to be done. Sharon and Shirley went through the list and put their names by what they wanted to do. Ardeth did what was left over, which always included mopping the kitchen floor, the least desirable of all the chores. When they finished a task they checked it off. Thinking about those times years later, Ardeth said, "I think that I just grew up with a sense of purpose and planning. I learned it from the crops, with Dad planting and harvesting and Mom buying and selling."

Shirley recalled, "Ardeth was the one who washed our hair, got us ready for school and helped us out. In our eyes, she and our brother, Kay, were perfect and could do no wrong. She was the model I wanted to follow. If I wanted to do something and my parents said, 'Ardeth never did that,' then I wouldn't do it either. I wanted to be like her."

Sharon's view of her older sister's help was more pragmatic. When Ardeth was getting ready to go away to school, Sharon started crying. Trying to comfort her, Ardeth said, "Don't cry Sharon, I'll be back!" Sharon responded, "I know, but who's going to mop the kitchen floor!"

Shirley also remembers the difficulties Ardeth had with finding her way from one location to the next. "I think Ardeth must have been given a choice before she was born—she could either choose to know east, west, north, and south, or she could know right from wrong. She chose right from wrong!" While Ardeth's moral compass is firm and certain, geography remains a challenge.

Both girls loved to watch their big sister get ready for parties and dances. They still remember getting into her bed when she was gone for the evening, knowing that she would sleep between them when she got home. They loved to wake up the morning following a dance and pull the confetti out of her hair while she was still trying to sleep.

BEHIND THE COUNTER

There were only two stores in town, *Greene's General Store* being one of them. Several miles northeast of town was the Hutterite colony. The Blood Indian Reservation was a few miles in the other direction. "We learned to appreciate different cultures, which was valuable to me in later years. I remember Mom saying, 'We need the Hutterites and the Indians, and they need us. That's what makes good friends.' The Hutterites brought their eggs and other goods to exchange. The Indians would get their treaty money and come to buy at the store. Many of the Indians couldn't write their names, so they would put an X on the line, and we would write their name by it. I still remember the incredible names. Maggie Dirty Face Plain Woman, Joe Cross the Mountain, and Tom Morning Owl were actual names of real people, and we learned to respect those names."

Ardeth remembers that certain Indians were always out of money, so they would leave their buckskin jackets as security, and her mom would let them have the groceries they needed. Then when their treaty money came, they'd bring it in and reclaim their jackets. The Hutterites, a religious group who dressed in dark colors, would not deal with banks at that time. They would bring their huge "grain checks" of three or four thousand dollars into the store. Her mom would take them to the bank, get them cashed and bring them back. "We had a safe in the back room of the store where we kept all the money. My brother and I were taught the combination on the safe at a very young age so that if Mom and Dad left the store, we knew how to get the money. It was a high trust for me, and I had a sense of major responsibility."

The little country store had products of all sorts: groceries, coal oil, gum boots, mouse seed, fly coils, bolts of fabric, thread, patterns, kegs of nails, pharmaceutical supplies, and fine English bone china! It also carried what her mom called "Ladies' Ready-to-Wear," which were the nicer dresses according to the standard of the time. These dresses were located in a small room in the back of the store to separate them from the regular, more ordinary clothing kept up front.

In addition to the family, a couple of ladies from town helped out in the store when needed. "Mom wanted us to look professional, so she had us wear uniforms—tan with red lapels and buttons. When we went into the store in our uniforms, we were uptown, first rate!"

June taught her children that it didn't matter how strong the blizzard was blowing or how cold it was, they opened the store

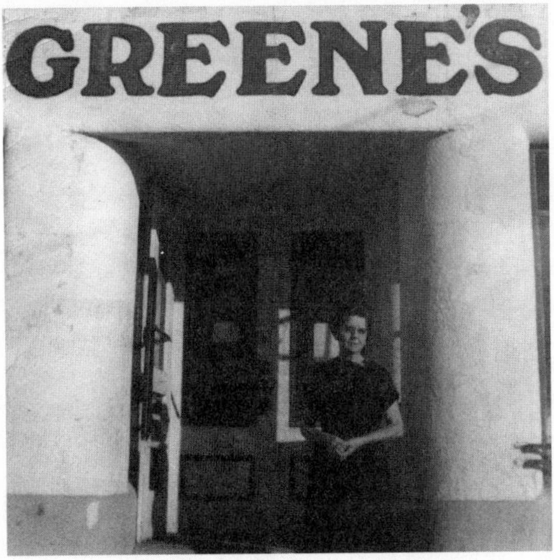

Ardeth's mother in front of Greene's General Store, which was located right next to their home

exactly at 8:00 A.M. and closed at 6:00 P.M. They stayed until the last minute, no matter what. If someone needed something after hours, June would always go out and open the store. She regarded each customer as a person of value and treated everyone with courtesy and respect.

Ardeth's mom ordered the items to stock the store; then an uncle delivered the groceries in his transport truck. Because they were unable to buy enough to fill the shelves, Ardeth said, "We learned to stack the shelves right to the edge so it looked like they were full, but there was nothing behind them. I never saw that as a facade. I saw it as having faith in the future. Mom always took pride in her good credit rating. She bought just what she could pay for. That was a great lesson. Never go into debt."

"I was in the store one time when the bread was delivered. As we put it on the shelves all I could think of was, 'Will we be able to pay for it?' I remember counting the money in the till, estimating the cost of the bread, and wondering if we had enough money. Even now, all these years later when I'm contemplating a purchase my husband, Heber, will say, 'Go ahead, we've got money for the bread!'"

CHAPTER TWO

A Heritage of "Believing Blood"

Paternal Ancestors

One of Ardeth's earliest memories, still vivid, is that of standing at the window of the farmhouse watching for Grandma Greene to come. When her grandmother came for a visit, she would walk three miles from town and then walk the three miles back. "That was such a highlight, when we could see Grandma Greene coming," Ardeth recalls. "She was a saint. She had long hair she would wash and brush and do up in a bun on the top of her head. As she grew older, she sewed an extra piece of material to the sleeve of her house dresses, giving them additional length to hide the growing plumpness of her arms. She wore glasses and always had a lace collar attached to the neck of her dress, secured with a decorative pin. Oh, I loved Grandma Greene! She was the one I saw as a perfect person, and I wanted to be just like her."

Grandma Greene began life as Adeline Allen on April 19, 1865. She was born in Syderstone, Norfolk, England, far from

Ardeth's grandmother, Adeline Allen Greene

the Canadian prairie town she would later call home. Her parents, Thomas and Sarah Cornwall Allen, reared their family of eight sons and two daughters on a large estate where Thomas worked as a blacksmith. The children gleaned in the grain fields during harvest time. Adeline's formal schooling lasted only four years, from 1870 to 1874, at which time she left school to work at home when her twin brothers were born. When she was fifteen, her father told her she would have to go to work in the fields. As this tedious work was not the job to which she aspired, she obtained work in the kitchen of a great house nearby, where twelve other servants were employed. Her ambition was to become a splendid cook, a goal she achieved.

During the time when she was employed as a cook, she and a fellow maidservant heard two Mormon missionaries teach of the Prophet Joseph Smith and the restored gospel of Jesus Christ. Adeline gained a conviction of the gospel's truthfulness and was baptized into The Church of Jesus Christ of Latter-day Saints on June 17, 1887, in the ocean at Brighton, England. With a strong desire to align herself with the Saints, she later left family and friends and endured the rigorous journey to Utah. She never looked back.

In her journal, she recorded an account of that eventful journey: "On August 29, 1889, I left my native land from Liverpool on the steamship *Wisconsin,* steerage passage with a company of Saints and sinners, a very unpleasant trip. There were storms at sea, and no conveniences, poor food. Had a wonderful convincing testimony that I was doing right, that I would arrive safely at my destination. During an especially rough night at sea, even though many were frantic, a peaceful calm influence sustained me. The elders came each evening to have singing and prayer with us. The hymn we sang that evening was, 'We Thank Thee, O God, for a Prophet.' I had never felt such happiness. It was a testimony to me I was doing right, leaving all and gathering to Zion."

Finally reaching New York City, Adeline next traveled to Norfolk, Virginia, on a large boat, where she embarked by train for Utah. The train had three coaches, "consisting of Elders, tourists and immigrants." Of her trip and subsequent arrival in Zion, she wrote: "Was in a railroad wreck, was injured and had to remain in Virginia for three weeks before continuing the journey. Arrived at Bountiful, Utah, October 5, 1889. Kind Brother and Sister Cole gave me a home until I could work. Fasted for the first time on the Prophet Joseph Smith's birthday, December 23, 1889."

Adeline left behind almost everything she owned as she

made her journey to Zion. Fearing that her decision to join the Mormons would meet with her parents' disapproval and that they would not sanction her decision to sail to America, she visited them one last time but mentioned nothing of her plans. Shortly after her arrival in Utah, she wrote to her parents, informing them of her journey. Their shock upon finding that their daughter had left home for a faraway land was expressed in the letter her mother sent in response to the news:

"My Dearest daughter, I received your letter quite safe but sorrow and surprised to see where you were got too. However and whatever on earth have caused you to go out of your own country and away from all your friends I cannot image. You say don't fret. How do you think I can help it when such a blow as that come. It struck me all in heaps and your Father was as bad when I told him. It does seem such a thing for you to be at home and not to say a word about it to anybody. . . . Your Father say of course if you had made up your mind to go we could not stop you and he should not wished if you was bound to go but he can't like the way you are gone in so underminded. He wish you had told him so he might have had a little talk with you about it and give you a little something to help you. You say you are happy but I can't think it for I am sure I could not have been happy to have gone into a foreign country and left you behind. You say you will come again but I don't think you will hesitate your life over the deep waters again."

This prediction by her mother proved accurate. Although Adeline kept up a correspondence with her parents until their deaths, as well as with some of her brothers, she never saw her parents or siblings again in this life.

Among the passengers on the voyage from England was Daniel Kent Greene, a young British missionary returning to his home in Utah. He also experienced the train wreck Adeline mentioned, which was caused by the collapse of a bridge over a stream. In that accident, all of her belongings were lost, including her pictures, treasures, and some lovely new clothes she had either purchased or made and was saving until after her arrival in Zion. Danny, who survived the train wreck unhurt, returned to New York with those who were injured. Although he was not acquainted with Adeline at the time, he carried her to the hotel room where the doctor cared for her.

Some time after returning home from his mission to England, Danny attended a social at the home of Brother and Sister Cole, where he was formally introduced to Adeline Allen. She soon became a favorite of both Danny and his family, and after four months of courting, they were married in the Logan Temple on March 26, 1890. They settled into a comfortable home that Danny provided for them in Smithfield, Utah, on a rented farm, where they lived for several years. Their home was surrounded by shade and fruit trees, and they had land to raise hay and wheat and have a garden. They were happy and felt fortunate to be near family and friends, able to make a living, and have opportunities for Church service.

For some time, Danny had desired to establish himself on his own homestead. After hearing of available land near the new Mormon settlement in southern Alberta, he began making plans to move his young family to Canada. Adeline, who was happy with their life in Cache Valley, did not share her husband's enthusiasm for pioneering. However, after much persuasion from

Danny, she finally agreed to go. They left with their two small children on April 28, and, after a difficult journey, arrived in Cardston on June 21, 1898.

Life on the Canadian prairie, with its long, harsh winters, was not easy for the young family. Upon their arrival, they found that the land for homesteading had been taken, and they had no money with which to buy other property. They spent their first winter in a poorly built lean-to room, where they suffered greatly with the cold. Danny, determined to have better living conditions for his family before another harsh Canadian winter settled in, hauled logs from the mountains and built a cabin about ten miles from Cardston. On October 3, 1901, while living in this home, they had a son, Edwin Kent (Ted), who would later become Ardeth's father. Because of his ability at handling horses, Danny was asked to drive the stagecoach from Cardston to Lethbridge, the nearest railroad station. He carried passengers and mail over the seventy-mile route. When the railroad came to Cardston, the need for a stagecoach diminished, and he found work helping farmers in the area.

Danny was recognized as one of Alberta's early settlers; he had a leading role in building up the wards of the Church, as well as the communities in the area. He was a spiritual man who taught his children by example. Daily family prayer and scripture study were part of his life. In 1909 he served a six-month mission in the Calgary area and helped to organize the first branch of the Church there. He was also a stake missionary for the Alberta Stake for a long period of time. In recognition of his service, he was invited by President Edward Wood to plow the first furrow as the Church commenced the construction of the Cardston Alberta Temple on November 9, 1913.

In 1915, the family purchased a home in Glenwood, about twenty miles from Cardston. Danny served as a stake missionary there for several years. His main desire was to live a worthy life and help his family to be good Latter-day Saints.

Early in 1919, he became ill, and it was soon discovered that he had cancer. After suffering through the summer and fall, he passed away on November 21, 1921. He was only sixty-three years old, but his hard outdoor pioneering life had aged him beyond his time.

Adeline lived on in their home for nearly thirty years. She lived to see all of her children marry in the temple and have families of their own, making her grandmother and great-grandmother to a large posterity. A favorite of grandchildren and great-grandchildren alike, she played games, told stories, and was a welcome guest in all homes.

That she attempted to share the gospel with family members in England is evident in letters from her brother, Ephraim. He wrote in 1941, "Let me thank you for the Deseret News's you have sent me and the magazines which I have received. . . . I have read them with a great deal of profit and insight concerning spiritual things, also the beliefs and faith of the Latter-day Saints. . . . Your doctrine if it was carried out by every one they would not go very far wrong. . . . I have been reading the addresses of some of your presidents delivered at the conferences and what wonderful addresses they are."

In another letter, in 1943, Ephraim said, "Most of the message delivered for your people I can say Amen to. It set a very high standard of living and carried out with all would bring the blessings described therein."

As Adeline grew older, she spent her winters in the home of one of her sons or daughters. When Ardeth was a teenager, Grandma Greene lived with her family for a time. "When I think of her," Ardeth says, "I think of her kneeling by her bed praying, or seeing her ironing her temple clothes. She was absolutely pure." Temple service was a very important part of her life, which did not go unnoticed by her granddaughter. Grandma Greene was faithful to the beliefs she had embraced as a young woman, diligently serving both her church and her fellowmen throughout her long life. She died on February 6, 1950, and is buried alongside her husband in the hilltop cemetery north of Glenwood.

Danny's parents, Evan M. Greene and Susan Kent, were among the early Mormon pioneers. Evan, Ardeth's great-grandfather, helped build the temple in Nauvoo and participated in the School of the Prophets. He was promised that his posterity would be blessed with believing blood. His wife, Susan Kent Greene, joined the Church at age sixteen after reading the Book of Mormon and gaining a testimony of its truthfulness. They settled for a time in Provo, where Danny was born on April 7, 1858. The family was later called to help settle Cache Valley in northern Utah.

Ardeth's paternal great-great-grandmother was Rhoda Young, sister of Brigham Young. She and her husband, John P. Greene, were given a copy of the newly printed Book of Mormon in 1830 by Samuel Smith, brother of the Prophet Joseph Smith. After they had received testimonies of the truthfulness of the book, they passed it on to Rhoda's brother, Phineas Young, who read it and immediately gained a testimony. Phineas then shared it with his brother, Brigham, who, after reading it, passed it to another sister, Fanny Young Murray. She, in turn, gave it to her daughter and son-in-law, Vilate and Heber C. Kimball. Thus was created the chain of events that brought about the conversion and baptism of both a future prophet and a future apostle of The Church of Jesus Christ of Latter-day Saints.

In April 1832, John and Rhoda Greene, Brigham Young, and all of the Young family, as well as the Heber C. Kimball family, were baptized into the Church. John and Rhoda became stalwarts in the early Church; and John was one of the six elders who were mentioned in the first verse of Doctrine and Covenants 84. He was a close friend of the Prophet Joseph and served as his bodyguard in Nauvoo.

Maternal Lineage

Ardeth's maternal grandfather, Edwin Jenkins Leavitt, and his identical twin brother, Edward, were born in Wellsville, Cache County, Utah, on September 25, 1875, to Thomas Rowell and Ann Eliza Jenkins Leavitt. When they were fifteen years old, Edwin and Edward left their home and family, bound for adventure and a new life in Alberta, Canada. They traveled by covered wagon, driving their cattle as they went. The trek took them six weeks, and they settled on land east of Cardston.

On April 10, 1901, Edwin married Julia Rebecca Pitcher, a Cache Valley, Utah, native whose ancestors had moved from England to Utah and later to Cardston, Alberta. Two weeks after giving birth to her second daughter, named Julia (June), Edwin's wife died on March 28, 1904. The grieving young father was left

Papa and Mamma Leavitt (as they were called)—Edwin and Nettie Leavitt. Ardeth's maternal grandparents lived across the street.

alone with a toddler, Laverne, as well as the infant, June, who would become Ardeth's mother. The two children were initially cared for by an aunt and then shifted back and forth between other family members for a time.

A welcome addition to the family came a few years later when Ann Jeanette (Nettie) Nelson became Edwin's second wife and mother to his two daughters. In time, four more children were born to them. About two years after their marriage, Edwin and Nettie moved to Glenwood, Alberta, where Edwin and his twin brother, Edward, who had married Ellen June (Nellie) Leishman, built identical houses on two corners of the same block. The Leavitts were very outgoing, strong leaders with vision, optimism, and confidence.

Edwin, always a good provider, was also interested in civic affairs. He was a member of the committee that helped bring the railroad to Glenwood, as well as serving as Glenwood's justice of the peace for thirty-nine years. The town's first telephone system was installed in a large room in his home where his wife and daughters were the telephone operators for thirty-five years. Music was another life-long interest. He sang in a quartet with his three brothers, led the ward choir for many years, and played the drums in several orchestras, handing down his musical talent to his family.

Mama Leavitt, as Nettie was called, was a good mother to Edwin's two older girls, as well as to her own daughters, and was absolutely the perfect grandma. There was never any indication that they weren't all one family. Never in all of Ardeth's growing up years did she ever hear the words *step-mother* or *step-sisters.* Edwin and Nettie's home became a hub of activities for the entire Leavitt clan. Ardeth recalled that everyone in Glenwood called Mama Leavitt "Aunt Nettie" and that people loved her for her nurturing kindness. "I felt safe in her home. . . . It was a fun place to take our friends, who were welcome guests. She always had cookies for us. . . . I determined that I would, likewise, have a home where people felt welcome and that I would always have cookies, especially for my children and their friends." That Ardeth succeeded in this desire can be attested to by both family members and friends, as well as by children, who frequently drop by for a visit and a cookie.

Family home evenings were held regularly at the Leavitt home. "Everyone took part and everyone else clapped and cheered. Even though I never felt as talented as my cousins, in Mama Leavitt's house I always felt like my grandparents, aunts, uncles, and cousins were cheering me on."

Both Leavitt grandparents were faithful Latter-day Saints and were active in Church service their entire lives. Their later years were spent in Cardston, where they passed away within two years of each other, Papa on August 19, 1953, and Mama on November 25, 1955.

Ardeth's maternal great-great-grandfather, Jeremiah Leavitt, born and reared in Quebec, Canada, married Sarah Sturtevant, who was raised in New Hampshire by Presbyterian parents. Sarah studied the Bible regularly and looked for a church like that described in the New Testament. When she heard of the Prophet Joseph's vision, she considered it of more importance than anything she had ever heard before. In 1837, Jeremiah and Sarah obtained copies of the Book of Mormon and the Doctrine and Covenants. Jeremiah wrote: "We had joined the Freewill Baptists and remained with them until we saw the Book of Mormon and Doctrine and Covenants and believed them without any preaching." They gathered with the Saints in Kirtland, Ohio, where they were baptized into The Church of Jesus Christ of Latter-day Saints. Three years before her death, Sarah wrote, "All I cared for was to know and to do the will of God."

From Kirtland, the Leavitt family went westward with the other Saints, eventually settling in Nauvoo, Illinois. In Nauvoo, Jeremiah and Sarah's son, Thomas Rowell Leavitt, met and married Ann Eliza Jenkins. Thomas and Ann Eliza became Ardeth's great-grandparents.

Forced from their homes by angry mobs in the winter of 1846, the Leavitts, with thousands of their fellow Saints, turned their faces westward in search of a new life. Eventually they made their way to Zion in the valleys of what later became Utah, where they were called upon again and again to aid in colonizing some part of the expanding empire.

By the time they finally settled down, the Leavitt families had helped to pioneer almost every corner of the territory, until their family ties stretched from Canada to California and many places in between.

Of the Noble and Great

Ardeth maintains a grateful appreciation for her heritage. While preparing a talk on record keeping, she reread portions of the journals of some of her ancestors, after which she wrote, "I have caught a spirit of gratitude for my valiant ancestors. . . . I express gratitude for such a heritage and plead for the valiancy and commitment to leave a life representative of those who have gone before and established a foundation on which to build. My ancestors are of the noble and great, and my earnest desires are to be the same."

In her first journal entry for 1981, she wrote the following:

Great-grandparents Evan Molbourne and Susan Kent Greene. Their daughter, Louisa Lula Greene (Richards) (standing) was the first editor of the Women's Exponent, *published from 1872 to 1914.*

"Tonight I have been reading my great-grandmother's journal—Susan K. Greene. In the front page of her journal, dated February 3, 1875, she wrote what I also would like to say expressing my feelings. 'I make this covenant to do the very best I can, asking God for wisdom to direct me in that I may walk with him in all righteousness and truth. I much desire to be pure in heart that I may see God. Help me, Lord, to overcome all evil with good. Susan K. Greene.' I wish to express the same thoughts and will look forward one day to seeing Great-Grandmother Susan K. Greene and hope that I can tell her I have followed her path, kept the faith and all of the covenants."

CHAPTER THREE

Growing Years

Reverence and Respect

In addition to family activities and work in the store, Ardeth's growing up years revolved around Church and school. On Sundays, she went to church with her family. The church building consisted solely of a recreation hall that could be divided into smaller rooms by curtains for the Sunday School classes. There was no chapel at the time. Ardeth's class was held in the basement by the furnace room. She later recalled, "I remember that it was dark and you could hear the furnace, but it was always warm."

In the Greene family, the children were taught that the Sabbath was a holy day, and they learned to show reverence and respect for this sacred time. With the exception of caring for the farm animals, all work was suspended, and the family enjoyed the Sabbath as a day of rest and worship. No activities were allowed that were considered inappropriate to do in their Sunday clothes, which they put on in the morning and took off at bedtime.

At times, refraining from their usual weekday activities on Sunday was difficult for the children. One Sunday Ardeth's younger sister, Shirley, came to the dinner table with her Bible open. She said, "Dad, I can't see anywhere in the scriptures where it says, 'Thou shalt not ride thy bicycle on Sunday.' His response ended the discussion: "It may not be in the scriptures, but that's how it is in our house." Ardeth recalled, "There was no use of an appeal to Mom because they always spoke with one voice."

From Ardeth's earliest years, her parents had taught her about the sacred nature of the temple. On April 4, 1939, she entered the Cardston Temple to be baptized. While she awaited her turn, she sat on a white bench looking up at the baptismal font, secured to the backs of the white stone oxen. She knew that she was in a holy place. A feeling of peace crept into her heart. She wanted always to have this feeling. Right then and there she decided that no matter what, she would always try to be good. She wanted to be worthy of the blessings of the temple forever.

When she was fifteen, she received her patriarchal blessing from Patriarch John F. Anderson. She was told that she would be surprised in the days to come at the blessings the Lord had in store for her. The blessing said that she would be guided in the selection of a mate. In addition, it stated that her life had been preserved for a wise purpose and that she had a bright future. That blessing has served as both a comfort and a guide throughout her life. It was recorded and transcribed by the patriarch's granddaughter, Elaine Lowe, who would later serve as a counselor to Ardeth in the Young Women general presidency

(April 6, 1987–March 31, 1990). Elaine Lowe Jack also became the general Relief Society president on March 31, 1990.

Primary was taught on a weekday afternoon, immediately following school. The schoolteachers led the children over the stile, across the street, and into the church house. Often, their schoolteachers were also their Primary teachers. Since most of the town was related in one way or another, more often than not these same teachers were also in Ardeth's extended family.

An event that had a great influence on her young life took place between the fall of 1944 and the spring of 1945. Because of World War II, there were no regular proselyting missionaries in Canada. Consequently, the Church invited older Church members to serve six-month missions where possible. Her father, who took personally any such request from the Church, considered the possibility with his wife. After much discussion, they felt it would be possible for him to be away from home for six months, and he volunteered. Subsequently, he was called to serve in an area just north of Edmonton in the Western Canadian Mission.

It was during the wintertime, and the task of managing the store and taking care of the chores fell to June and her two oldest children, Kay and Ardeth. Although her dad was only about ten hours away by automobile, he never came home during that time. How much she missed him was recorded in her diary of March 13, 1945: "Oh, I'm so homesick for Dad. If he'd only hurry home I'd be in heaven. When I feel sad and alone it's too much but when Dad is here it is so much easier."

About a year after completing his missionary service, Ardeth's dad was called as bishop of the Glenwood Ward. At the time of his call, a new church building was badly needed. Other nearby communities in the same situation were building the cultural hall first and then adding on the chapel later. Athletics were a very high priority, and the thinking was that you could hold church in a cultural hall but you couldn't play basketball in a chapel. As the bishop, her dad took a different approach. He decided to build the chapel first and then add the cultural hall. This decision met with a great deal of opposition, even among some of his closest friends, but he held firm and the chapel was built first. Later, many agreed that building the chapel first had had a great impact for good on their small community.

While Ardeth's dad was an inspiring example of Christian service, her mom helped to make it possible. For example, during the time that Ted served as bishop, he was very busy helping to build a new meetinghouse. He gave turkeys to the Relief Society sisters to cook and serve to people who would work on the chapel. He also gave a cow to a new family who was having a difficult time. "Mom always did behind-the-scenes things, and we were always cheering Dad on. It was not until later we came to realize that Mom was always in the wings, playing a major role."

Since Ardeth and her brother and sisters were out-of-doors with their dad on the farm, sometimes for hours at a time, he was the one who had time to listen to them. "As I look back, I think the reason we had so much time with Dad was because Mom made it possible by staying in the store, helping to provide the resources for our clothes, our education, lessons, and a variety of other activities. Dad was always attentive to helping Mom in the store, but she was the one who kept it going."

School Days

Ardeth looked forward to the time when she would be old enough to go to school. She wanted to do well like her brother, Kay, who was three years older. He was bright, capable, and talented, and she wanted to be as smart and as well regarded as he was. Full of anticipation, she set off on the first day, eager to learn. It was a memorable experience, but unfortunately not in the way she had hoped. Her first mistake came when she called her teacher "Aunt Rosanna." In front of the entire class, her aunt stated that in school she was not to be addressed as "Aunt" but as "Mrs. Greene." Embarrassed, but intent on doing well, Ardeth was excited when the students were asked to write their names on the blackboard. She knew she could do that. Proudly she printed, in capital letters, "A R D E T H," the only way she knew how to write. Her teacher immediately erased her name, telling her that it wasn't right, and replaced it with "Ardeth"—capital A, followed by lowercase letters, which, to the small girl, didn't look like her name at all. Ardeth was devastated, and felt as if that correction was a confirmation that she wasn't as smart as the other kids.

Because the school was small, there were two grades in each class. The older students corrected the papers of the younger ones. Ardeth and her cousin, Colleen, were in the same class, even though Colleen was a year older. Many times Colleen corrected her younger cousin's spelling papers. Ardeth remembers that she always had mistakes, which made her feel that she wasn't as smart as Colleen.

Even as a child, she noticed the difference between the capable, well-prepared teachers and those who were less effective.

At times, there were also unavoidable situations that contributed to her feelings of scholastic inadequacy. During her third-grade year, the teacher became ill and was forced to give up her position. Ardeth and her classmates were moved up to the next class even though they had not completed the year's work. When the new school year began, they were still in the middle of the previous year and never felt like they were quite able to catch up. Ardeth later reflected, "I never learned to spell, and spelling is still a problem for me."

Puzzled as to how to overcome this deficit, years later as an elementary schoolteacher she came up with a creative solution. She told her young students, "I'm not really good in spelling, so every word I write on the board that you have a question about, I want you to look up in your dictionaries. Every time you correct a misspelled word, you'll receive two extra points in spelling!" That idea resulted in benefits for both teacher and pupil. The students gained points and the teacher became more comfortable with what she was writing on the board. Ardeth told them, "We work together on this. You help me and I'll help you."

Ardeth's own school experiences helped her many times when she became a teacher. For instance, when she first began teaching elementary school, she noticed that learning the intricacies of long division continually eluded one of her young students. Because of her earlier struggles in school, she could follow her student's thought patterns. She could recall every wrong way to think about solving the problem and was very patient with the child. As she later remembered, one day her young pupil just exploded, saying, "I've got it, I've got it! I'm not dumb after all!

Finally, you said it right!" Finding the key to unlocking the minds of her students was an extremely rewarding quest.

Difficult experiences were not always limited to the classroom. A trauma that occurred when she was in the third grade remains vivid. One day after school, riding her bike down the steep hill at the side of the school building, she rode headlong into a barbed wire fence stretched across the bottom of the hill. Bleeding profusely from a large gash on her neck, she was near panic. One of the teachers who came to her aid assigned another student to help her get home. Upon seeing the blood, the girl became terrified and tugged on Ardeth's hand, urging her to run faster, saying, "Hurry, hurry! You're bleeding to death! You're going to die!" Although she didn't die, she still carries an indelible thin white line on her neck as a memento of the occasion.

As her school days progressed into weeks, into months, and then into years, Ardeth's feelings of scholastic inadequacy deepened. By the time she was in the sixth grade and approaching the beginning of junior high school, she felt increasingly insecure about her ability to learn. A bout with yellow jaundice (hepatitis) kept her out of school for an extended period of time during the sixth grade. When the final report cards were handed out at the end of the year, Ardeth had failed the grade. She was devastated. All of her friends would be going on without her, and she would have to stay behind with the younger students. She closed her report card so no one could see her disgrace. Her parents were out of town, and she was taking care of the store. "I remember as vividly as if it were today," she recalled. "All of the kids came into the store saying, 'What did you get? What did you get?' I remember thinking, 'I can't reveal this to anyone.'"

When her parents returned she divulged the disturbing news. They immediately went to her rescue. Her dad approached the principal, offering to tutor his daughter to help her catch up with the rest of her class. The principal agreed that she would be allowed to enter the seventh grade if she could prove herself by the beginning of the next school year. All summer long, she and her dad worked to complete the lessons she had missed during her long illness and recovery. "I spent a lot of time with him, learning, practicing, studying. I worked with him on the farm and he would drill me. He made me feel like I could do it." She recalled that although her dad had never graduated from high school and his spelling was as creative as hers, they worked diligently to enable her to rejoin her schoolmates. Finally, she was able to master the requirements and was permitted to move from the sixth to the seventh grade on schedule. Years later she remembered what a traumatic season that was for her.

FROM FAILURE TO TRIUMPH

Although school and studying occupied a good portion of her time, academics were by no means her only activities. The high school, housing grades seven to twelve, was in an old brick building one block from the elementary school. Since each class was small, everyone had opportunities to participate in a variety of activities. They sang in choirs, acted in plays, and played in the town band. As neither Ardeth nor Colleen played an instrument, they became the band majorettes. Colleen's mother, an accomplished seamstress, made their uniforms—red and white satin dresses with short skirts. Tall hats and tall boots completed their outfits. They took their roles seriously. They practiced and practiced under the lilac bush in Colleen's front yard until they could throw, catch, and twirl the baton to their satisfaction.

In the summer of 1946, Glenwood Band was invited to play at the famous Calgary Stampede. This was the ultimate in recognition. The band played yearly at the Raymond Stampede, but since the Calgary Stampede was larger and more selective, the excitement ran high. Going to Calgary, which was three hours away, was a big trip. When Ardeth and Colleen arrived in town, they became separated from the band members and got lost. Frantically they searched for the parade starting point. Out of breath and near tears, they finally arrived only to find that the band had begun their march without them and were well along on the parade route. Running to catch up, they were finally able to step into their accustomed places at the head of the band and

Ardeth and three of her cousins as the Glenwood Band Majorettes. Clockwise from top: Connie Leavitt, Ardeth, Medra Beaves, Colleen Prince. One brother and six additional cousins were also in the band.

marched along, with both their knees and their heads held high. Ardeth was embarrassed and felt as if she had failed once again.

Many years later, she was engaged as a speaker for a group of women gathered at a large conference facility in Calgary for a motivational program. As she pondered returning to the place where she felt she had blown it years earlier, she decided to redeem herself of her past performance. She discussed with her husband, Heber, what she could use as a substitute for the long-discarded twirlers' baton. He purchased a dowel approximating the size of a baton from a lumber yard for her to use. But in the rush to check her luggage at the airport, the dowel was left behind in the trunk of the car.

From her hotel room the evening before the speech, Ardeth called the hotel concierge, telling him of her need for a substitute baton. Unable to come up with a solution, the concierge asked the hotel engineer for help. A short while later, Ardeth answered a knock on her door. There stood the engineer with a smile on his face and a "plumber's friend," minus the rubber end, in his outstretched hand. After thanking him most sincerely, she locked the door and practiced her twirling skills with the makeshift "baton."

Prior to the meeting the next morning, Ardeth placed the baton out of sight behind the speaker's podium. Feeling uncertain as to whether or not she should use it, she proceeded with her talk, entitled "Doubt Not, Fear Not." Standing before the sea of friendly faces, her courage emerged, and she determined to follow her plan. She related the occasion when she had experienced a sense of failure in their city. She explained to the audience that it had remained in her mind for these many years, and with their indulgence she would like to close the door forever on that experience. As she began telling her story, she reached behind the podium and brought out her "baton." First smiles, then laughter erupted from the audience as they recognized the substitution.

She began twirling as she spoke, first one hand and then the other, to the side, in front, and behind her back. Then, in a simulated maneuver, she pretended to throw the baton in the air and catch it. The supportive response encouraged her, and she moved to the side of the podium and began to march in place, back straight, eyes forward, head held high, and knees, now not so high. With her baton raised triumphantly in the air, she received a standing ovation. It was an effective way to connect with the audience in acknowledging that everyone has experiences they would like to resolve so they can move on.

Friendships

One of Ardeth's early experiences with friends occurred during World War II. She helped to form a club whose purpose was to collect tinfoil to assist the war effort. The club members met after school to wrap the collected foil in balls. After some months, thinking her cousin Colleen had been president of the club long enough, Ardeth suggested the club members vote and appoint a new president. She was sure she would be elected. But when the vote was taken, they had voted Ardeth out of the club!

"They didn't know about parliamentary procedure, and I didn't know about winning votes," Ardeth relates, "but I used the best resources that I knew at that time. I went into the back room of our store where we kept all the supplies and took some O'Henry candy bars and distributed them to all of the club members. I bought my way back into the club. Then I learned that when the candy is gone, so is the loyalty! I discovered that there were better ways to win friends."

As she grew older, Ardeth's circle of friends included both girls and boys who enjoyed a variety of social events together. A favorite activity was attending the movies, which were shown every Thursday at the church. "I went to a show called *A Star Is Born,*" she recorded in her diary in February 1946. "My cousin, Keith, came and sat by me just because I had some popcorn. It was a grand show." Three weeks later, shortly after her fifteenth birthday, she wrote, "Saw the cutest show called *State Fair.*" Another time she recorded that she and her friends went to see a movie called *Shine On, Harvest Moon,* but there was a power failure and they couldn't see it.

Often the young people attended dances, picnics, or carnivals in nearby towns. On one such occasion, Ardeth and her brother, Kay, attended a stocking dance in Hillspring, about nine miles from Glenwood. "We wore wool socks and danced to the phonograph. Then we roasted wieners in the fireplace. It sure was fun." Even though he was three years older than Ardeth, Kay often took his younger sister to the dances. On one occasion, the two won a jitterbug contest. "He always included me, which made me feel grown up."

Ardeth never had a serious high school romance, but she did enjoy the company of the young men. One teenage diary entry records: "Never had so much fun in all my life. Went to dance in Cardston and danced with all the boys I wanted to. Wasn't I lucky!" On another occasion, she was looking forward to a special event—a big carnival in Hillspring. She and Colleen were going with two friends. Her anticipation of an exciting evening was dashed the next day. She recorded: "My date phoned to tell me he's sorry, but he has to play for a dance tomorrow night. After doing my hair and everything! If disappointments build character, this little girl's going to have a mighty strong one."

In Ardeth's diary, her name was often linked with that of a young man, though the names frequently changed. In one entry, she confided: "Cleon and I, Connie and Jack, and Nita and Ken all played hooky from school today. Sure had fun!"

Many years later, just prior to the beginning of the Calgary Stake conference, Ardeth, who was then serving as the matron of the Cardston Temple, was seated on the stand next to Cleon, her former school chum, now the stake patriarch. As they were quietly chatting, Ardeth asked, "Did you ever think that we would be sitting on the stand together, preparing to speak at a stake conference?" Cleon responded, "You'd better watch what you say!" She replied, "I will if you will!"

Not long after the stake conference, she came across three prize-winning ribbons Cleon had given her after winning them at a track-and-field meet when they were teenagers. She had tucked them away where they had long since been forgotten. When she saw them again, with his name printed on them, she looked for an opportunity to return them to him. Knowing that he regularly attended the temple, she took them with her. The next time she saw him there, she told him she had something that belonged to him that she wanted to return. He was surprised when she handed him the ribbons. Together they remembered that long-ago day and enjoyed recalling the importance of childhood friends and memories.

It's Obedience

Two days prior to Ardeth's fourteenth birthday, a social and dance was planned to celebrate the anniversary of the organization of the Relief Society on March 17. Everyone looked forward to these special occasions, especially the young people of the town. Church policy was that youth under fourteen could not attend the dances, but everyone else was sure to be there. Even though her fourteenth birthday didn't come until two days after the event, Ardeth was certain her parents would let her go. When she realized her dad's intention to adhere strictly to the rule, she pleaded with him, saying, "Dad, it's only two days! Would you keep me home from a dance that we only have twice a year—to celebrate Christmas and Relief Society? Everyone is going! It's just two days!"

Her dad replied, "It has nothing to do with the dance. It's obedience. You wouldn't break your obedience to wait until you are fourteen for two days would you?"

Ardeth said, "Yes, I would!"

Her dad was quiet, but firm. "It's not the dance. It's obedience."

She didn't attend the dance.

Star

One of Ardeth's most enjoyable activities was horseback riding. She loved the sense of freedom it gave her. One of her dreams was to have her own horse, and she saved her money for what seemed like a very long time. A few days after her thirteenth birthday, she and her dad attended an auction where she found just what she wanted: a brown filly with a white star on her forehead. Since her savings were less than the amount needed to compete in the auction, her dad agreed to make up the difference. He continued to bid until the horse was hers. Not long after she wrote: "The horse isn't hardly broke yet, but I wanted to ride her anyway. Well, I got on and was really having a swell time till I got thrown off. And you should see my jaw. It's as big as a mountain!"

Being thrown didn't deter the plucky youngster from getting back on her horse, and in time she and Star became the best of friends.

"I loved that horse," she recalled. "Star and I would ride through the open fields, and I remember the wind blowing in my face and feeling like I was on top of the world. I think I found a feeling of something that I could do when I was not doing well in school. I didn't have a lot of leisure time, but having the horse was really important to me."

Her dad, who knew how much having a horse meant to

Left: Ardeth's horse, Star, named for the star on her forehead. Right: Ardeth in her buckskin beaded jacket. Her dad painted the fancy design on her boots.

Ardeth, wrote: "There was no greater thrill [to Ardeth] than to dress for a good horseback ride. She would canter over the grassy hills with a soft breeze in her face, or just saunter along with a good friend who was on her own pretty sorrel, while they talked of the last dance party—or maybe the one coming up!"

On her fifteenth birthday, Ardeth's mom and dad gave her a beautiful white buckskin jacket. It was a surprise gift custom-made by someone on the Blood Indian Reservation. Tucked inside the jacket was a note from her parents: "Here's to the gal with the darkest of hair of all of the gals in our beautiful lair. So put on the buckskin, not forgetting the britches, and ride with the best; there is no need for switches." That beautiful "gal with the darkest of hair" and her pony, Star, became a familiar sight as they seemingly flew across the Canadian prairie.

GORDON KAY

Ardeth felt a close bond with her brother. She often accompanied him while he did the chores, just because she liked to talk to him. On one such time they were both sitting on one-legged stools in the barn. Kay was milking a cow, and she was encouraging him to squirt milk into the open mouths of the barn cats encircling her. If he had complied with her pleadings, he later said, there wouldn't have been much milk in the bucket!

When Kay left home to attend college in the fall of 1946, Ardeth wrote, "I'm going to miss Kay a heck of a lot." While he was away at school he began using his first name, Gordon. A year later, he left to serve a mission in Australia. Long after, he wrote how unexpectedly seeing his sister on a newsreel helped him through a bout of homesickness. "One unusual experience occurred when I was half the world away, in considerable distress. Missionaries were allowed to attend movies then, and it was quite routine to show news clips and special features before the main event. My mission started with disruptions, first working in northern California for two months awaiting ocean passage, then being seasick the whole month of travel across the Pacific on a small troop ship just after World War II. I was desperately homesick the first weeks in Sydney. The movie started with film footage of the parade that opened the Calgary Stampede in 1946, and who was playing the Colonel Bogie March, with teenage majorettes strutting before the band? Yes, our Glenwood Band! Seeing Ardeth in her uniform, twirling a baton, lifting her knees high, along with three of our cousins, was like a breath of village air. My homesickness melted, and if it started to return during the three years I was away, I remembered Ardeth's strut and twirl."

Following his mission release, Kay returned home and worked at a variety of jobs to obtain enough money to attend school. Not intent on marriage at the time, he said, "I dated my attractive sister. Ardeth had an eye single to the thought of Elder Kapp, a missionary in Canada who was billeted at our home during an excursion to the temple in Cardston. We must have seemed an unlikely couple at the annual Gold and Green Ball and other social events that year—brother and sister dating."

HER OWN TALKS

Ardeth's initial introduction to public speaking was by giving what were called "two-and-a-half-minute talks" in Sunday School. However, the first talk she gave that felt like a real talk to her was when Kay came home from his mission. He was asked to speak in a sacrament meeting in a nearby ward, and he took her along to speak with him. Giving talks was always a frightening experience, but Ardeth participated when she was asked. On one Sunday, shortly after she turned fifteen, she noted in her diary that she "had to give two talks on Beehive work tonight. I was scared to death but got along okay, I guess."

She loved to read the talks given by Richard L. Evans as part of the Tabernacle Choir's Sunday morning broadcast, *Music and the Spoken Word.* She practiced writing and tried to write a talk like the ones Elder Evans gave. She kept writing until finally she had written a little book of her own talks, dreaming that some day she would be asked to give a talk someplace! Little did she know that as the years went by and her confidence in her speaking abilities increased with experience, she would become a prolific and much sought-after speaker throughout the Church. Eventually, a few of her talks and articles were included in two of her books, *My Neighbor, My Sister, My Friend* (Salt Lake City: Deseret Book, 1990), *The Joy of the Journey* (Salt Lake City: Deseret Book, 1992), and others.

A Sacred Pilgrimage

The summer Ardeth was fifteen, her dad and the father of her friend, Orva Lybbert, took the two teens and four of their girlfriends on a pack-horse trip up to the head of the Canadian Rockies. "We had a big pack-horse, as well as our own horses, and we rode for ten days. We camped every night and never saw any other human beings. We were just in nature with a lot of wildlife." This exploration of the rugged mountains that kept watch over her prairie home was a life-changing event for the young girl. Her discovery of the majesty of God's creations made a profound impression on her youthful heart. She later wrote about her experience:

"Once into the mountains we began to see and feel and experience things we had not even anticipated. It was as if scales were falling from our eyes as the colors, shapes, sounds, and smells crowded in to be part of this great adventure. The silver drops of dew left on the freshly washed leaves in the morning, the bubbling song of the crowned kinglet of midday, the shadows of the evening advancing along the rocks, and the whispering pines at night all added to this vision that was opening up before us. . . .

"As if visiting a friend's splendid home, we tried to partake of all the beauty around us—to look, admire, and understand the value of such precious possessions; to take nothing with us; and to leave things as nearly undisturbed as possible. The value of everything seen was enhanced because of the beauty and appreciation awakened within the heart of those who were prepared to receive what was there to share. . . .

"Our mountains were never the same to me after that. Our packhorse trip had turned out to be a pilgrimage, a journey to a sacred place. It was in the mountains that I saw the sun filter through the leaves like rays of heavenly light bridging heaven and earth and casting a celestial glow that revealed only the beautiful and sacred—the majesty of all God's living things. And He was there, secluded yet very near" (*Echoes from My Prairie* [Salt Lake City: Bookcraft, 1979], 26–27, 33).

Ardeth often drew from these early experiences later when she taught and spoke to young women throughout the Church. Reflecting on the source of her ability to teach from her own experience, she is quick to give credit to her parents' guidance in helping her to learn from the commonplace, everyday activities with which she grew up. "In the store there was always much to do which involved working with other people. I observed how Mother unfailingly treated every individual with courtesy and respect. On the farm, it was just Dad and me. We would survey ditches and build fences. Dad would always say, 'Keep your eye on the horizon. Don't look down.' It seemed to me that there was a lesson in every part of life."

NEW HORIZONS

Even though school continued to be difficult for her, Ardeth studied hard for exams, always hoping that "it would do some good." After she failed the sixth grade, she spent the summer making up the work and caught up with her class. Her continuing efforts paid off. At the end of the next year, she recorded: "I passed with all A's except one and that was a B. Pretty good, eh?"

However, as she began high school, in September 1946, her feelings regarding her scholastic abilities had undergone little change. She still felt as though she wasn't as smart as her classmates. On the first day of the new fall term she recorded, "Started school today. I hope I like it." Her next comment was revelatory: "Shirley started this morning. I feel sorry for her to think she has thirteen years ahead."

Late in the summer of 1946, when she was fifteen, her dad said that if she would work hard to get good grades he would take her to Salt Lake City for the October general conference. As Ardeth had never been farther from home than the three-hour trip to Calgary, she was very excited at the prospect. Accordingly, on October 1, she and her dad set out on their trip to Utah. Her mother stayed at home to work in the store and care for her two little sisters. They drove as far as Pocatello, Idaho, the first day and spent the night with Kay, who was then a student at Idaho State University. That evening Kay took her to a school dance, where she had a wonderful time. The next day, they stopped to see both the Idaho Falls and Logan temples, which she pronounced as "grand!" Finally arriving in Salt Lake City, she looked upon the majestic Salt Lake Temple for the first time. "Oh, what a beautiful temple!" she recorded in her journal.

She had been taught to view the temple as the university of the Lord. On one occasion she walked around the Cardston Temple grounds with her parents. They explained to her that instead of worrying that she was dumb, she should focus on being good. Then one day, if she was obedient in keeping God's commandments, rather than simply walking around outside of the temple, she could go inside. There she would learn all she needed to know to return to her Heavenly Father. If she was obedient, they said, she could become an honor student in the Lord's university. Although it might be possible to get a degree from one or more universities of the world, if she were to miss the temple, she would miss the highest degree in the celestial kingdom.

On October 4, 1946, Ardeth attended her first general conference in the Salt Lake Tabernacle. Sitting with her dad in the north balcony, she watched attentively as President George Albert Smith stood at the podium, ready to conduct the conference. She was almost overcome with the realization that she was actually seeing the prophet. She also saw the organ and heard the Tabernacle Choir sing "Come, Come, Ye Saints." Thirty-eight years later she stood at that same pulpit to address a general conference.

Two days later they headed for home, stopping again in Pocatello to spend time with her brother. After spending the next night in Helena, Montana, they arrived safely home. "Back in good old Alberta today on these rough old roads," she recorded, "but am sure glad to be home, although I had a wonderful time."

Returning to school the next day, Ardeth had to work hard to catch up on her missed schoolwork, but she didn't mind. The trip had been worth it. It would also prove to be a turning point in her young life. The experience helped her anticipate that things would eventually turn to her good. It was from this point in her life that she began to see beyond the end of the road that she viewed through her kitchen window.

Although she knew her studies were important, Ardeth sometimes justified procrastination. One winter evening, with nothing else to do, she decided to spend the evening studying when a note was delivered from Colleen. The note read: "Dear Ardeth, I've got an idea. Why don't you come down and we'll pop popcorn and then study together. Bet we could accomplish a lot. Mom and Dad are going to town and I couldn't possibly stay alone. I'll get Mom to leave a recipe for that candy to go on the popcorn and will you put some peanuts on the bill and bring them down? We can eat and study like fury. Of course you'll stay all night. Be sure and put up a good argument to your Mom." Ardeth's subsequent diary entry chronicled the evening: "Planned to stay home and study tonite. Colleen's mom and dad went to town so she said come down and make candy, popcorn and study. I went down and stayed all night. The candy was good, the popcorn was swell. (We didn't study.)"

WINTERS

Winters in Alberta are long, snowy, often windy, and bitter cold. During the winter of 1947, Ardeth recorded in her diary that the roads were blocked so that no one could get in or out of town. The weekly movies were cancelled, as were dances, parties, and, occasionally, Church meetings. "It was so cold today," Ardeth recorded on January 29, 1947, "33 degrees below zero. Some winter." On these occasions, staying home and making their own fun was the best option for her family. As Ardeth wrote in her diary two days later, "I wanted to go to town to the Sadie Hawkins dance but it was 25 degrees below, so Aunt Laverne and Uncle Jim, Aunt Lamoine and Uncle Jack, Mom and Dad and Colleen and I stayed home and played Rook."

Another year she did go to the dance in subzero weather. In *Echoes from My Prairie,* Ardeth told about that eventful, life-threatening night. She and her date had traveled through very cold weather to the social center in Cardston for a Christmas dance. When the dance was over it was forty degrees below zero.

"The Indian reservation lay between our town and Cardston," she recalled. "There were very few houses sprinkled across this vast area—no other building, no trees, nothing to break the harsh wind that swept across the road against the snow fences, carving cavities in the high drifts.

"About three miles out, we spotted a car along the side of the road. The danger to life and limb on a night such as this would never allow anyone to consider passing someone up, not anyone.

. . . Without wasting time for talk, two couples who turned out to be our friends crowded into our car. . . .

"Their gas line had frozen up. It was decided that we should turn around and go back to Cardston. If a garage was still open, we could get something that would thaw the gas line and take care of that problem.

"Before leaving town the second time, I went into the garage and called home. . . . I explained the details of our plight but assured [Dad] that everything was going to be all right. But just in case of trouble, we checked our watches and determined about what time we should arrive home. If we were not on schedule, he should come to our rescue.

"Again we started out across the reservation. The wind chill continued to lower the temperature. We reached our friends' car, but their efforts to start it were in vain and continued attempts only increased the danger to all of us. Without any discussion we crowded together in one car, grateful for the added warmth of so many bodies, and headed for home."

They traveled only a few miles farther when their own car froze up. "While we watched the snow swirling in front of the windshield, we listened to each other's suggestions as to what we might do. The side windows were already frozen over. Yet we felt a great sense of relief, there in the quiet of the car, when I reminded everyone that I had called home."

After they had waited a few minutes, an old truck pulled up. Some Indians from the reservation hooked a chain to the bumper of the stranded car and pulled it to the turnoff.

"At the turnoff they unhooked their chain from our car, and

we thanked them most sincerely. As they drove out of sight, threat of the cold again weighed on us. We waited.

"'How long do you think it will be before your Dad will get here?' questioned someone in the backseat.

"'Well,' I explained, 'if he waits until the time we should have been home before he leaves, we'll have to wait at least another half hour.'

"While no one complained, we all felt that it would be a long half hour, even huddled together under the two blankets we always carried during winter travel. With our fingernails we tried to scrape a small opening in the frost-coated windows so we could watch for any sign of car lights coming from the west.

"I kept thinking how glad I was that I had called home, and yet I knew that even without the call, if we were later than we were expected to be, Dad would be out after us. . . . I remembered the time some years before when dad had come after me because it was late. But that time it was a summer party and I didn't need him. In fact, I was so embarrassed I thought I would die. Tonight, I knew that his coming would allow us to live. Reports of people freezing to death while stranded along the country roads at this time of year were not infrequent.

"'Your dad is coming!' someone shouted, 'I can see his lights!'

"We were sure no one else would be coming in this direction on a night like this. I realized that Dad had not waited to come to our rescue. He must have left home right after my call, waiting only long enough to warm up his car before taking off across the reservation. . . . As the lights drew closer we began singing,

'For he's a jolly, good fellow,' assured now that our safety and comfort were only minutes away.

"A man got out of his car, his bulky parka almost obscuring his face, but there was no question that it was my dad. . . . We all piled into his car, even more crowded now with nine people, and safely returned home.

"Later, I thought about what might have happened if the telephone lines had been down, as they sometimes were during severe winter storms, but then I realized that Dad would have been there when we needed him anyway. He always knew where we were and when we should be home, and he came after us if we weren't there" (*Echoes from My Prairie,* 85–88).

A Landmark Experience

Ardeth occasionally suffered with painful earaches, but neither she nor her parents were concerned that they were anything but temporary infections from which she would quickly recover. One of these occurred in the spring of 1947, shortly after her sixteenth birthday. Her parents were away on a long-anticipated vacation in California. The children were left in the care of Grandma Greene. Her mom and dad had been hesitant to leave. Ardeth had a cold, and they knew she would have to spend time in the store. However, she said her cold was much improved and encouraged them to go. They were rarely able to have a holiday, and it had been planned for some time. She assured them that she would be fine, and she would have help in the store. She could lie down on the cot in the back room if necessary.

Her parents had been gone only a few days when she developed a serious ear infection. The pain in her ear became unbearable. The local doctor explained to her grandmother that her condition was serious and required immediate surgery. Her aunt and uncle rushed her to the hospital in Calgary, three hours away. As they drove past the Calgary City Cemetery, she thought: "I'm probably going to die, but I hope Mom and Dad won't feel guilty about being gone."

The doctors rushed Ardeth into surgery immediately. Kay was the only one of her siblings old enough to recognize the seriousness of the situation. Left at home with his two young sisters, he desperately prayed that she would live through the surgery. Her aunt and uncle stayed with her until her parents, who had been informed of her condition by telephone, reached her side sometime the next day. They had driven all day and all night, not even stopping at home. Tired and worried as they were, she could feel their love and concern as they spoke with her and held her hands. Her father placed his hands on her bandaged head and pronounced a blessing, which immediately filled her with a wonderful feeling of peace. Her mother also explained that she would arrange to have her name placed on the prayer roll of the Cardston Temple. Although Ardeth had never heard of the temple prayer roll, something in the tone of her mother's voice assured her that all would be well. She hoped she was worthy of having her name written in the temple.

The type of surgery that she underwent was life-threatening. The doctors told her parents that the infection had been so severe that if she lived there was a high chance she would lose her equilibrium as well as the hearing in the infected ear. Since she didn't understand what "equilibrium" was, as she began to recover her main concern was that her head had been shaved on one side! "My hair was very thick and very long. I combed the remaining hair over to the other side, but it just wouldn't stay!"

"Within weeks I could walk steadily, and my hearing was back to normal. Instead of losing my hearing in the infected left ear, it has remained stronger than in my right. . . . Since that frightening experience years ago, I have become acquainted with another kind of hearing, not with my ears but rather in my mind and my heart. Through that traumatic experience in my youth, I have a better understanding of how I was saved from what I feared might be a premature funeral" (*The Temple, Our Home Away from Home* [Salt Lake City: Deseret Book, 2003], 45–46).

Years later, as matron of the Cardston Temple, Ardeth watched over the prayer roll in the very temple where her mother had placed her name so many years before. Observing those who paused to write the name of a loved one in need of a special blessing, she could testify, from heartfelt experience, to the power of prayer.

Although profoundly grateful for the success of the surgery, she again found herself in the unwelcome and all-too-familiar situation of falling behind in her studies. Her recovery following the surgery stretched over a period of several weeks. After her return to school she recorded, "I'm so far behind and so discouraged I don't know what to do. They say a quitter never wins, and a winner never quits." But by the end of the school year, she had failed to complete the required classes necessary to move on to the twelfth grade. Her parents pondered a solution that might help her catch up.

She quickly regained both her health and her optimistic attitude. The school year ended, and she once again enjoyed the dances, movies, parties, and picnics that were so much a part of her summertime. She returned to her work in the store and helped with the farmwork. The family also prepared for Kay's departure to serve in the Australian Mission. As happy as she was for his willingness to go, she knew that his leaving would create a void in her life.

MISSIONARIES

An unexpected event eclipsed everything else that happened that summer. On a Saturday afternoon in late June, with Ardeth excited at the prospect of attending a dance that evening, her dad approached her with a special request. Four missionaries were coming for dinner. Since her mother was in the hospital with pneumonia, he asked if she would consider skipping the dance in favor of fixing supper for them. Reluctant to miss the weekly social event, she searched for an alternate plan. Assuming her father was referring to the stake missionaries, she thought her grandmother would enjoy the company of the older gentlemen. "What about Grandma, Dad? If she could come, she could fix their supper and make them feel welcome."

"Yes, she could," he replied, "but it wouldn't be the same."

"Oh, why doesn't he just say I can't go?" she thought. "How can I be mad at him when he leaves the decision up to me?"

Quite certain that no one had ever been called upon to sacrifice so much, she reluctantly agreed to his request. With the attitude of a martyr, she prepared a meal of tomato soup and grilled cheese sandwiches.

Years later, Ardeth wrote about that evening in one of her books: "With the last of the sandwiches prepared, . . . I heard a car drive into the yard. I walked to the window to see the cause of my weekend deprivation. Could it be? I blinked my eyes once and then again. Dad hadn't told me. I didn't know. I wondered if he had known. The thoughts of missing the dance that had crowded my mind until I could think of nothing else suddenly dissipated. I hurried to the bathroom just off the kitchen and combed my hair, grateful that it still looked nice. Did I really look sixteen? I wondered. Maybe just a little older, I hoped.

"Wanting to appear casual, I returned to the kitchen just as the missionaries came through the side door, . . . four handsome knights in shining armor—courageous and bold, righteous and hungry. Dad, I thought, I'll always do what you want. Just ask anytime.

" . . . Although I had somehow lost my appetite, everyone else seemed to enjoy his supper. . . . The consensus was that the sandwiches were delicious; and someone even said the tomato soup was good, which relieved me very much.

" . . . After supper, while I cleared the table and did the dishes, our guests sat around the table visiting with my family—all except one guest, that is. One of the missionaries helped me dry the dishes" (*Echoes from My Prairie,* 74–75).

Her diary entries are brief but revealing: "We had four Mormon missionaries come for supper tonite. Elder Kapp, Elder Nixon, Elder Kjar and Elder Watson. All wonderful men." The following day, a Sunday, she reported: "Elder Kapp and Elder Nixon stayed overnight. Elder Kapp asked to take our picture. He's certainly wonderful. And gave a grand talk. We had six missionaries speak in church tonight." On Monday morning she wrote: "The Elders left this morning. Mom's in the hospital and

I cooked for them. Elder Kapp thought it was O.K. We made a date to meet at the B.Y. in 1949!"

After the missionaries left, she returned to the bedroom where they had slept, looking for anything that might possibly serve as evidence that Elder Kapp had actually been there. In the wastebasket she spotted laundry labels from his shirt. She knew they were from his shirt by the location of the laundry printed on the labels, which corresponded to the field of labor where he was serving. Rescuing them from the basket, she tucked them away in a corner of her dresser drawer. In the privacy of her room, she often held them in her hand as a visual reminder of their first meeting.

In his journal, Elder Kapp recorded his version of their first meeting: "Met the bishop's daughter. She is cute and fun but kind of young."

A Missionary and a Testimony

After what seemed like a very long time, a letter addressed to "The Greene Family" was delivered to their mailbox. "Got a real nice letter from Elder Kapp today with some pictures of he and Elder Nixon," Ardeth wrote. Elder Kapp had also included the picture he had taken of Ardeth and her family as they stood on the steps, waving good-bye to the missionaries. Ardeth persuaded her mother to let her write a letter to Elder Kapp and thank him for sending the pictures. June was reluctant about letting her daughter write to the missionary. Although she yielded to Ardeth's request, the letter was written under her watchful eye and was signed by the whole family.

For several weeks Ardeth waited excitedly for the mail. Finally, her patience was rewarded. A letter came from Elder

Kapp, thanking her for writing the thank-you letter! Scribbled in very small letters on one corner was a message meant for her eyes only. Her heart sang as she read the words: "See you at the Y in 1949!"

One year later, Ardeth accompanied her father to the annual missionary conference held in Cardston. They were invited to sit near the front of the chapel. Elder Kapp, then serving as a district president, was sitting on the stand. Although no words of affection or attraction had ever been spoken or written between them, her heart beat faster as her eyes dared to glance at him during the opening song, which she remembers singing earnestly, "I Need Thee Every Hour."

The testimonies borne by the young elders filled the room with a spirit that was indescribable. "As I left the chapel located on the second floor of what was called the Social Center, right at the top of the stairs was a large picture of the Prophet Joseph Smith. I had not remembered seeing it before. That day, the overwhelming feeling of the reality of the restoration of the gospel and the importance of the Prophet, Joseph Smith, was so real that it felt like the picture was speaking to me. I hurried to the car without speaking to anyone. When I got home, I went to my bedroom where I could be alone. I didn't want to ever lose the feeling that had completely consumed my full attention."

ANOTHER CHANCE

The summer passed, and Ardeth struggled to catch up with her classmates. With so few students in each grade, subjects were taught on alternate years. There was no opportunity for making up a failed class the following year. Partly as a result of her prolonged absence from the ear infection the previous spring, she was not prepared to go on with her class to the twelfth grade. Again, she was devastated. The only solution seemed to be for her to sit out the school year.

Once again, she was faced with the prospect of her classmates going on without her while she remained behind to study with the younger students the following year. Once again her parents approached the principal regarding ways to help her catch up to her classmates. His response: "Don't be concerned about it. She's not college material anyway!" If she had needed further confirmation of her inability to learn, this was it. Although she could see no favorable solution, her parents consoled her by saying, "If they don't have any more confidence in you than that, you need to have a fresh start. We'll do what we have to do."

Not knowing what her parents meant by a fresh start, Ardeth was both surprised and excited when they arranged for her to complete her senior year at Brigham Young High School in Provo, Utah. There she could make up the work she had missed during her illness. In order to complete all of the credits needed for graduation, she would have to take a correspondence course in addition to attending the classes taught during the school day.

Although frightened at leaving home so soon, she was determined to succeed with this new opportunity she had been given. "I don't know how my mom and dad ever, first of all, decided that they could afford it; second, that they trusted me that much; and third, that they were willing to give me a chance when my history didn't really justify it," she later recalled. "I went to Provo feeling like my parents were laying everything on the line to give me another chance, and I didn't have a lot of confidence that I would ever be successful."

CHAPTER FOUR

B. Y. High

Away from Home

Early in the morning of September 3, 1948, Ardeth and her dad set off for Provo, Utah, where she would attend Brigham Young High School for her senior year. "I had an awful feeling in my stomach when I realized each turn of the wheel was taking me farther from home," she wrote in her journal that night. Ardeth was uncertain about this new adventure. She was aware that her parents were making a sacrifice to give her another chance with her education. She knew they believed in her. But she didn't have a lot of confidence that she would vindicate their trust.

Although nervous about this new adventure, she enjoyed the travel and recorded: "This is the first day of my trip, and so far it has been grand. I only hope I will enjoy my stay in Provo as much as I have enjoyed the first day. What if I get lost after Dad leaves!" Arriving in Provo the following evening, she wrote, "Provo is a beautiful little city and the school buildings and campus are just wonderful. Things are going swell as long as Dad's here, but I guess when he leaves it will be a little hard to keep from getting homesick." By the time her dad left for home a couple of days later, Ardeth was both excited and a bit frightened at being on her own. "As a kid I always longed for such a chance. But it seems funny—I have no desire to do anything I haven't done before."

Arrangements had been made for her to live in an off-campus apartment with a group of girls who were attending Brigham Young University. Since high school began several days before the start of college classes, she stayed in temporary housing while waiting for her roommates to arrive. Even though she was the only high school student among them, she wanted to be part of the group. Moving into the apartment a few days after her school had started, she wrote, "The other girls arrived tonight and they're all nice people—a lot of fun. Four out of the eight of us are writing to missionaries."

Even though she was happy in Provo, she couldn't help thinking about what was happening at home. "Tonight in Waterton, Mart Kenny is playing for a big dance. Gee, I'd like to be there, but still I'm glad I'm here." Letters from home as well as those from a certain Elder Kapp eased her homesickness and helped her adjust to her new community. "Golly, Provo is a wonderful place. I sure wish Mom and Dad would move down and bring our house. I have been in Provo just one week tonight and it's wonderful!"

On her second Sunday in Provo, the ward Sunday School superintendency visited Ardeth and issued a call for her to teach a Sunday School class. As they visited for a few minutes, each of the men expressed appreciation for her willingness to accept the call. They also said they felt she would work well with the young people in her class and, given her diligence and enthusiasm, she would become an outstanding teacher. "I told them I was thankful for the opportunity and would be glad to accept the call."

The much-anticipated first day of school arrived. "Today was my first day of school and I was really frightened because I didn't know how to register or what subjects I needed." She was also afraid she would get lost (which she did), but by the end of the day, she was able to record: "Everything worked out swell and I got all the courses I wanted. I think school is really going to be swell this year. . . . Met a lot of new kids and had a perfect day."

Even though the first day went better than she had anticipated, she couldn't help noticing some differences between herself and the other students. She had dressed simply in a white cotton blouse and a plain navy skirt, only to find that she looked different from the other girls, most of whom were dressed in plaid skirts, with the particularly stylish girls wearing the highly coveted Jantzen sweaters and Joyce shoes. She thought to herself, "Wow! If I could ever dress like that I would think I was the fanciest girl in the world!"

Ardeth's experience in making new friends was limited, since she had never been around anyone other than those she grew up with, many of whom were relatives. She wasn't sure how to go about making friends with her new schoolmates. Knowing only one other person in the whole school, a girl from Cardston, she was lonely and homesick. She wasn't part of any group and felt that she didn't fit in anywhere. Even if they had asked her, she didn't have the money to do the things that the other kids did.

Although she worried about fitting in and having friends, each day of school seemed better than the last. "Today we started our classes and they're just wonderful. The teachers just seem to be one of us." Then a few days later: "Another wonderful day of school. It just seems like a holiday instead of school." Viewing school as something to be enjoyed was an about-face for Ardeth, but she found herself enjoying her classes and was determined to be successful in her studies.

BE A FRIEND

As the days passed, Ardeth's desire for friends increased. Although no one was unkind to her, she nevertheless felt a long way from home—alone and lonely. It seemed that everyone else had friends and belonged in some way. She wondered how she could get in. Finally, she decided to take the problem to the One she knew could help her. Kneeling at the side of her bed, she poured out her seventeen-year-old heart to her Heavenly Father. Night after night she prayed for friends—girlfriends, boyfriends, friends young or old, member or nonmember. She pleaded, "Heavenly Father, if you'll help me get through school and help me to have friends, I promise that I will try to do what is right in every way. Please help me know how to have friends." She knew that if she would be totally obedient to the commandments, as she had been taught, her Heavenly Father would make up the difference.

At the end of one such prayer, the feeling came over Ardeth that she should *be* a friend. The thought came to her mind that there may be others who felt as lonely as she did. She thought, "Maybe I should try to forget about myself and be a friend first. I can smile, and I can say 'Hi' to everyone I meet." Ever obedient to the promptings of the Spirit, she set out to put her new idea into practice. She began to focus more on being a friend than on having one. At first it was difficult to extend herself in this way, but the more she did it, the easier it became.

Soon she found herself being included in activities with her fellow students. The initial weeks of the term brought a series of "firsts." Among others, she attended her first football game, went to a zoo for the first time, and had a date for her first high school dance.

CHALLENGES

Her first telephone call from a boy remains vivid in her mind. Her roommates all enjoyed an active social life. Their boyfriends were in and out of the apartment, escorting their dates to games, dances, and parties. Finally, a male voice asked to speak to Ardeth. Her excited roommates crowded around so as not to miss a word of the conversation. The caller was a boy from school. He asked, "Would you go to a movie with me?" Since it was a Sunday, she asked, "Today?" He responded: "Well, sure. You can go to church first."

Conflicting thoughts crowded her mind. She had been praying that she could have a date. Was this an answer to her prayer? But it was Sunday. Did it really matter that much? She so much wanted to have friends and to be accepted. Would her parents, who had put such trust in her, find out? Maybe she could go and then repent afterwards. Then she thought of her promise to her Heavenly Father that she would always try to do what was right. She remembered that he had said, "I, the Lord, am bound when ye do what I say" (D&C 82:10). Whether her parents would know or not, she knew that she had to remain true to what she had been taught and knew to be right. Despite her desire to be accepted, she knew her answer had to be "No." She was afraid that he might never call again, and he never did. But she had been true to herself and to what she had been taught. She determined then and there that she would never let her parents down, nor would she break her promise to her Heavenly Father. She later reflected that this experience was as hard a test as she had ever had.

Ardeth's parents had provided enough money to allow her to finish her schooling away from home, but there wasn't much left over for extras. She remembers walking past an ice cream parlor on her way home from school, thinking that if she really saved her money, she might be able to buy an ice cream cone the following month. Even though she wished for a little more money, she appreciated the opportunity her parents were giving her to prove herself and to graduate from high school on schedule.

Despite these challenges, school and all of the accompanying activities seemed to grow more and more exciting for the young Canadian. "I went to a big football game tonight with Ken, a friend from home who is attending Brigham Young University," she wrote. "It is really pretty to see huge bands march around at the stadium." A few days later she recorded, "Another week of school and it's been swell."

Ardeth was happy to see her parents when they traveled to Utah in October for general conference. They drove to Provo to pick her up, then returned to Salt Lake City, where they stayed for a few days. In addition to conference, the trio attended the reunion of the Western Canadian missionaries. "I really had a nice time, met several elders I know and lots who said they knew

Elder Kapp. Sure is nice to be with the folks again." A highlight of general conference was the opportunity to shake hands with Richard L. Evans, whose talks she had so admired. When her parents left for home, she wished that she could return with them for a few days. But the short time she spent with them had buoyed her spirits.

FINDING FRIENDS

Fall term sped by, and before she knew it, Ardeth found herself on the way home for the Christmas holidays. As excited and happy as she was to be with her family and long-time friends again, she found, to her surprise, that she was also eager to return to Provo and her increasing circle of friends at B.Y. High. At the beginning of the new year, she was so busy with school work and school activities that she scarcely found time to chronicle her days in her journal. Her efforts to be a friend were bearing fruit as she now found herself part of a large group of friends.

Elder Kapp as a young missionary. After meeting the bishop's 16-year-old daughter, Ardeth, he recorded in his journal, "Met the bishop's daughter. She is cute and fun but kind of young."

In February she wrote, "On the 12th we had a large assembly at school for the purpose of choosing a queen for our Sweetheart Ball. Out of twelve girls up for Queen, a very good friend of mine was chosen, and I, along with another girl, was chosen to be an attendant." As a result of her increasing popularity, her schedule was filled with parties, dances, games, and Church activities. She enjoyed her friends, which included both boys and girls, as well as the social activities they attended.

Ardeth also delighted in her Church activities, particularly the Sunday School class she was teaching. Striving to magnify her calling, she tried to always prepare lessons that would teach gospel truths to her students.

A Growing Testimony

As Ardeth matured socially, she was also maturing spiritually. Her testimony continued to grow in significant ways. In a talk she gave many years later, she said, "Let me tell you about an old set of scriptures that my mom and dad gave me when I turned seventeen. I had read the Book of Mormon before, but one day it was different. Perhaps I was more in tune with the Spirit, or maybe I had studied more diligently and prayed more fervently. I was young, but I wanted to know for myself if the Book of Mormon was true. On that particular day I came to the part about faith in the thirty-second chapter of Alma. As I finished that chapter, I experienced a feeling that I recognized as a witness from the Holy Ghost—I knew the Book of Mormon was true. I wanted to stand up and shout. I wanted to tell the whole world what I knew and how I felt, but I was alone. So with tears of joy streaming down my face, I wrote on the margin all the way around the page the feelings in my heart at that moment. I made a big red star in the margin on the top of the page and wrote, "May 31st, 7:30 A.M. This I know, written as if to me." Then I wrote in the margin on one side, "I have received a confirmation. I know the Book of Mormon is true." Across the margin on the other side I wrote, "One month ago I began fasting each Tuesday for a more sure knowledge. This I know" (Ardeth Greene Kapp, *I Walk by Faith* [Salt Lake City: Deseret Book, 1987, 29).

A LETTER FROM DAD

As much as she missed her parents' constant companionship, she had not realized the extent to which they missed her until she received a letter from her dad a few weeks after her visit home for Christmas. The letter was written with a great deal of nostalgia that reflected his increasing awareness that his oldest daughter's life was on the brink of a major change and a realization that she might never live at home again for more than just a short period of time.

"Dear Ardeth," he wrote, "We have known each other for a long time, and I'm sure that at one time I had very little competition. Those were lovely years and I look back on them now as some of the finest in my life. There was no thought at that time there could be another one come between us (so to speak) and I anticipated your wishes with a great deal of joy and satisfaction and hope that I would always be able to satisfy them. . . . Since you have been gone from me so long, I have come to wonder with a kind of regret if I will ever again be so important to you.

"Love is a grand thing and whatever the future may bring I will always cherish the years when we were so much together. I recall carrying you around in my arms and pinching those chubby cheeks, making braces for those ankles which had a tendency to bend. . . . Watching the development in poise and movement as dancing lessons progressed, and then when you were requested to add color to the band by marching out in front with a lovely smile and smart step. How I looked upon you with such possessive pride.

"I taught you to ride a horse, and only once, which I regret now, did I find time to go with you into the grand and glorious mountains to drink the streams and ride the trails, milk the deer, and make camp in a rainstorm.

"I also taught you to drive a car, which you do in no mean fashion, even to trusting the lives of four fine missionaries in your care.

"Well, these are things which I remember with so much love and affection. I'm sure you will understand my feelings toward young upstarts who come barging in with such a possessive air. Honestly, I don't believe I would be able to stand it if it wasn't for the life and love of your dear mother. She was a lovely girl, much like your own sweet self, and so loyal, as I know you to be.

"Then there is another thing which means so much to each of us and that is the gospel of our Lord and Savior. I recall helping you learn memory gems and little talks and encourage you to take advantage of your opportunities. How well you have done this is evidenced by your attitude today and the joy you find in these principles. And to now see you showing your appreciation by accepting responsibility in Sunday School teaching.

"You can see what I mean when I say that when some young upstart wants to beat my time, I want him to be a real, genuine, down-to-earth, up and coming young man worthy of the title 'Latter-day Saint.'

"Right now in my mind's eye, I see a dark-eyed daughter, dark hair flowing under a sombrero, of a lovable, lovely young lady in green breeches and buckskin jacket with a fine brown filly at her side, anxious to take her for a canter across a green meadow or on a hill situated against the skyline of life.

"Guess it must be me that's homesick."

He signed the letter, "Lots of Love to my Darling Daughter, Dad."

DAD WAS RIGHT

About a month later Ardeth recorded: "Speaking of excitement! I was at the dentist's and Lorna and Margaret dashed down to tell me Kapp was in town and had come down to the house twice to see me, also went to the library and couldn't find me." Although she had often thought about the message printed on the corner of a long-ago letter, she could scarcely believe that he had returned from his mission and their meeting was about to become a reality!

Urging the dentist to complete his work as quickly as possible, she arrived home just in time to answer the phone and hear his voice. "He said he would be down at 7:00. Golly, I was so excited!" Promptly at 7:00 P.M., Heber arrived with his friend, Max. This was their first meeting outside the mission field, and Ardeth was truly happy to see him. Heber was living with his family in South Weber, near Ogden, Utah. Since he had no car of his own, he had ridden to Provo with his friend, hoping to spend time with her before returning home. That evening, as luck would have it, she had a date to the junior prom. Though disappointed that she was unable to spend more time with Heber, she recorded: "It was sure grand to see him again. He hasn't changed at all. He and Max have to go back to Ogden tonight. I went to the Prom and had a nice time, although I had a hard time trying to keep my mind on the dance. My date is a nice kid, but Kapp's sure got something."

As anxious as she was to speak with him again, days went by without any word from Heber. At the end of two weeks he still had made no further contact. Ardeth decided to fast all day Sunday and pray that he would try to see her again. On Sunday evening, Heber, who had again come to Provo with his friend, called and asked if they could get together and talk. They visited for much of the evening.

Since Heber was serving a full-time mission at the time of their first meeting, most of their interaction had taken place via the postal service. Other than through their letters, they had had no opportunity to broaden their friendship. Although he was now home, there were still almost a hundred miles between them, making a steady courtship difficult. Heber either had to catch a ride with a friend, ride the bus, or hitchhike his way to Provo, which he did on occasion. He made his way down as often as circumstances would allow. Since money was scarce, their dates often consisted of walking and talking.

Just prior to spring break, Heber called and asked if she would spend Easter weekend with him and his family at their home in South Weber. Wishing to have no deception about his late request, he confessed to having invited another girl first, but after the girl cancelled at the last minute, he decided to ask Ardeth. As she had been wishing for the opportunity to become better acquainted with the young man she knew mainly by correspondence, she agreed to go.

They traveled by bus to Salt Lake City, where they met members of his family who took them the rest of the way to South Weber. She was happy to get acquainted with Heber's mother, not realizing that it would be their only meeting. Even though Sister Kapp was ill, she accompanied them into the mountains for a picnic. Ardeth and Heber enjoyed a variety of events with his family, including church on Sunday. "Heber's family is very nice. They have a nice home and I really enjoyed myself," she recorded in her journal.

April general conference came shortly after Easter. As was their custom, Ardeth's parents traveled to Utah to attend the sessions. This provided an opportunity for them to become better acquainted with Heber, who by now was frequently making the trip to Provo.

REWARDS

Not long after her parents' return home, Ardeth began to realize that graduation was only a few short weeks away. At the conclusion of each school year, B.Y. High School selected one boy and one girl as the representative students for the year, chosen by vote of the students. "Much to my surprise, I was fortunate enough to be the one, and had my picture in the yearbook. I felt it was a great honor, especially since it was my first year at the school. However, it was a thrill which I only hope I was worthy of. I desire to live an exemplary life that I might be worthy of being called the Representative Girl of such a wonderful high school."

A school newspaper writer was lavish in praise of the newly

elected representative. "There is nothing foreign about Canadian-born Ardeth Greene. Her friendly nature and sparkling personality have been a welcome addition to 'Y' high and our only regret is that she waited till her senior year to come here to school. In the recent election, . . . Ardeth was chosen from the senior high and her reaction to this election was, 'the biggest surprise of my life, but I feel very honored and hope I am worthy of it.'

"Ardeth . . . thinks Provo is wonderful . . . and claims the B.Y. student body to be 'the friendliest bunch of kids you'd ever want to meet.' Music, food, sports, dates, dancing, school, all make up most of Ardeth's likes, but she emphasizes her one dislike—insincere people. Ardeth is looking forward to graduation but feels bad about having to leave her many friends. She plans to attend the college to study elementary teaching."

The participants for the graduation program were selected from the ten students with the highest scholastic standing, of which Ardeth was one. Her desire had been to do well enough in her last year of her high school to justify her parents' trust in her. She had done this and more, achieving things she had never even dreamed of at the beginning of the year.

The last few days of school were spent in preparation for graduation day. She also received her first yearbook and enjoyed exchanging autographs with her friends as they said good-bye to each other. One observation in her yearbook would prove to be accurate: "I don't need to wish you luck, for someone as wonderful and intelligent as you will never need luck. Your own effort, your achievements, your excellence in all things will speak for you wherever you may be."

Representative Girl at B.Y. High School, May 1949

Another inscription from a boy who was finishing his junior year read: "I was thrilled to see you immortalized in the halls of old "Wye" high as Representative Girl. It is an honor you truly deserve and we all hold up our standards to try to match yours. You have a wonderful soul that is your most prized possession. I hope you will always remember 'Digger,' Dallin Oaks." More than thirty years later, Elder Dallin H. Oaks was sustained in general conference as a member of the Quorum of the Twelve Apostles on the same day that Ardeth was sustained as the general president of the Young Women.

Ardeth's parents arrived in Provo the day before graduation to be with their daughter at this momentous time. "Needless to say, I was extremely glad to see them and especially on such a glorious occasion," she noted. As Ardeth had been keeping frequent company with Heber since the Easter weekend, she invited him to attend her graduation. The long-anticipated day was full of excitement, culminating in the graduation exercise itself. "Graduation started at 8:00 P.M. at the Joseph Smith Building. The audience was all standing as the graduates slowly marched up the aisle. . . . As I walked along it was a feeling I will never forget, yet one I can never describe. To see Mom and Dad sitting there, and Kapp sitting with them. . . . Believe me, it wasn't easy to keep the tears back."

The commencement address was given by Oscar A. Kirkham, a member of the First Quorum of Seventy. His message became a motto for Ardeth's life: "Build a seaworthy ship, be a loyal shipmate, and sail a true course."

Heber escorted her to the graduation dance, which marked the official end of her high school days. After the dance they went for a drive, reluctant to have this special day come to a close. She later recorded: "The dance was very nice, and after we went for a little drive. It was then I was sure my feelings toward Heber weren't just respect and admiration."

CHAPTER FIVE

Heber

With the completion of school, Ardeth looked forward to spending the weekend with Heber before she and her parents returned home to Glenwood the next week. On Saturday evening, Ardeth and Heber drove in her parents' car to Saltaire, a popular open-air dance pavilion on the edge of the Great Salt Lake. "We had a very wonderful evening, a grand time dancing. Just being with Kapp was wonderful."

After the Sunday meetings the next day, they went for a drive. Knowing it was her last evening in Provo, it was difficult to say goodnight, as they each realized they were also saying good-bye. They discussed the circumstances of their first meeting nearly two years earlier and how they had kept in touch through letters since that time. "Although we were really strangers except for the acquaintance of one day, it hardly seemed possible we hadn't known each other all our lives." They finally parted with the hope that Heber would be able to visit Glenwood in the summer. In the meantime, they had to be

Heber, 1950

content with letters, which Ardeth hoped would come often. The letters did come, and through those letters, their feelings for each other deepened.

In July, Heber telephoned to tell her of the death of his mother. Ardeth wired flowers "in the hope that it would help in some small way." She observed in her journal, "It is at such times we really appreciate our gospel, and among his many admirable qualities I do feel I value his love and appreciation of the gospel more than anything else."

Heber's paternal and maternal grandparents both joined the Church in Holland, where his father was born, and immigrated to Utah. They settled in Weber County, where his mother was born. Heber was eight years old when his father contracted tuberculosis. Eventually, it spread to the entire family, except for the baby. Young Heber fasted and prayed for his father's return to health. After his prayers, he was impressed with the feeling that his father would not live but that things would be all right. The following spring, his father passed away, leaving his mother with nine children, the oldest of whom was thirteen. At the time, the family's only means of support was a vegetable farm, attended to by the children.

When Heber's mother was diagnosed with tuberculosis of the kidney, she entered a TB sanatorium in Ogden for treatment, leaving the four older children, including Heber, to care for themselves as best they could. The younger children were placed in the homes of relatives. Eight of the nine children were diagnosed with tuberculosis of the lung. Doctors determined to remove the mother's infected kidney, believing that this would cause her health to improve and enable her to care for her family. Incredibly, they removed the wrong kidney, leaving her with failing health and the need to accept welfare to assist in the support of her family.

Despite his mother's many trials, Heber remembered her indomitable spirit and her wonderful sense of humor. She seemed always to be singing, and her positive attitude carried the family through many difficulties. She trusted completely in her Heavenly Father's promise of the great blessings that would come to the faithful who were obedient to his teachings. Her children were blessed by following her example of unswerving devotion. Even though living on welfare, with only pennies to get by on, she always insisted on paying her tithing. Her bishop, wishing to help ease her burden, gave it as his opinion that, considering her situation, no tithing was expected from her. She felt differently, knowing that she and her family needed the promised blessings.

When he was eighteen, Heber joined the United States Navy

and served until the end of World War II. Shortly after his return home, his older brother received a mission call. Although Heber was eligible to serve, his bishop had not issued a call to him, thinking that his mother would wish to have him at home to help in caring for the family. His mother spoke with the bishop, assuring him that her desire was for both sons to serve missions. Shortly thereafter, Heber was invited to submit his missionary application. Although very ill at the time, his mother was given a blessing in which she was promised that she would live until her two sons returned from their missions.

When Heber was asked if he had a preference as to where he might serve his mission, he responded that since he didn't like the cold, he would be happy to go almost any place except Canada. Subsequently, he received a call to serve two years in the Western Canadian Mission. In the true spirit of "I'll go where you want me to go," he accepted the call and ultimately became a leader in the mission, serving as a branch and district president. For a time, he even filled the role of branch Relief Society president! Since his mission was being financed by family, neighbors, and friends, he viewed the funds as sacred and determined to be the best missionary he could be. In this, he was successful.

A few months after Heber's return, his mother told her family that it was time for her to go. At her request, Heber gave her a blessing of comfort and peace. Within a few days she quietly slipped away.

PROMISED

Not long after his mother's passing, Heber wrote Ardeth that he was planning to travel to Glenwood for the visit they had both hoped for. Not only did she look forward to seeing him again, but she was also excited for her family and friends to become acquainted with the young man she had spoken of so often. On the appointed day, Monday, August 1, 1949, she and her dad drove to Lethbridge to meet Heber's bus. From the moment he arrived until his departure twelve days later, their time together was idyllic.

At first they were content to sit on the lawn and talk and just enjoy being together. The day following his arrival they took Sharon and Shirley to the river, where they all enjoyed a swim. When Heber suggested that they go to a dance that evening in Waterton, Ardeth was somewhat reluctant. The band wasn't as good at the beginning of the week as it was on weekends—nor were the dances as well attended. Heber had never been to Waterton, and she wanted everything to be at its best when he saw it for the first time. However, since he seemed anxious to go, she agreed.

Arriving at dusk, they drove up the hill by the Prince of Wales Hotel, where they looked out over Waterton Lake. In the twilight evening the lake looked especially beautiful, with a full moon just beginning to appear above the points of the mountains that bordered each side of the water. As they stood there, heart spoke to heart and spirit to spirit, and by the time the lake was fully bathed in the moonlight, Heber Kapp and Ardeth Greene had pledged to become companions for eternity. She knew that the prayers she had offered from her youth about choosing a mate had been answered. He slipped a small but beautiful diamond ring on her finger. She loved the ring, but even more she loved what it signified.

Encased in their own special cosmos, the newly betrothed

couple joined the dancers in the open-air dance pavilion. How appropriate it was that the band was playing a song that was special to them, the words to which made a connection with their hearts: "I'll Be Loving You, Always" by Irving Berlin.

As the music ended, they spotted her cousin Colleen among the dancers. She was the first to hear their happy news. They didn't stay long at the dance, but soon returned home. There Ardeth woke her mom and dad to share the happenings of that special evening. After telling other family members the next day, Ardeth was pleased to note that "it just seems like Heber fits in so well and is loved by the whole family." The only exception was her little sister, Shirley, who was miffed to think that Ardeth would leave the family to go off with a stranger!

The days rushed by, and on Saturday, Ardeth and her dad drove Heber to Lethbridge to meet the bus that would take him home.

The newly engaged couple were reluctant to separate. Their wedding was planned for the following June, still a long way off. However, their sadness at parting was tempered by the realization that it would be for only a month. Ardeth had decided to return to Provo in September to enroll as a student at Brigham Young University.

The young couple spent every weekend together. On Sundays Heber and Ardeth would often attend the homecomings of some of his missionary friends, which gave them the opportunity to visit a variety of wards. When they visited his home ward in South Weber, he was often asked to speak or to teach a Sunday School or priesthood lesson. She was proud of how capable he was.

When the quarter ended in December, Ardeth returned home to Glenwood. Heber joined her for Christmas. They had decided that she would not return to school the following quarter. Her dad had asked her to stay at home to help her mother, who had been ill. She was also looking forward to February, when Kay would return from his mission. After Heber returned to Utah, she was again sad to be apart from him and anxiously awaited his letters, which were long and frequent. One friend remarked that much of their courtship had been by correspondence course. Ardeth responded, "How true—but what a wonderful correspondence!"

An unexpected but very exciting event for Ardeth occurred as her family made plans to welcome Kay home from his mission. Upon his release from the Australian Mission, and following a tour of Europe, he was to drive a new car home for their dad. Immediately upon finding out that his route would take him through Ogden, she had the idea that she should go to Utah to meet him. No small part of her plan was the thought that she would also be able to spend a few days with Heber. Accordingly, in early February, she boarded a bus bound for Ogden. Fierce winter weather set in and heavy snow forced the bus to travel slowly, and sometimes to stop altogether. She arrived three days later than planned. However, her joy at being reunited with Heber made up for the arduous travel.

She was anxious to see Kay, who she knew had arrived in Provo. Heber drove her immediately down to meet him, but since they didn't know where he was staying, they were unsure how to find him. Much to their surprise, as they were driving along Main Street she spotted Kay driving along the same street! Kay caught sight of her about the same time she saw him, and both cars stopped while the brother and sister had a joyous reunion in the middle of the street. After a brief stay in Utah, Ardeth and her brother drove home to Glenwood, where Kay was warmly welcomed by family and friends.

FOR TIME AND ETERNITY

Ardeth returned again to Utah with her parents to attend the April general conference. She admitted to not making the trip solely for the conference. She and Heber spent a few days together making wedding plans, then said good-bye once again. This time their reluctance in parting was tempered by the realization that when they met again, it would be for an appointment in the Cardston Temple. There they would be united not only for time, but also for eternity.

Heber drove to Glenwood in his recently purchased used car, arriving just two days before the wedding on June 28, 1950. Although it is traditional to charge women with pre-wedding jitters, Heber contributed his share of nervousness. The day before the wedding, Ardeth noticed that his usual calm demeanor had given way to a slight agitation. Repeatedly, he insisted that he needed to find his tithing receipts. When she inquired why he wanted them at that time, he replied that he must have them to go to the temple. She replied that she thought he only needed his temple recommend. He sheepishly agreed that is what he had meant! Through subsequent years of constant temple attendance, she has teased him asking, "Are you sure you have your tithing receipts?"

The day of the wedding, Ardeth was surrounded by her parents, grandparents, and other family members and friends. Heber felt fortunate that his brother and sister-in-law were able to make the trip to Canada to be with them for their special day. The group gathered in the chapel of the temple where President Willard Smith, who was to perform the sealing, asked Heber to speak. As always, Ardeth was impressed by the remarks of the young man she was about to marry. She was so thankful for that first meeting which had led them to this day.

After the temple ceremony, the newlyweds, joined by their family, gathered in front of the temple to have the special occasion recorded by photographers. More than fifty years later, dressed in white clothes, they again posed for pictures in the same place, this time as president and matron of the Cardston Temple.

Ardeth's parents had planned a wonderful wedding reception to honor the young couple. Since it was a lovely summer day, they set up tables on the lawn at the side of their house, where a variety of beautiful flowers were in bloom. Wedding receptions in Glenwood typically involved the whole town. Announcements were posted on the store windows, inviting everyone. In keeping with tradition, Ardeth's parents planned and served a full-course dinner for all of their guests.

Bobby Blackplum, a friend from the Indian reservation, wanted to honor the couple. He provided two horses that pulled a wagon complete with a cover on top to make it seem more like a carriage. Everyone insisted that the newlyweds get in and drive around the block along the graveled road. Ardeth in her wedding dress and Heber in his new suit climbed aboard to the cheers of their neighbors and friends. Although Heber had worked on a farm for much of his life and could competently handle a horse, Ardeth's dad was unaware of his ability. Worried that his new

Wedding day, June 28, 1950

son-in-law wouldn't know how to guide them, he held the bridle and led the horses and carriage all the way around the block with half of the town following.

When the reception ended and the young couple prepared to leave, everyone followed them out to their car, where they found that pranksters had wedged their luggage in the front seat so as to separate the newlyweds from each other. Undeterred, Heber started the car, prepared to roar off in a cloud of dust. When he put his foot to the gas pedal, the engine roared, but the car didn't move. Again, pranksters had been at work, mounting the automobile on blocks to ensure that it would stay put. As everyone laughed, the blocks were removed, and finally they made their getaway.

A few days later, they headed for Utah. When they reached the border separating the United States and Canada, they had to unpack all of their wedding gifts and declare them at customs.

In addition, they were surprised to learn that Ardeth would have to pay a $50 immigration fee to enter the country. Since she was moving so far away from home, her parents thought she should have a little nest egg to take with her in the event of an unexpected emergency. So, before leaving home, she sold the horse her father had given her back to him for $50, the exact amount she now needed. None of them had foreseen that the emergency would happen so soon. Since it was the only way she could legally enter the United States, she surrendered her precious resource to the immigration official. Years later, she joked that she had given up her horse, her maiden name, and her Canadian citizenship for Heber.

As she prepared to move from Canada, the home of her birth, her mother gave her wise counsel concerning citizenship in her new country. She pointed out that those in Glenwood who had moved from the United States but had never become Canadian citizens were never able to vote or otherwise participate in the governmental process. She counseled her daughter to become a citizen of the country to which she was moving. She told her of the importance of being a loyal citizen, having the right to vote, and becoming a part of the United States of America. Although it was a three-year wait before she could apply for citizenship, Ardeth followed her mother's counsel and, in 1953, became a United States citizen. Her grandparents had all been citizens of the United States, living in Cache Valley, Utah, before migrating to Canada.

Nevertheless, she continues to remember her roots. Years later, while working together in the Young Women office, she and fellow Canadian Elaine Jack took occasions to celebrate and remember the heritage of their birthplace. They often got together on July 1, Canada Day, to sing their national anthem, "Oh Canada!" Many years after her move, Ardeth was invited to speak at the BYU Canadian Studies lecture series. She was asked to address what it meant to be born a Canadian and then to become an American citizen. Studying and pondering her response, she thought of the route Americans had taken to become a nation. They had won their independence by revolution to fulfill their motto: "Life, liberty, and the pursuit of happiness." Canada, whose motto is "Peace, order, and good government," had gained its independence by evolution, rather than by revolution. There are strengths in both governments. But for her, the future lay in the United States.

Toward the end of their long drive from Glenwood, the young newlyweds stopped at Maddox Restaurant in Brigham City, Utah, a short drive from their new home in Ogden. With the only money they had left, they ordered one chicken dinner and split it between them. They had no money for a tip.

In spite of the fact that they had no money and, in addition, had taken on part of the debt incurred by Heber's mother's illness and subsequent death, nothing could deter them from their conviction that everything would be all right. They had been sealed in the temple, where they were promised all of the blessings that would come from remembering to seek first the Kingdom of God. Their first home, a tiny basement apartment in Ogden, awaited them. They were happy, excited, and on their way to a bright future.

CHAPTER SIX

Life Together

The Dilemma

Christmas was approaching and Ardeth was puzzled. She did not have a single cent with which to purchase a gift for her husband. How could she earn extra money? Even though they budgeted carefully and lived frugally, there was no money for extras, not even for Christmas.

As she glanced around their tiny home, she reflected on their first few months together. Her only request regarding a place to live was that it be clean and safe. The basement apartment that Heber had secured prior to their marriage met that requirement, but it had little else—it even lacked furnishings. The owners had divided it, by a curtain, into two small rooms. One room held a bed, which they could get to only by walking sideways. The other room contained two laundry tubs that were used every Wednesday by their landlady on her weekly wash day. The room also served as their kitchen and living area, having a small counter space, a stove, and a refrigerator. A wooden screen closed off the bathtub and toilet from the rest of the room.

After they moved in, Ardeth was full of anticipation, wondering who their first visitor might be. A bill collector from the mortuary was the first to knock at their door. He also was the first to address her as "Mrs. Kapp," which only slightly compensated for the reason for his call. Heber and his brothers had assumed responsibility for the debt incurred by their mother's hospital bills and funeral arrangements. While she fully supported their decision, Ardeth occasionally felt anxious, but never discouraged, about how they would be able to satisfy that obligation. And she still prayed for a way to earn enough money to buy Heber a Christmas gift.

The Solution

Ardeth enrolled in a cosmetology course at Weber College in Ogden. She thought that having an occupation she could engage in at home would be helpful when they began the large family they anticipated. One of the girls in her class mentioned that she had landed an evening job plucking turkeys at a cannery across the tracks on the west side of town. She invited Ardeth to come along, assuring her there was plenty of work. Here was an answer to her prayer! She didn't hesitate. Plucking turkeys was something she had done growing up on the farm at home, and she knew she could do it. In spite of Heber's hesitation, she went with her friend to the cannery for their first evening of work.

She was surprised to find that she was required to purchase a leather apron before commencing work. Since she had no money, the employer agreed to deduct the cost from her first paycheck. The next surprise came when they entered the large area where they were to work. The smell was nauseating, and the steam and heat from the scalded turkeys was almost unbearable. Except for Ardeth and her friend, none of the employees spoke a word of English. As the turkeys were lifted out of a vat of boiling water, they were hung on hooks suspended from an overhead conveyer belt. Each worker was assigned a bird to pluck. The feathers piled up like dirty snow on the cement floor. Since their pay was calculated by the number of birds plucked, speed was of the essence. This was definitely not like plucking turkeys at home!

By the time the others had finished their turkeys, hers was still only half cleaned. The supervisor took it from the conveyor belt and placed it on a rack, instructing her to stay there until she was finished. She felt like a schoolchild who was told to stand in the corner. At the end of the evening she had not earned even enough to pay for the apron. When she returned home and Heber asked how the work had gone, she replied. "Fine. Just fine." She took care to hide her fingers, which were blistered and sore from the boiling water. Returning the next evening, she muttered her mom's slogan to herself: "A quitter never wins, and a winner never quits." She was determined to be a winner, not a quitter.

At the end of her third day, Heber insisted on picking her up after work. When he came in and saw the conditions in which she was working, he absolutely refused to let her return. He paid what was still owed on the apron and took her home. They weren't *that* poor! Now, whenever she and Heber confront a challenge, they look at each other and say, "Well, you could be plucking turkeys!" Somehow that makes everything look brighter. She still has the apron.

ADJUSTMENTS

Although she was very much in love, Ardeth found that adjusting to married life was sometimes more difficult than she had supposed. Having come from different backgrounds, she and Heber approached things in different ways—as is typical in most marriages. One example was their approach to special occasions. In the Greene family, there was a celebration for every occasion. A birthday was not complete without cake and a party. Because of his mother's poor health and meager income, Heber had never had a birthday party until he was on his mission, when the mission president's wife surprised him with a cake. In Ardeth's family, she and her sisters always got a new dress for Christmas, whether they needed one or not. No one ever went to a Christmas dance in a dress they had worn before. Heber couldn't understand why Ardeth would need a new dress just because it was Christmas!

This and other differences of opinion were troubling to Ardeth. On the one hand, she felt she must be wrong because Heber was older, had served in the Navy, been on a mission, and was wiser and more experienced. On the other hand, it went against her sense of integrity to do something his way if she didn't feel right about it. She couldn't just let go of what she thought was right simply to please him. However, if she did everything his way, there would never be disagreements or differences of opinion.

Because of their love for and trust in each other, they were able to explain their differing feelings in areas of potential conflict. They could trust the other's intent, though their differences were not always easily resolved. They learned that there are always new challenges to be worked through. Early in their marriage, it was easy to feel that when they had differing opinions, one must be right and the other wrong. They later came to learn that their differences often added to the richness of their relationship. As two people seldom see eye to eye on everything, differences didn't always have to imply right or wrong.

As Ardeth explains: "In some cases our interests are different, but our values and eternal goals are always the same. It is in our sameness that we continue to build our relationship, not our differences. While the desire to be at one with each other is great, to always assume your idea is wrong can begin to undermine your confidence and self-worth. There must be unity without sacrificing identity. One of the important discoveries is to learn that you don't have to be right all of the time. This insight often comes after years of molding, testing, giving, and sharing." As the years go by, they continue to learn that opportunities for growing and for sharing both differences and similarities are ongoing.

HIGH FASHION

In addition to part-time work at Sears, Heber attended Weber College. He was grateful for the G. I. Bill provided to war veterans to help fund his education. Ardeth finished her course and received a Utah state license in cosmetology. At the same time, Heber finished his two-year degree at Weber. They both received Associate Degrees on June 1, 1951, and walked across the stage together. Even though no family members were able to come to celebrate with them, they were happy that they had achieved their goal.

As the child they hoped for had not yet come, Ardeth pondered employment possibilities. Heber asked where she would like to work if she could work anyplace in town. Her immediate response: "Samuels." At that time, L. R. Samuels was the most prestigious women's dress shop in Ogden. She couldn't imagine having the courage to walk into the store, much less ask for a job. Even though she had some retail experience from working in her mother's small country store, she didn't feel qualified for such a position. Heber thought that applying would be a good experience for her, even if she didn't get the job, so she decided to try.

They rehearsed how she might approach the manager at Samuel's. She would explain that she had some experience in selling, that she was impressed with his store, and that she believed she could sell the merchandise. On the day she applied, she was so nervous that she paced back and forth on the sidewalk across the street for over an hour, rehearsing her presentation in her mind before gathering the courage to go inside. She approached the first sales clerk she saw, asking to speak to the manager. After she was introduced, the manager asked what experience she had, and she told him of her work in her mother's store. When he asked if she could start work on Monday, Ardeth could hardly believe she had heard him correctly. She ran to the Sears store where Heber was working and excitedly told him of their good fortune. He was as excited as she was!

She was put to work in the downstairs budget department. Eager to show herself a hard worker, she enthusiastically greeted every customer who came downstairs. As time went by, she sensed a coolness from the other clerks. Not understanding their behavior, she was puzzled and troubled. Finally, the supervisor called Ardeth into her office and explained that because the sales clerks worked on commission, it was important to take turns waiting on the customers. That was the first time she had ever heard of sales commissions. Embarrassed by her mistake, she apologized, saying that she was just trying to do her very best. She also apologized to her coworkers, and they soon became friends.

In a short while she was moved upstairs to work in the higher-priced clothing department, or as her mother would have put it, in the "better dresses." In this case, the better dresses were Jantzen sweaters and skirts, plus the popular Joyce shoes—the desirable, high-end clothing items of the day. Just handling the beautiful clothes was exciting to her, and she was confident she could easily sell them. In her plain but serviceable navy skirt and white blouse, she was very aware that she didn't dress as fashionably as the customers she served. Shortly after she was moved upstairs, a new policy was instituted among the employees. Scott Dye, the store's manager, announced that the top salesgirl for each of the next several months would be awarded an entire Jantzen outfit, complete with the coveted Joyce shoes. Although she allowed the other clerks their share of the customers, Ardeth worked very hard and earned the top spot every month. After she had been awarded several beautiful new outfits, the policy was discontinued. It wasn't until years later that she realized Mr. Dye's strategy. He had provided a way for her to improve her appearance and increase her confidence without confronting her about her limited wardrobe. It was a kindness for which she was grateful and which she never forgot.

Occasionally, during a slow time in the store, Ardeth would

slip into a dressing room and try on maternity clothes, imagining what it would be like when she had the need for such apparel. Months had gone by since their wedding, and many of their friends had begun their families. Worries began to creep in regarding their failure, thus far, to realize their hopes of parenthood. Part of the heritage each of them brought to their marriage was faith in the Lord. At an early age, Ardeth adopted a verse from Proverbs as her own personal guide: "Trust in the Lord with all thine heart; and lean not unto thine own understanding. In all thy ways acknowledge him, and he shall direct thy paths" (Proverbs 3:5–6). Although trusting, she was troubled.

Because of her continued success at Samuel's, Ardeth was offered a job as an assistant buyer for her department. She and Heber discussed the opportunity at length before coming to a decision. As the new position would require travel, and therefore time away from home and husband, the prospect held little appeal. She declined the promotion.

MOUNTAIN BELL

While she waited for the longed-for family, Ardeth decided to pursue a different type of employment, although she was unsure what that should be. A Samuel's customer, Clarice Williams, with whom she had become friends, was employed at Mountain States Telephone Company. Impressed with Ardeth's enthusiasm and skill with people, Clarice suggested that she apply at the phone company, mentioning the profitable opportunities the company offered. Since the doctor with whom she and Heber had been consulting had suggested that she spend less time on her feet, she decided to follow her friend's suggestion and apply at the phone company.

Looking over her application, the manager, Carlos Yeates, asked what she could do. She responded, "I'm not sure!" She was quick to add that she would try to do anything she was asked. Mr. Yeates gave her a letter to type. She had never taken a typing class and her hunt-and-peck method was not fast. It seemed to take forever to get through it. Timidly, she waited for him to look over the letter, after which he said with a smile, "Well, we've found one thing you can't do!" He referred her to Howard Berg, the business office manager, thinking she could be employed as a service representative. Although the department had no opening at that time, the manager was impressed with her contagious enthusiasm. He offered to put her to work temporarily in the basement searching through the "dead files." She was asked to search through mounds of paper looking for unpaid bills that could be turned over to a collection agency.

After spending her first day on the job, alone in a windowless basement room with only the glare of a single hanging light bulb to pierce the darkness, she was tempted to never come back. Again, the words of her mother—"a quitter never wins"—was her only inducement to return the second day. Although she disliked the work intensely, she was determined not to quit before she had completed it. Within a couple of weeks, she was invited to attend a special training program for prospective service representatives. Upon successful completion of the training, she was moved into the business office. She enjoyed her work, and gained valuable training that would benefit her in years to come.

In the meantime, Heber had begun working full time at Sears, where the manager, who was impressed with his abilities, encouraged him to enroll in the company's management training program. Although he was grateful for the offer, his real desire was to receive further education and become a teacher. Accordingly, he and Ardeth made the decision to move to Salt Lake City. He would work toward a degree in education from the University of Utah and continue part-time employment with Sears in their Salt Lake store.

THE GREENE GIRLS

The summer following their marriage, Ardeth and Heber began a tradition that continued for many years. They invited Sharon and Shirley to spend part of their summer vacation with them in Ogden, where they planned to keep them busy having a good time. During the day when Ardeth and Heber were at work, the girls often purchased tickets at the Egyptian Theater and spent most of the day watching the same movie over and over. In the evenings after work, Ardeth and Heber took them swimming, hiking, or to picnics in the park. Their stay always included at least one visit to a nearby amusement park, where they tried to go on all of the rides. They also spent one evening each summer enjoying the pioneer musical, *All Faces West.* On one occasion, Ardeth took them on a shopping spree, lavishing $28 on each sister to spend as she liked. When they returned home with their purchases, Heber was happy to take a seat, providing an appreciative audience for their fashion show.

As the years went by and the girls grew up, the visits continued to be a highlight of each summer for all involved. Occasionally, Sharon and Shirley brought a friend from home to share in their fun. When Sharon graduated from high school in 1957, she and Shirley moved to Edmonton, where they lived with their brother, Gordon Kay, and his family. Sharon attended the University of Alberta, and Shirley completed her last year of high school. Upon Shirley's graduation, the two sisters moved to Provo to attend BYU.

Wanting the girls to become involved in school and make new friends, Heber told them they were always welcome to visit, but not to come before Thanksgiving. This proved to be wise counsel, and before long, new friends, especially boys, became of particular interest, and they found college life too exciting to leave. However, they still relied on their big sister to come to their rescue when needed. On one occasion, Sharon called to report the excitement of a very special evening for which she desperately needed a new dress. Ardeth, who had purchased a sewing machine for such emergencies, told her to choose the color and the pattern and she would do the rest. The beautiful new dress was completed in time for Sharon to wear on that special occasion.

After two years at BYU, Shirley returned to Canada to complete her education at the University of British Columbia. Somehow, most of her clothes were lost in transit and her expenses were more than she had anticipated. To make matters worse, she had taken her favorite article of clothing, a wool skirt, to the dry cleaners, where it had been lost. And if that wasn't enough, her last five dollars were stolen. She didn't know how she would ever manage.

In the meantime, while looking at skirts in a department store, Ardeth felt impressed to buy one and send it to Shirley, along with a blouse and a necklace. A couple of weeks later she received a letter from Shirley, detailing her tight financial situation and her earnest prayers for assistance. On the day that she had been reimbursed twenty-five dollars for the loss of her wool skirt, which gave her the badly needed cash, she returned home to find that a package containing the new skirt and blouse had come in the mail. Accompanying the package was a note which read: "I saw this skirt in ZCMI the other day and it reminded me of you. The blouse is on loan and you may keep the necklace."

For several years Sharon had dated a young man with whom she was becoming serious. His undesirable conduct was of great concern to her parents, who had been praying for an end to the relationship. During one summer break she was employed at Banff National Park, a resort town near Calgary. At the end of one workday, she returned to her apartment to find a letter that Ardeth had felt an urgent need to write, expressing her concern for her sister's future. Sharon later recalled: "What I remember about that letter is how much she really loved me and wanted me to be happy. I don't remember exactly how she said it, but she expressed her feeling that the only way to be happy is to be good. Somehow that letter turned me around and I knew what I needed to do to be happy." Over the years, Sharon has remembered how that letter made a difference in the direction her life took. "It touched me so deeply that I determined I would end the relationship. It took me a while, but it was from that time on that I knew I had to end it. I often look back on those times and think how different my life would have been if I had married that guy."

Ardeth has never left behind her feelings of protectiveness and concern for the well-being of her younger sisters. She has taught them lessons over the years which have served them well.

And she in turn has learned great lessons of life from these cherished sisters. Their continued close friendship is a joy to them and to their families.

CHAPTER SEVEN

Changes

Ward YWMIA President

In the summer of 1952, Heber and Ardeth purchased a cinder-block home in a new, low-income housing area in Kearns, just west of Salt Lake City. The houses, all occupied by young couples like themselves, had been constructed virtually at the same time, and all looked alike. Until she became more familiar with the area, it was a challenge for her to keep track of which street they lived on and who lived in which home.

Shortly after their move, the Kearns First Ward was created, and Ardeth was called to be the ward's first YWMIA (Young Women Mutual Improvement Association) president. She was excited to serve in this new calling. She reflected on the promise given in her patriarchal blessing that she would be surprised in the days to come at the blessings the Lord had in store for her. She felt certain that this calling fulfilled that blessing.

After her acceptance of the call, the bishop asked her to find two counselors and submit their names to him. Since she didn't know anyone in the area, she walked up and down every street, knocking on doors, introducing herself, and getting acquainted with her new neighbors and fellow ward members. In the course of meeting many new people, she selected two women to be her counselors. As requested, she gave their names to the bishop. As she did so, she realized that she had only their names, with no accompanying addresses or telephone numbers! Without any other means of identifying them, she retraced her original tour of the neighborhood to obtain the addresses and telephone numbers.

HERE WE COME!

Heber graduated from the University of Utah in June of 1954, with a degree in secondary education. That fall, he accepted a position teaching social studies at Valley Junior High School in Taylorsville. As the end of the school year approached, he heard of better salaries available to teachers in California. He and Ardeth decided that he should apply for a position at a school near Long Beach. When he was offered the job, they sold their home, packed up their belongings, and moved to the town of Lakewood. In the meantime, Ardeth had applied for a position at the Pacific Telephone Company in an office in Compton, not far from their new home. Coming with a glowing recommendation from the Mountain States Telephone Company, she was hired immediately.

On the first Sunday in their new ward they were greeted by a member of the bishopric, who invited them to an interview with the bishop. Within a few days, they were given callings, Heber as a counselor in the YMMIA and Ardeth as a counselor in the YWMIA. Later that year she was called as the president. During their first Sunday meeting, a call was issued for volunteers to assist at the cannery sometime during the following week. They volunteered but were surprised that more people did not agree to take the assignment. Upon completion of the work, they better understood the reluctance of their fellow ward members. The smell of the fish they canned saturated their clothing, their hair, and, most especially, their hands, where the odor seemed to seep even underneath their fingernails! They reeked of that special perfume for longer than either of them cared to remember. It was a long time before they could enjoy eating tuna fish again.

Their home was close to Disneyland, giving them frequent opportunity to serve as unofficial tour guides for friends and family members who came through the area on vacation. Since they generously offered their small apartment for overnight accommodations, they sometimes found themselves sleeping in the reclining seats of their car to allow room for their guests. That only added to their enjoyment of entertaining family and friends, who were always welcome.

Both Heber and Ardeth worked diligently in their callings. One highlight of their service came in the form of an unforgettable experience while working on a ward roadshow. After competing and winning in their stake, they found themselves scheduled to compete with a ward in Hollywood. Hollywood! Just the name was exciting! Part of the desired scenery for their Hawaiian theme was a banana tree. Ardeth's competitive spirit suggested that she should settle for nothing less than a real banana tree. Accordingly, she approached her neighbors and, in her most persuasive manner, convinced them to cut down one of the real banana trees in their backyard for this important event.

Anticipating audience delight at their realistic stage prop, they loaded the tree in the back of a borrowed truck and set off, with their young cast members and crew following, bound for the nation's movie mecca. When they arrived at the ward building, they jumped out of the truck, prepared to assemble the set for the production. To their dismay, they found that between the heat of the California sun and a severe wind, the tree was in such bad shape that it could not be used. The production went on, sans tree, and without winning the competition. However, they were not lacking in effort, and the memory of performing in Hollywood brought its own reward.

HOME TO UTAH

Some time during their move to California, Heber and Ardeth had each had the distinct impression that they would not be staying in California beyond Heber's contract for the school year. They both had the feeling that they belonged in Utah. On their drive home to Glenwood for Christmas in December of 1956, their route took them through Utah. They stopped in Farmington, where Heber visited with the superintendent of the Davis County School District.

Although they fully enjoyed their stay in California for the remainder of the school year, by the time the last day arrived, they were packed and ready to return. It was then that Ardeth realized she was more homesick for Utah than she had realized. Heber had been offered a contract to begin teaching at South Davis Junior High School in Bountiful in the fall of 1957. They located an apartment near the junior high school where he was to teach, and within a few weeks of their moving in, she was once again called as the ward YWMIA president—this time in the Bountiful Third Ward of the Bountiful Stake.

DREAM HOME

It was while living in California that Ardeth and Heber first began to talk about building their own home. Although Heber had no previous home building experience, they determined that if they were ever to afford the home of their dreams, they would have to build it themselves. With no drafting experience or knowledge of how to draw house plans, Heber nevertheless began drawing rudimentary plans on butcher paper stretched out across the kitchen table. They pasted the plans to the bedroom ceiling of their small apartment for more careful study. In her mind, Ardeth heard a slogan her father had repeated over the years: "He who builds no castles in the air, never builds them anywhere. Have a dream and go after it."

Heber began to visit homes under construction and carefully observed every phase of the home building process, from the foundation to the roof. Some of his time was spent laboring on an expansion of their ward building, which gave him practical experience. With scrap wood obtained from the church construction, they built a tiny scale model of the home they had so carefully planned on paper. Ardeth completed the interior with miniature furniture she fashioned from the scraps.

Shortly after their return to Utah, they put a down payment on a building lot in the neighboring town of Centerville. Night after night they studied their plans until they knew them by heart. They worked, dreamed, saved, and planned, anxious for the day when their finances would be adequate to turn their dreams into reality. Frequently visiting their newly acquired property, they placed large rocks around the perimeter of their planned home, envisioning what the finished product would look like. They outlined each room with the rocks, then walked in and pretended to look out the windows, memorizing the view from every angle. Soon they became well acquainted with the variety of seasonal moods visited upon the area—summer, fall, winter, and spring. Both sunny days and starlit nights found them in their "home," until they knew the landscape and the climate by heart. Every detail was as clear to them as if it were already built.

DELAYED DREAM

In the spring of 1958, Elders Spencer W. Kimball and Mark E. Petersen of the Quorum of the Twelve Apostles visited their stake conference. After interviewing Heber, Elder Kimball called him to be a member of the high council of the Bountiful Stake. "I didn't want to be on the high council," Heber recalled. "I thought that high councilmen were a bunch of old men, and I was too young for that! Most of all, I was just plain scared. How could I be a high councilor? People would look to me and expect something I couldn't deliver." At the time of his call, Heber mentioned to Elder Kimball that he and Ardeth were planning to build a home outside of the stake boundaries. Elder Kimball simply stated, "I think you should accept this assignment." Heber didn't remember anything further about their conversation, but he concluded that when they were ready to build their home, the stake president would release him from his calling on the high council.

A few months following the call, they were ready to begin

building their home. Anticipating his release, Heber visited with the stake president, Stanford Smith, informing him of their plans. He was startled at President Smith's response: "I didn't call you to the high council. The Lord did. You'd better talk with him about it." From their earliest remembrances, both Heber and Ardeth had been taught to seek the Lord's counsel in their lives through prayer and then to listen for the answers. Most important, they had been taught to follow that counsel when it came. They had often studied the scripture in Doctrine and Covenants 11:12: "Put your trust in that Spirit which leadeth to do good—yea, to do justly, to walk humbly, to judge righteously; and this is my Spirit."

When Heber shared the stake president's advice with Ardeth, she thought, "I don't know if I want to ask the Lord." She was afraid that she already knew what the answer would be, and she was also afraid that she would not like it. After seeking to know the Lord's will, the impression came that they should sell the lot and remain where they were, allowing Heber to continue serving on the high council. The purchase price for a building lot within their stake boundaries was considerably more than what their lot had been. Feeling like their sacrifice must be similar to that of the pioneers who had left their homes to move west, Ardeth nevertheless knew what they must do. They put their property up for sale. It sold immediately. All she could think about was that they were saying good-bye to their dream.

THE SUNSHINE CLUB

With their move to Utah, Mountain States Telephone Company was happy to hire Ardeth back in their Salt Lake office. In time, the training department manager advanced her to the position of training instructor for the new service representatives. She was happy for the promotion but soon realized that training new representatives was no easy task. For one thing, it was difficult to teach them to be excited and convincing as they tried to sell customers on the idea that one black telephone with a twenty-five foot cord, centrally located in the hallway of their home—and on a party line—was good service! They were working in an area where large numbers of new homes were constantly under construction. The necessary lines and cables for more advanced telephone services were not available. There were countless customer complaints, making it difficult for the service representatives to maintain a positive attitude.

Finally, in an attempt to boost morale among their coworkers, Ardeth and some of her friends at work decided to form what they called the "Sunshine Club." To gain admittance, each person had to agree to go all week without uttering a single word of complaint, substituting positive comments for negative ones. Those who agreed to the rules were admitted to the club. The members had such a good time that soon others asked for admission. Years later, their particular work division was still remembered and referred to as "The Sunshine Club."

Shortly after the club's organization, Ardeth was asked to accept the position of business office supervisor. When she tried to explain that she felt unqualified for such a position and knew nothing about the BOP (a huge book on business office practices), the business office manager told her that what she lacked in knowledge she made up for in enthusiasm, and she could learn the rest. She accepted the position.

In addition to the good times that were shared among its members, those in the Sunshine Club enjoyed many lasting friendships. In the fall of 1961, Ardeth completed requirements for the Golden Gleaner award, at that time the highest honor given to the young women of the Church. She was to receive her Golden Gleaner pin at a special evening presentation. She made herself a pretty pink dress for the occasion, and expressed to her fellow Sunshine Club member Irene Boede her wish for a pair of pink shoes to go with the dress. They chatted about it for a few moments, but Ardeth knew that, given the cost, the pink shoes were not really a possibility. Nothing further was said about the shoes.

SHOES OF FRIENDSHIP

Shortly after their conversation, a package from a prestigious ladies' shop in Salt Lake City was delivered to Ardeth at home. Curious, she quickly unwrapped the box and removed the lid. There she saw a pair of pink shoes. But these were no ordinary shoes! Irene had rescued them from her garbage can. She spray-painted them with cheap pink paint, covered the holes in the toes with bright pink bows, and paid the store to deliver them. The next day, everyone at the office was abuzz with the story of the pink shoes. That gift became the focal point of a friendship that lasted for a lifetime.

Ardeth kept the shoes, waiting for the appropriate time to return them. At Christmastime, she dyed them red and green, lined the interiors with velvet, filled them with fresh holly, and gave them back to Irene. Irene loved them, and so did everyone at the office.

The following March, they reappeared at a birthday party for

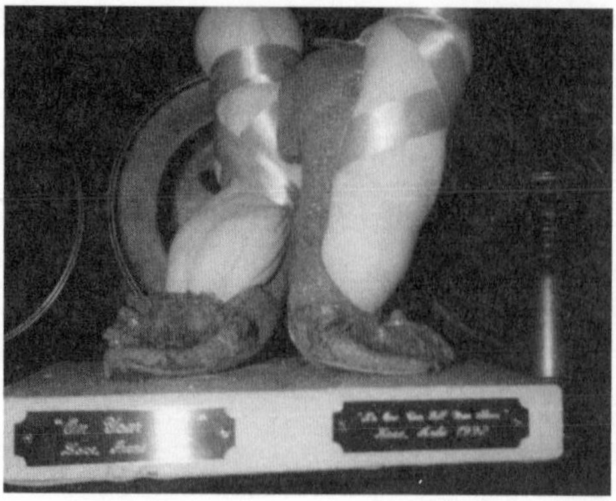

These are the shoes as they were found in the box presented at the Lambda Delta Sigma social (see pages 125–26).

Ardeth. This time green ivy plants were growing out of the dirt which now filled the shoes, creating an interesting planter box.

Ardeth pondered her next move, and waited. The perfect opportunity came a couple of years later when Irene announced that she was transferring with the telephone company to work in Hawaii. At her farewell party the shoes served as a centerpiece for the refreshment table. Ardeth had carefully lined them with tinfoil, which she hoped rendered them sanitary enough for the hors d'oeuvres she placed in them. After the party, she gave them to Irene as a going-away gift.

Two years after Irene's move, Ardeth received a call from her explaining that she was coming for a visit and asking if Ardeth could pick her up at the airport. Excitedly waiting at the gate, Ardeth was quick to spot her friend. In a very large straw hat with an oversized brim, Irene attracted the attention of many. The edge of the brim was decorated with dangling shells from the islands. And mounted strategically on the top were those shoes! In full view of many curious onlookers, Irene removed the hat and ceremoniously placed it upon Ardeth's head.

After further contemplation, Ardeth asked Heber to build the shoes into a sturdy set of bookends. He bolted them firmly to the wood and broke off the heads of the bolts so they could not be separated from the bookends. Then he sprayed both shoes and bookends with bronze paint. Ardeth sent the new bookends to Irene with a note that read, "Encase your memories in lasting bronze!" She felt certain that she had seen the last of the shoes.

Shortly after their move to a new home several years later, Ardeth opened the front door to see a huge package on her doorstep. It had been mailed special delivery and was marked, "Fragile." The postmark read "San Francisco," which was a clue, since Irene had been transferred to San Francisco some years earlier. Upon opening it, Ardeth discovered that, somehow, Irene had rescued the shoes from their imprisonment in the bookends. They were now attached to the center of a large, framed square of linoleum. An attached note read, "Dig this crazy linoleum and keep on walking!" The note further mentioned that on her flight from Hawaii, Irene had explained to the crew that the wrapped package was an original oil painting and must be given preferential treatment!

About five years later, Irene, who had been undergoing kidney dialysis treatments, was planning to visit Salt Lake City for a few days. Ardeth invited all of their old telephone company friends to a party in her honor. She carefully planned the menu, giving close attention to the dessert. Purchasing an oversized angel food cake tin, she removed the shoes from the picture frame, bent them around the inside of the pan, and tied them together with a string. Then, anxiously hoping that they would survive the baking, she covered them with two packages of cake mix and slid the pan into the oven. The cake came out looking normal, as she had hoped. Removing it from the pan, she placed it on a beautiful plate and sought the skill of a professional cake decorator to give it her most artistic design.

Irene, the guest of honor, who was in frail condition, arrived at the party first, followed by all of the old friends from the telephone company. Everyone chatted excitedly around the dinner table, catching up on the news. Toward the end of the party, someone asked what had ever happened to those crazy old shoes. As if on cue, Ardeth announced it was time for dessert and invited everyone to sit in a circle. She placed the elegantly decorated cake close to Irene so that she could more easily see the message written on the top: "We love you, Irene." Everyone exclaimed over the beauty of the cake, and someone asked what flavor it was. Ardeth explained that the cake was made from a very special recipe she had picked up in her travels. Another asked what it was called. Ardeth explained that it was called a "tushu" cake.

Handing a silver cake knife to Irene, Ardeth prepared to videotape the action. Cutting a cake that was at least eight inches deep was difficult because the knife didn't reach all of the way through. Finally, one strong sawing motion cut through the string, the cake erupted, and two old straw shoes burst out. When the laughter died down, Ardeth told Irene that on the hard days of her treatments she could play the video and remember that she had finally been gotten the best of. Irene responded that figuring out how to return those shoes would extend her life!

In 1986, the twenty-sixth floor of the Church Office Building was the setting for the annual Lambda Delta Sigma social event of the year. Ardeth, then the Young Women general president, was to receive the "Elect Lady" award from the

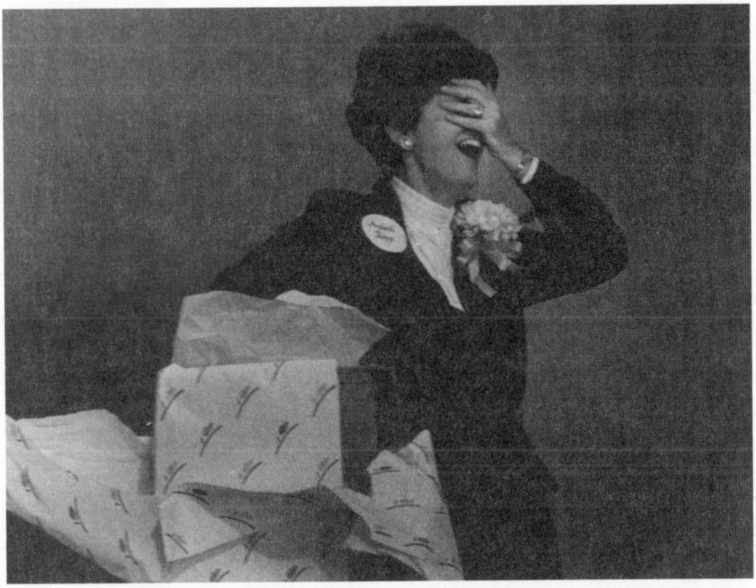

The presentation of the shoes at the Lambda Delta Sigma social

national Church sorority. Present at a luncheon in her honor were more than three hundred coeds and their leaders from the Intermountain West. Many of Ardeth's family members and friends, as well as her counselors in the Young Women general presidency, were also in attendance. The theme for the special occasion was "On Your Toes." Each round table had been beautifully decorated with a centerpiece of pastel flowers. Artistically mounted in the center were two small satin toe shoes in dance position. Irene knew of this event, as well as the theme Ardeth would address. She called Ardeth's sister, Sharon, and gave her specific instructions for preparing the infamous shoes and when to present them.

Following an impressive presentation by dancers from Ballet West, Ardeth stepped to the podium to address the audience. Before she could begin, she was handed a large box wrapped in decorated paper and tied with a purple bow. Thanking the attendees for their thoughtfulness, she tore off the paper and lifted the lid. Gazing at the contents, she shouted, "Oh, no!" Nestled in the box were a pair of pink straw shoes, mounted on a platform and designed to look like ballerina slippers. An inscription on the platform read: "On Your Toes. Love, Irene." The bewildered audience looked to her for an explanation, and to their delight, she explained the "shoes of friendship." These shoes had now been exchanged for over twenty-five years.

When Irene passed away a short time later, Ardeth took the shoes to a florist, briefly explained their history, and requested the creation of a floral wreath to include them. Members of Irene's family later retrieved the shoes from the cemetery and returned them to Ardeth. In a letter written to honor Irene and sent to the members of the old Sunshine Club, Ardeth wrote: "This is not the end. Friendships that survive through the years will not end with this life, but will continue on in other times and places. I will keep the shoes for now, but Irene will see them again, and our sunshine club will never end."

CHAPTER EIGHT

"Lean Not unto Thine Own Understanding"

LONGINGS

Ardeth's picture of her life as an adult had always included a family of her own. In her mind she would be living in a little house surrounded by a white picket fence. Her yard would have lots of flowers, especially sweet peas, hollyhocks, and gladiolas along the fence. And to complete the picture, no fewer than eight children would be running in and out the door, climbing the fence with the flowers, growing up under their parents' watchful care.

Having no children was something she had never contemplated, nor had Heber. When a baby did not arrive as soon as they had hoped they began to feel anxious, but not overly concerned. They still lived in anticipation of the time when the longed-for baby would be added to their family. Every month they thought that it would be only nine more months before that glorious event. Every month they were disappointed.

Time marched inexorably on. Babies came to the homes of

their friends. Why not to them? That question remained unanswered. They found that they had to decide whether to share in the joy of their friends' children without becoming envious, or withdraw inside themselves. Desiring to continue their friendships, they chose the former course of action. They tried to rejoice in each new birth; they refused to let their own heartache prevent them from sharing in the happiness of others.

Once, during an overnight camp-out with friends who had small children, Ardeth found herself in tears just at the sight of the young mother wiping her child's nose. Running into her tent, she sobbed out her longing for a little nose to wipe. Even the smallest things reminded her of their childless state. Again, she wondered how long they would have to wait.

After visiting doctors and undergoing a series of tests, they received the devastating news that it would take a miracle for them to ever have children. Since they believed in miracles, they maintained a positive attitude regarding their eventual parenthood, fully believing that their desire for a large family would not be denied. They trusted that their Heavenly Father had heard their petition and would grant their deeply held longings for children.

Their emotions ranged from hopefulness to doubt. They remembered the commandment, given as part of their marriage covenant, to multiply and replenish the earth. Another thought came. Perhaps they were not worthy or righteous enough to qualify for the blessing of children. It was difficult for them to be able to explain their feelings, even to each other, much less to family and friends. Ardeth struggled with her emotions. If she wasn't to be a mother, what was she to be?

"I will forever remember the day a child new to our neighborhood knocked on our door and asked if our children could come out to play. I explained to him, as to others young and old, for the thousandth time, that we didn't have any children. This little boy squinted his eyes in a quizzical look and asked the question I had not dared put into words. 'If you are not a mother, then what are you?'" (*My Neighbor, My Sister, My Friend* [Salt Lake City: Deseret Book, 1990], 121).

Not for Now

After countless times of fasting and prayer, they requested a special blessing from a member of their stake presidency. Following the blessing, they attended the temple in the attitude of fasting and prayer, yearning to know the Lord's will in their behalf. That day they left the temple with a feeling that they would not be blessed to have children born to them in mortality. They had long since learned to listen to the whisperings of the Spirit, and they could not deny the promptings they had been given. Difficult as it was, they would accept it. But now they desired to know why. Why would they not be given children to teach and to love in mortality? Were they unworthy? Would they not be good parents? Why would the Lord withhold this longed-for blessing? Ardeth agonized over her thoughts.

Then came the day that Heber was called to be a bishop. Finally she was convinced that their childless state was not because of unrighteousness.

Friends and family members began suggesting adoption. Surely this would be the answer. Knowing that the Lord could put babies in the families where they were supposed to be, she had no reservations about adopting a child. Again, they took the matter to their Heavenly Father, repeatedly addressing the question in fasting and prayer. Each time they experienced a stupor of thought. Ardeth later said: "If you get a stupor of thought instead of a confirmation, you have to decide whether you're going to go against that principle you've learned about being guided by the Spirit and say, 'I'm going to do it my way,' or, 'then we must wait.'" They did not receive a confirmation that they should adopt.

"From my own experience, I've learned that the only lasting peace is the peace that comes when we strive to follow the Lord's will concerning our opportunities in life. To do that, we must consider our alternatives, formulate a decision, and take it to the Lord. Then, as President Dallin Oaks observed when he was president of Brigham Young University, 'When a choice will make a difference in our lives—. . . and where we are living in tune with the Spirit and seeking his guidance, we can be sure we will receive the guidance to attain our goal. The Lord will not leave us unassisted when a choice is important to our eternal welfare'" (*My Neighbor, My Sister, My Friend,* 125). They learned that they must be willing to bend not only their knees, but also their wills.

One of the most difficult aspects of their childless state came in the form of questions and comments from family members and friends. It was difficult to explain that although they loved children and longed for their own, they had received a different answer. The perception by some that they were selfish and chose not to take on the responsibility of rearing children hurt deeply. Comments were made that if they would adopt they could learn to love children. Doctor friends said they could get a baby for them. Still, they felt that they had received direction and must be obedient. Even so, they wondered why.

One evening when Ardeth was alone she contemplated the possibility that she would never bear a child in this life. Suddenly, a scripture that had great meaning to her as a young girl came echoing into her mind: "Trust in the Lord with all thine heart; and lean not unto thine own understanding. In all thy ways acknowledge him, and he shall direct thy paths" (Proverbs 3:4–5). The words were not new, but the message came as an answer to a fervent prayer.

The next question for which Ardeth sought an answer pertained to what she could do to live a fulfilled life. "One night, as my husband and I were reaching for that 'kindly light' to lead us 'amid the encircling gloom,' we read a statement from President David O. McKay: 'The noblest aim in life is to strive . . . to make other lives . . . happier'" (*My Neighbor, My Sister, My Friend,* 126).

Ardeth explained: "These words were like a beacon in the dark. They became a motto, a guiding light. That night, speaking I think by inspiration from the Lord, the patriarch of our family said to me, 'You need not possess children to love them. . . . The world is filled with people to be loved, guided, taught, lifted, and inspired.'" Heber also observed that what matters most is how you respond to the situation. Some time later, while studying the New Testament, the message in 2 Corinthians 1:3–7 came like a voice from heaven: "Blessed be God, even the Father of our Lord Jesus Christ, the Father of mercies, and the God of all comfort; who comforteth us in all our tribulation, that we may be able to comfort them which are in any trouble, by the comfort wherewith we ourselves are comforted of God. For as the sufferings of Christ abound in us, so our consolation also aboundeth by Christ. And whether we be afflicted, it is for your consolation and salvation, which is effectual in the enduring of the same sufferings which we also suffer; or whether we be comforted, it is for your consolation and salvation. And our hope of you is stedfast, knowing, that as ye are partakers of the sufferings, so shall ye be also of the consolation."

Ardeth has delivered comfort and hope to countless childless couples through her writing, her public speaking, and hundreds of letters. She has come to know, in a personal way, that when the Lord comforts us in our tribulation, we are able to offer that same comfort to others.

Her Life Is the Lord's

Ardeth and Heber realized that if they were to learn important lessons about unselfishness and sacrifice that their friends with children were learning, they must put themselves in situations where they could serve. They began to say yes to almost every request to speak and to teach. It wasn't long before they had many opportunities to serve and to sacrifice. Ardeth's niece, Shelly, observed that when Ardeth realized she wasn't going to have children, she completely turned her life over to the Lord. "I hardly ever see her doing something for herself. She's out on speaking assignments, visiting friends, preparing talks, serving in the temple. She is always serving. I think she must have thought, 'If I am not going to be a mom at home with my kids, then my life is the Lord's. I am going to do all I can elsewhere.' And she does."

Even so, there have still been times when she has dealt with restless, uncertain feelings accompanied by the desire to know if her life is acceptable to Him. She recorded in her journal in 1980: "I keep thinking of my blessing that tells me I'll know the Lord's will concerning me. I so want to fill the measure of my creation and do what it is I'm supposed to do. I've thought over the years that not having children would finally be a closed subject that was accepted and no more thought about—but I guess those feelings will always be there. More than anything else in the whole world, I'd like to have a family—children—grandchildren and be a homemaker—a good neighbor and friend. Sometimes I feel lonesome inside."

Not one to dwell on her feelings of lonesomeness, Ardeth strives to bring solace to those who may be experiencing similar feelings by continuing to accept requests to speak to childless couples across the country. She answers countless letters, seeking to bring peace and comfort by sharing her confidence and faith in Heavenly Father's plan for each individual. Her thoughts, both written and spoken, have brought peace to many. "We who do not have children can wallow in self-pity—or we can experience 'birth pains' as we struggle to open the passageway to eternal life for ourselves and others. I bear testimony that instead of wrapping our empty and aching arms around ourselves, we can reach out to others. As we do so, one day we can even be able to hold our friends' babies and rejoice" (*My Neighbor, My Sister, My Friend,* 127).

In His Own Time

The peace, comfort, and eternal perspective obtained by Ardeth and Heber did not come quickly or easily. She explained: "I don't know how long it will be for others who have similar longings. For us it was years. But one day we did gain an eternal perspective, and we felt peace, not pain; hope, not despair. I would have liked so much to have received that insight years before, but I know that had that happened, I would have been deprived of the growth that comes from being comforted by the witness of the Spirit after the trial of my faith.

"If I have any comforting message for others, it is this: Peace of mind comes from keeping an eternal perspective. Motherhood, I believe, is a foreordained mission. For some, this glorious blessing may be delayed, but it will not be denied. Motherhood is an eternal reality for all women who live righteously and accept the teachings of the gospel" (*My Neighbor, My Sister, My Friend,* 127–28).

Because Ardeth has experienced feelings known only to women who have remained childless, and because she speaks openly and eloquently about them, she is able to bless the lives of many others.

Typical of the comfort her message brings to those who deal with feelings of despair when confronted with the possibility of childlessness are the thoughts expressed in excerpts from the following letter:

"My oldest daughter battled infertility for several years. . . . [She] demonstrated . . . a determination that she was not going to be defined by her condition and often commented that she was in the good company of Sister Ardeth Kapp. Many times people would say to her: 'You just need to have enough faith.' Hasn't Sister Kapp had enough faith? Sister Kapp's life continually shows that faith is not what you demonstrate to get what you want—it is what you demonstrate no matter what you get. . . .

Had [Sister Kapp] had a house full of little ones, . . . my daughter might not have had the example that she so desperately needed to see her through her own period of adversity."

As the years pass, Ardeth is able to share in the joy of the families of her friends, even though the feelings are sometimes bittersweet. "Each year, the Christmas cards sent by friends increase in size to accommodate pictures of their expanding families. For now, our family picture remains the same—just the two of us. My desires for children of my own remains strong, and I think that's all right. Even though I accept the will of the Lord, I would not wish for us to ever lose our desire for a family." In the meantime, Ardeth and Heber have complete confidence in the promises of their Heavenly Father. They have been assured the blessings of a family in His own way and in His own time.

CHAPTER NINE

To Their Good

A Dream Renewed

Following the sale of their lot in Centerville, Ardeth and Heber continued to serve wholeheartedly in their callings in the Bountiful Stake. A few months later, they became aware of a lot for sale on Center Street in Bountiful. This property, within their stake boundaries, seemed to be perfect for them. It had an even better view than the lot which they had sold. Even though it was more expensive, they were surprised to find that it was still at a price they could afford. They made the decision to purchase the lot and were able to pay for it more quickly than they had thought. Within a short time it was completely paid for.

Not long after, Heber began to seek a construction loan. Since he planned to build the home himself, he took his drawings with him for the loan officers to look over. Although they tried to be polite, a couple of them laughed at his sketches. He was turned down in his request by four different lending institutions. A fifth loan officer asked to keep the plans so that he

Ardeth and Heber officially break ground for their first home, July 1959

could study them. Calling Heber into his office a few weeks later, the officer asked about his construction experience and how many homes he had built. When Heber replied that he had no experience and had not built even one home, the officer asked him why he thought he could build this home. Heber's response was, "I just know I can." The loan officer told him that the lending institution had fifteen criteria that needed to be met before they would make a loan. He said that Heber did not qualify in any of the areas. Despite this, they were going to give him the loan, though they were not sure why.

On July 23, 1959, just over a year after Heber's call to serve on the stake high council, construction workers operating heavy-duty equipment dug a hole for the basement of the Kapp's future home. Earlier, Heber and Ardeth took a shovel to their lot for their own ground-breaking ceremony. They rejoiced together that what had once seemed a setback had turned to their good.

Because of their previous careful planning, they were well acquainted with each detail of their future home and were able to begin work immediately.

They were determined to build as much of the house as they could by themselves. They went as far as they could, then drove to construction sites looking for homes that were at a similar stage. There they noted what had to be done next. For example, they carefully studied how to put the plate on the concrete foundation so that they could begin the framing process. They found there was always someone willing to answer their questions if they were willing to ask. They worked early in the mornings, each stopping to go to their jobs when the time came. Heber returned again in the afternoon after school, and Ardeth joined him at the end of her day with the telephone company. In this way, step by step, they completed each stage of construction from the foundation to the roof.

Their budget for the completed structure included money they had set aside to be used on interior furnishings, including carpet, window coverings, and other accessories. Ardeth, who had always been interested in fabric, texture, and design, took an extension course in interior decorating so she could plan the furnishings herself. However, they found that even the best planning and budgeting sometimes fail to take into account the often hidden costs inherent in home building. By the time all of the essential elements of the home—the foundation, walls, and roof—were completed, there was little left for interior furnishings. Ardeth lamented to Heber that the foundation alone cost more than what they had planned to spend on furnishing the inside, and you couldn't even see it! However, they both realized that a firm foundation, although unseen, was necessary to the integrity of the whole structure. Nothing would be compromised by delaying the desired furnishings for a time.

When the home was completed, an article in the Mountain States Telephone Company newsletter chronicled their accomplishment: "Talk about do-it-yourself! Ardeth Kapp, business office supervisor, Commercial Department, and her husband, Heber, did just that. Working evenings and weekends, they built their own house from bottom to top. The couple designed and drew their own plans for the split-level, six-room house, which covers 1600 square feet and is complete with utility room and a full basement.

"Ardeth pitched in and did her part of the work by doing all the wall papering and staining the cabinets in the kitchen, not to mention the tarring of the foundation. In addition, she helped her husband with the lathing, flooring, electrical work, shingling, and painting. During the construction period, she was also taking an extension course in interior decorating, which enabled her to plan the interior. She is now fashioning some of the draperies. Actual construction of the house was started in August, 1959, and as of May of this year, the do-it-yourself house is 'home' to Ardeth and Heber Kapp."

They moved into their new home in May 1960, approximately a year and a half from the time when they thought they had buried their homebuilding dream forever. It was a testimony to them that the Lord was watching over their lives. Once again, what had been seen as a setback had a purpose. A phrase found in Doctrine and Covenants 90:24 became a firmly entrenched slogan: "Search diligently, pray always, and be believing, and all things shall work together for your good." With faith, trust, and obedience, their blessings had been multiplied.

YOU MUST RETURN

Ardeth often reflected on a promise in her patriarchal blessing: "Your life has been preserved for a wise purpose." Through life's highs and lows she took comfort from this quiet whisper. Then came a time when she felt that her life was at a standstill and that she was going nowhere. Feeling that she would not be blessed with a posterity in this life, she struggled to find and then to fulfill the purpose of her creation. With each new Church calling or while assisting Heber to fulfill his callings, she thought, "This is the wise purpose." Still, deep inside, she felt uncertain, at times almost despairing. She wept, she fasted, she prayed, deeply and often. She continually sought to know her Heavenly Father's will concerning her life.

On March 14, 1960, her mother's birthday, she returned to Glenwood to attend funeral services for her aunt. Standing at the grave site, her coat turned up around her neck for protection against the biting wind, she felt a sense of urgency about something, although she didn't know what. Then in her mind she heard a gentle whisper: "Time is passing. You must return to school and get your degree." It had been over ten years since she had last been a student, just prior to her marriage. Why should she now have the feeling that she must return to school? She felt excited. Although she didn't know the purpose, an exhilarating sense of peace and direction came over her.

Returning home, she discussed the experience and her feelings with Heber. She felt that if she was to be obedient to the promptings she had received, she must return to school immediately. Ever supportive, Heber agreed, although he suggested she wait until summer was over and enroll for the fall quarter. Her friends at work, however, thought she was crazy. Here she was, they told her, the employment and personnel representative, interviewing and hiring college graduates who were hoping for a chance to some day have a job like hers. She had the highest position possible for a woman in the telephone company at that time. Her idea of returning to school made no sense to them at all.

Although she couldn't logically explain it to others, and even though returning to school at age thirty hardly made sense even to her, she had learned to follow the promptings of the Spirit. She knew she must be obedient. When she expressed to Heber the urgency she felt to begin her studies immediately, he agreed that she should enroll for summer quarter at the University of Utah. Reluctant to have her leave, her boss advised her that if she would continue to work full-time, the telephone company would pay for a portion of her tuition.

She transferred her eight hours of credit from Brigham Young University and began that summer, taking three classes of five credit hours each. In addition to her employment, she continued to serve as her ward Young Women president. Heber provided continuous support, and even though she was very busy, she had a confirming feeling that she was doing the right thing. She was also very happy in her dream home.

For Only a Year

In 1961, shortly before the end of summer quarter, while Ardeth was at school, Heber answered a knock at their door. A man standing on the porch said that he and his wife had been admiring their home while visiting friends across the street. He asked if it was for sale. Jokingly, Heber responded, "Well, I suppose anything I have is for sale at a price!" He soon found out that the man was very serious. He and his wife had sold their home in Ogden and had to be out within two weeks. Heber explained that he could not sell without his wife's consent. Nevertheless, the would-be buyer was serious enough that he was writing out an earnest-money check just as Ardeth returned from school. By the time Heber had a chance to give Ardeth an explanation, the man was back with his wife to tour the home. After looking through it, they said that they liked everything about the house and wanted to buy it. Almost before Ardeth had time to realize what was happening, she and Heber had sold the home they had occupied for only a year! Even though it had happened unexpectedly and very quickly, Ardeth felt that it was right. Heber told her that by selling this house they would have enough money to build another one. He just hadn't expected that they would have to begin thinking about building again so soon.

From Ardeth's perspective, the move could hardly have come at a worse time. In the midst of preparing for finals, she now found herself needing to find a place to live. They located an apartment across the street from their church house. Within two weeks they were moving out of their home as the new owners were moving in. Although still in the same stake, the apartment was in another ward, which meant that Ardeth was released as the ward Young Women president.

While Heber continued serving on the stake high council, Ardeth received an assignment to teach the MIA Maids in her new ward. There were ten fourteen-year-old girls in the group, and she wanted to become acquainted with each one. She eagerly plunged into planning lessons and activities. On their first meeting together as a class, one of the girls announced: "You don't have to bother to call and ask for my attendance. Just mark me absent at sacrament meeting, 'cause I never go and I never intend to" (*Miracles in Pinafores and Bluejeans* [Salt Lake City: Deseret Book, 1977], 23). To Ardeth's surprise, she found that many of the others were less than enthusiastic about attending Mutual, giving the excuse that they were too busy with school. But she was not satisfied with their excuses, and she carefully set about to change their attitudes.

I Made Them a Deal

"I made them a deal," Ardeth recalls. "I told them I was also busy with school. Trying to graduate in three years, I was taking a maximum load at the University of Utah, including summer attendance. In addition, I was working full-time. If they could show me they had more studies or more tests and were busier than I was, they were excused. If not, they had to come because I would be prepared to teach them." The girls compared their studies and their time pressures with those of their new teacher. In the end, they all came.

By the time her MIA Maid girls were of age to become Laurels and move out of her class, they had all become good friends. In addition, they each felt a strong connection with their leader and were reluctant to change. After some discussion, and without Ardeth's knowledge, the girls approached the bishop with an idea. Could their teacher please advance with her class?

Although it was unusual, the bishop agreed to their request. The girls were elated, and the MIA Maid teacher was equally pleased.

Over their time together, Ardeth and the girls she taught shared experiences that bound them together with fond memories. After three years together they had become a close-knit group. They decided to come up with something they could leave as a legacy for those coming after them. Their stake was in the process of raising funds to be used for building a recreation center, so they decided to put on a fashion show, sell tickets, and give the money they earned to the stake president to help with the new building. With no funds and no experience, they enthusiastically forged ahead.

Ardeth recalls how the program developed:

"Plans were made, committees were assigned, and a report-back meeting was scheduled. After that, each meeting became an

Ardeth with her Mia Maid class at a gathering in the mountains

enlargement and expansion of the original plan. It was when the girls decided on a luncheon for all of the girls and women in the ward, in addition to the fashion show, that they had to expand their resources. One of the girls began to break the barrier that seemed to limit their dreams when she proposed an idea: 'Why don't each of us have our moms serve on the committee we're responsible for?' Some thought it was a great idea and readily volunteered their mothers' help. Others were more hesitant. 'I don't know if I want to work on a committee with my mother. We don't really get along all that well.' But when the strength of these expanded resources was considered, it was unanimous that every girl would at least ask her mother and report back next week.

"By the time of the next meeting every mother had agreed to help—including one mother who had seldom been inside the Church but who now agreed to be a member of the committee of which her daughter would be chairman. With their [mothers] now involved, the girls continued to enlarge upon their plans. One suggested that they should invite the whole stake. Another recommended that they build a big ramp to extend from the stage out into the cultural hall. Someone else thought that the ramp should be covered with red carpeting with large plants lining both sides.

"Realizing not only their limited resources, but also the labor which would be needed, one by one the girls began volunteering their fathers, each assuring the others that her dad would help. One of the fathers had never been involved in *any* Church activity, but the girls remained undaunted. The dads, who all agreed to help, were not the only men who were recruited.

Mothers began volunteering their sons and fathers recommended priesthood quorum members. By this time, ticket sales had increased to the extent that the size of the ramp had to be shortened to allow room for more and more tables.

"With such interest in the event, the program committee . . . decided such an elaborate affair would surely justify a celebrity to announce the fashions and to be the show's moderator. The girls learned that Rosemarie Reed, an internationally known fashion designer, was visiting in Orem, Utah. . . . They contacted her and she accepted their invitation" (*Miracles in Pinafores and Bluejeans,* 23–26).

Ardeth was anxious that the whole experience be a positive one in every way for her young charges. She later remembered that in the midst of the furor of preparation, she sent a silent prayer heavenward, which she repeated every day until the event was completed: "Heavenly Father, if you'll help me to lead these girls successfully through all of this preparation to a successful outcome, I promise I'll never get myself involved in such a big project again!" It was a promise she was destined not to keep.

"Throughout the weeks preceding the event, the only detail that remained constant was the date, and when it finally arrived, the events unfolded as planned and with all of the girls' dreams fulfilled. Mothers and fathers, brothers and sisters were there to support their Laurels. The stake presidency, members of the high council, and many fathers took their places as waiters just as the girls had envisioned, each dressed in black pants, bow tie, and white shirt, and with a towel over the left arm" (*Miracles in Pinafores and Bluejeans,* 26).

The following Sunday morning, the Laurels and their

teacher met with the stake presidency and high council at the stake center. It was a very special experience for each girl. The class president presented $700 to the stake president, explaining that it was a gift from this ward Laurel class to those who would follow them.

An article in the *Church News* titled "Triumph in Fashion" spotlighted the event. While the article gave a glowing report of the show, the real triumph was known only in the hearts of each of those who had participated. As each girl gave a report to the stake president, the event was finally summarized: "*When we had our family behind us, supporting us and working with us, we had fun in working together. And it seemed as though there wasn't anything we couldn't do*" (*Miracles in Pinafores and Bluejeans,* 26).

Not long after the fashion show, Heber and Ardeth completed building their second home. The move took them to another ward in their stake, and she was called as the second counselor in the stake Young Women presidency. Although she was happy for the opportunity to serve in this new calling, she was reluctant to have the close association she had enjoyed with "her girls" come to an end.

"That Same Sociality"

Throughout the years, Ardeth and the girls in her class have remained friends. They plan get-togethers as time and distance allow. On January 8, 2005, the women held a luncheon in honor of their former teacher. Looking back over forty years since the beginning of their association, they sat in a circle to reminisce. Each voiced a common thought. While they have forgotten many of the lessons she taught, they have not forgotten her love for them. A special bond still connects them to her and to each other.

One former Laurel, Marsha Gurr Richards, now a member of the Young Women general board, does remember a specific lesson. "Ardeth told us that happiness depends more on what happens on the inside of us than what happens on the outside. She said that Heavenly Father has a plan for our lives. She shared her personal philosophy that even though we may not understand it at the time, all things will work together for our good. Those two thoughts were so profound to me that I recorded them on an index card and taped the card to my closet door where it remained until I married. Thirty years later, my mother gave me a manila envelope containing papers of mine that she had found. Inside, I found this card, now brittle and yellowed with age. Memories flooded back as I began to realize that indeed, all things, even the hard ones, had worked together for my good."

Another former class member recalled Ardeth saying that the lessons given would mean more to them as they grew older. She found that to be true. One remembered how Ardeth decorated her classroom, often bringing fresh flowers to make it more attractive. Taking note of how effective that was, she finds herself doing the same thing in her teaching profession.

As they continued reminiscing, their thoughts turned to the fashion show. They laughingly recalled that Ardeth kept the money they had earned in a pillowcase on her bedroom shelf until it was presented to the stake president. They also remembered how their parents had appreciated being involved in helping with the preparation for that big event. One mentioned that

Ardeth (center) reunited with her Mia Maid and Laurel class

her parents felt as though Ardeth loved them as much as she loved their daughter. She honored their roles as mothers and fathers. This feeling of love and support helped turn them back toward the gospel, and they gradually realigned themselves with the Church.

Ardeth said that at the time she worked with those young women, she was beginning to realize that she would not have children of her own. Those girls helped to fill a void in her life, and she loved them. However, she received an impression that she should not try to take the place of their mothers or in any way come between them and their families. Carefully heeding that prompting, she helped to forge bonds between the parents and their children, which had a profoundly positive impact on all of the families.

The only former class member who was unable to be in attendance at the luncheon wrote Ardeth a letter. "I want you to know how much you have meant to me throughout my life," she said. "Your influence when I was one of 'your girls' was so positive, and I know led me to make choices that will have eternal blessings. I remember one particular lesson where . . . we were all acting rather like the teenage girls we were, and were not being very attentive. You stopped the lesson and informed us that you were working, going to school, and had many things to do, just as we were all involved. You were making the effort to be there to teach us, and that if you could put in the time, we ought to be able to do the same. Dead Quiet. You gave us a wonderfully prepared lesson, but the only lesson I remember from that night was that I never wanted to do anything to disappoint you. Many times in my life I have thought of that night, and hoped sincerely that you would never be disappointed in the direction my life was going."

Ardeth said that she always had a feeling in her heart that their loyalty to the gospel would sustain them. And it has. Even though all have had trials and challenges, all ten of the former young women are actively engaged in Church service, with strong testimonies of the gospel. As that special reunion drew to a close, with everyone obviously reluctant to part, Ardeth said, "This day is priceless." And then she quoted a favorite scripture: "And that same sociality which exists among us here will exist among us there, only it will be coupled with eternal glory" (D&C 130:2).

A Little Miracle

In response to an article in the *Church News* (January 15, 2005) that chronicled the reunion of Ardeth and her former class, Ardeth received the following letter from a brother in Virginia.

"Dear Sister Kapp: It feels a little strange writing a letter to you about such a brief incident long ago, but the recent article in the *Deseret News* about your reunion with your Laurels prompted me to write.

"In the mid-1980s, I was a struggling returned missionary living in Bountiful. One day you came into the store where I worked. It was natural to recognize you because of your prominence as Young Women's general president. . . . I remember thinking, 'This is kind of neat—wonder what she's really like?'

"I was at a very real low point in my life at the time, having recently lost my mother and my best high school friend to illnesses. Even more difficult was the struggle I was experiencing in my personal and spiritual life—I certainly qualified as one of the 'walking wounded.' As you came through the counter and I rang up your purchase, we struck up a conversation. . . .

"That's when something happened. I don't know what you said to me, if it was unspoken, if you asked my name, or any of the details. But I knew from your demeanor that you sensed a need in me and that you cared about me. There was an unspoken expression of love and confidence and concern. As you left, I remember thinking, 'She knew. She knew how low I am. How could she know that?' I also felt the Spirit of the Lord.

"After you left, I felt uplifted not just for that day alone, but that little experience, along with some others, gave me the courage to continue on. I have a family now, and a great life in the Church. I look back on that period, and there are a handful of things that stand out now as turning points. One of them is this brief minute with a complete stranger—a little miracle. Thank you."

Ardeth, who over the years has received countless letters containing similar expressions of gratitude observed, "We can never know when someone needs a smile or a kind word. By striving to be spiritually in tune, we can be the means of lifting another without even realizing it." And the effects of such a kindness can have long-lasting and even life-changing effects.

CHAPTER TEN

Seek Learning

By Study

Ardeth continued to work full-time at the telephone company and to take the maximum number of classes at the university. Any spare time was taken up with homework. After one hard evening of studying, she went into the kitchen to reward herself with milk and donuts. She remarked to Heber, "In the next world I want to be thin and smart." In his humorous way, Heber responded, "If you'd quit eating donuts and keep on studying, maybe you could be thin and smart in this world!"

At times Ardeth felt discouraged when her grades failed to measure up to the high standard she had set for herself, and she experienced the insecurities that had stalked her during grade school. On one occasion, the professor of her class in public administration posted the scores of a test on the board. Ardeth was devastated when she realized that her score was the lowest one. During this and similar times she did the only thing she knew to do: she prayed hard and studied harder. Her hard work and preparation paid off. The public administration professor, Dr. Arthur Wiscombe, realizing her discouragement at having received the lowest grade in the class on the first test, called her after the next one. Since she was not at home, he left a message with Heber—she had received the highest grade in the class! She was ecstatic. That call was just the boost she needed. It gave her new confidence.

While contemplating a major, Ardeth entertained the idea of obtaining a degree in elementary education. Some time after she began her university studies, the bishop of her ward, who was also a superintendent of schools, commented on the wonderful rapport she had with the young women of her ward and added, "We need people like you in education. Please think about teaching school." She felt that if she was not to have a family, teaching school would give her the opportunity to work with children and to tutor, understand, and love them. The bishop's counsel came as a confirmation of what she should do.

"My Philosophy"

While enrolled in a philosophy class in 1962, Ardeth fulfilled an assignment to write a paper regarding her personal beliefs, a one-page, hand-written essay simply titled, "My Philosophy of Life."

"Life, to me is a rich experience with a definite purpose," she wrote. "Its purpose is to strive for self-mastery. One should strive to live life in the fullest sense. This would be achieved by making a maximum contribution to the betterment of society, and being mentally prepared to recognize all experiences in life as a possible schooling situation. Even the most unpleasant events can serve as a challenge to one's sense of inner balance and the ability to be in command of one's own conduct.

"Since I feel an assurance of a pre-existence and a life after death, the relative uncertainty of mortal life does not detract from efforts toward self-mastery, since life will continue on in a situation where these accomplishments will be of added value. Although I have many unanswered questions relating to life, I am grateful that the magnitude of the universe is not limited to man's understanding, and that a Supreme Being exists, giving purpose to life."

"ALSO BY FAITH"

As she moved closer to graduation, her studies continued to be a challenge, in part because of her full-time work. So, in the fall of 1963, she terminated her employment with the telephone company. When her credits were evaluated for graduation, projected for the following spring, it was discovered that she was three hours short of the required number. Since she was already registered for the maximum number of hours allowed, she enrolled in a home study course in English literature. She wrote the papers for the entire course between Christmas and New Year's Day. Since she could hand in only one lesson per week, she numbered them and turned them in weekly over the course of the quarter.

With graduation drawing near, her transcripts were reviewed and her advisor saw that she had failed freshman English. Often her professors would write comments on her papers like, "good thoughts," "creative ideas," or "good sequence." One professor added, "But how did you ever get through freshman English?" Ardeth assumed this was a reference to her creative spelling. She admitted to her advisor that she had never retaken the class because she couldn't fit it into her schedule. Going over her grades, the advisor commented, "You could not have as high a grade point as you do and not know English." The requirement was waived and, much to her relief, she was cleared for graduation.

By attending classes all year round, she completed all of the work for a bachelor's degree in three years. In addition, she graduated cum laude. It was a testimony to her of the truth of the scripture in Doctrine and Covenants 88:118: "Seek learning, even by study and also by faith." She studied diligently, but she also sought her Heavenly Father's help to increase her understanding. Study and faith were both essential parts of her learning.

During her last quarter, Ardeth was a student teacher at the Stewart Training School on the University of Utah campus. Following graduation she was asked to remain at the school as a full-time teacher. Though flattered by the offer, she accepted a position as a fourth-grade teacher at Oak Hills Elementary School in Bountiful, located near her home. She felt that teaching the children of her friends and neighbors would be a wonderful opportunity.

A few days prior to graduation (which occurred on June 8, 1964), one of her friends told Ardeth to pray for rain on graduation day. When quizzed as to the reason, the friend only said, "Just pray for rain." Although Ardeth did not comply with the request, with graduation day came a pouring rainstorm, and the commencement exercises, which were planned for the football stadium, were quickly moved indoors.

That evening Ardeth learned the rest of the story. Another friend had made arrangements for a helicopter pilot to fly a banner reading, "Yay, Ardeth!" over the football field during the commencement. Ardeth, who already felt conspicuous because she was older than the majority of the graduates, was happy to have dodged the extra attention the stunt would have produced.

A Sister, a Move, and a Wedding

Not long after Ardeth and Heber had moved into their new home, Sharon went to live with them while she completed her student teaching. After graduating from BYU, she obtained a teaching position at an elementary school in Bountiful and continued living with them for the next three years. Sharon maintained an active dating life and later remembered her sister and brother-in-law shepherding her through many courtship traumas. She said, "It seemed like we had our best talks just as we were kneeling for prayer each night. It has been an eternal blessing for me to be tutored by these two great people during my early twenties when I was choosing an eternal companion and observing how a good marriage works." In the course of time, Sharon became friends with a young man from Bountiful named Ralph Larsen. The two had initially met at BYU. After Ralph left to serve a mission in Germany, Ardeth encouraged her to keep writing to him, which she did.

Ardeth and Heber had lived in their second home for close to three years when they were again approached by would-be buyers asking if they would sell. An agreement was made, and following another period of apartment dwelling, they were ready to move into the home Heber completed just following Ardeth's graduation. In addition, Sharon was to be married on July 2. Her courtship with Ralph Larsen had resumed following his mission. In remembering that hectic time, Sharon said, "With everything else that was going on, Ardeth planned a wonderful open house for us a few days following our marriage in the Cardston Temple. She hung baskets of daisies around the rafters of their new garage. All of the bushes and greenery they were going to plant were set around the yard in their pots. I look back on that time and wonder how in the world she did all that!"

CLASSROOM TEACHER

In the fall of 1964, Ardeth began her teaching career with a group of fourth graders in Room 16 at Oak Hills Elementary in Bountiful. She had carefully set her goals for these students: "To see that every child felt good about himself, and, with increased confidence, have opportunities for reaching his potential" (*The Gentle Touch* [Salt Lake City: Deseret Book, 1978], 2). Since school had been difficult for her, she wanted to help her students enjoy learning. It could even be said that she wanted them to have fun! Her innovative teaching methods were memorable as well as fun. One geography lesson serves as an example.

Knowing that geography had no seeming relevance to the world of nine-year-olds, Ardeth decided to try an approach that she hoped would help capture their interest and make the learning fun. She told the children about her plan for an imaginary airplane trip which would take them across the state as they learned about the geography of Utah. The students were formed into groups who were to become experts in their designated areas. One group was assigned to make large maps of the major land formations. Another studied rainfall reports. Still others became knowledgeable regarding industry and tourism in the state. Some of the boys were assigned to research the fishing, hiking, and boating opportunities. Everyone had a part.

Large charts were prepared that would show the areas they were to study, as if they were seeing them from the air. Each group of students was to serve as guides for the various areas on which they had become experts. Finally, Ardeth prepared her classroom to look as much as possible like the inside of an airplane. The desks were arranged in rows. Seat belts, airsick pills, and even brown paper bags (in the event the pills didn't work) were all part of the enactment. As the trip would take the entire school day, stewardesses from the class were assigned to make arrangements with the cooks in the kitchen for lunch to be served in flight. After much discussion regarding the coveted position, one student was assigned to be the captain of the plane. His voice, giving explanations and instructions regarding the flight, was recorded. Sounds of the plane taking off, as well as in flight, were recorded with the help of a hand mixer.

As the day for the flight over Utah landmarks drew near, the excitement level in the class grew higher and higher. The students were eager for the day to arrive. One evening, shortly before the big event, Ardeth answered the phone in her home. An anxious parent nervously rehearsed her concerns for the safety of her child during the trip. Trying to ease her fear, Ardeth explained that they really were not going to leave the classroom. The mother responded, "But Patty said she had a ticket and was going to meet the plane and . . ." As Ardeth explained the plan, the mother became satisfied and even enthused about the trip. In fact, if there had been room, she might have even been willing to join the flight! Ardeth later wrote, "The following day—

watching Patty lean steadily to the right in her seat as the captain's voice explained over the increased volume of the engines that we were climbing over the high Wasatch Mountains, and if we looked to the right, we could see the heavily populated area below—I wondered if her mother might still question the reality of our flight when Patty reported her day's experience with the study of geography" (*The Gentle Touch,* 75–76).

Before beginning her first year of teaching, Ardeth was concerned about how she might handle potential discipline problems. She pictured herself walking up and down the aisles strumming a guitar and creating an atmosphere where everyone could have fun and be involved as they sang together. During the summer before school began, she took guitar lessons and learned to play five chords. When the children would begin to get restless, Ardeth would pick up her guitar and walk down the aisles strumming a few chords, and everyone would join in singing.

One evening, a mother of a student called and asked Ardeth if she would come to a party she was having to play her guitar and lead group singing. Ardeth insisted she really didn't play the guitar very well. The mother responded, "My daughter says you do." Ardeth explained that she knew only five chords and that her repertoire of songs was from the fourth-grade music book. She also told the mother that the students sang so loudly that they didn't know whether she was playing or not. The woman thought Ardeth was only being modest, but Ardeth was finally able to convince her that she couldn't play for her party.

As she continued to gain experience as a teacher, Ardeth quickly came to realize that the success of her class as a whole depended on her understanding the uniqueness of each child.

Recognizing this, she decided on a plan. Rather than conducting an interview or a conference, she determined to become acquainted with each child by having a *visit.* As she continued these visits, the children gradually came to trust her enough to allow her entrance into their hearts. At times, some would admit to her their difficulties in a particular area of learning. When this occurred, she would respond: "Is that something you would like me to help you with?" Often the children seemed surprised at their teacher's offer of help, expecting, it seemed, to be chastised for having the problem. Once the offer was accepted, the student came to feel that the help was that of a friend following through on a promise made, rather than of a teacher prodding.

As the seasons passed and the months slipped away, Ardeth realized that the goals she had so carefully planned prior to the beginning of the school year had been amplified. Her visits with the children had helped her to see that her goals should be determined by their goals, their needs, their special interests, and their accomplishments.

In response to an assignment to write about their fourth-grade year, one of her students wrote: "This year was the funnest year ever. [My teacher] taght me the very most and she gave me help in arithmitic like no other teacher. . . . And She alwas makes you feel good. If you come in late she wouldn't scream and say, 'You bedder not be late again, or I'll send you down to the princibal.' She only says, 'Glad you could make it,' or something nice like that. Bye" (original spelling retained).

Years later, Ardeth expressed her philosophy of good teaching, gained from her own experiences in helping children to learn: "I believe that if a teacher is ever to be allowed into the private, sacred realm of a child's heart, where lasting changes take place and lasting imprints are made, a sensitivity to the inner spirit of each child and a reverence for teaching moments is required. This sensitivity is difficult to teach, but is unquestionably the most important quality to be learned" (*The Gentle Touch,* 4).

In recalling her classroom experiences, she said: "I wonder why it is that the sense of smell can return a total experience to the consciousness even better, I think, than sight or sound. It is in the recollection of that smell of chalk dust; warm, sweaty bodies after recess; school lunch; and poster paint that even the emotion of a teaching experience not recalled for years is relived with such clarity as though it were occurring for the first time."

THE BISHOP'S WIFE

On July 28, 1966, Heber was called to be the bishop of their ward. Ardeth, who was serving in the stake YWMIA presidency, recorded her thoughts regarding her husband's new assignment. "Another milestone in our gospel experiences. Heber will be a good bishop. He is a good organizer, is efficient, is patient, and loves and lives the gospel. It is a real blessing to have such a wonderful husband. The stake president stressed that this calling was for both of us and I'm anxious to be a good bishop's wife, although I don't know just what that entails." Then she added, "At least no one can criticize the bishop's kids."

Ardeth and Heber were humbled and grateful for the support and love that was expressed to them by their ward members. One little boy told Heber that he liked him because he was fun, he was funny, and he was good. A little girl proudly brought them a squash from their family garden. Still another member brought two large, homegrown melons, taking care to let Heber know that he had reserved the largest ones for "the bishop." They were impressed with the respect and honor that were given to the calling of a bishop. At this time, Heber was still teaching junior high school. He loved working with young people and helping them learn.

In the fall, Ardeth returned to the classroom for her second year of teaching fourth graders. She supervised two interns from Brigham Young University. About this experience she said, "We learned together that the focus for effective teaching in the elementary schools is not on the subject but the child. We decided that when people ask, 'What do you teach?' the answer should be, 'I teach children.'"

Although she enjoyed working with the college interns, she most enjoyed teaching young pupils in a classroom of her own. After one day's work she wrote: "School was most enjoyable today. Although I'm supervising two BYU interns, I've had one class to myself for a couple of weeks. The greater joy is in teaching, not supervising."

Instructional Television

Toward the end of her second year of teaching, Ardeth was offered a position as a teacher for the Utah Network for Instructional Television. Sharon was a teacher for an educational TV program, and as the two sisters enjoyed opportunities to work together, Ardeth decided to join her. They enjoyed doing several shows together before Sharon moved to St. Louis, Missouri, in August of 1966, where Ralph would attend dental school.

Ardeth wrote and produced two educational television

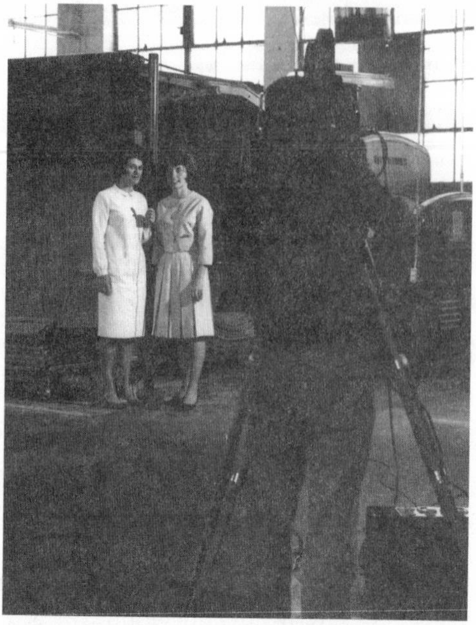

Ardeth (left) and sister Sharon (right) during filming at Utah Woolen Mills for their TV program, "Let's Take a Field Trip"

programs for children: "Let's Take a Field Trip," and "Cultural Kaleidoscope." Again, she wanted to make the learning enjoyable and as realistic as possible. For one of the "Kaleidoscope" programs, she came up with what she thought was a great plan. One of her former university instructors, Dr. Elliot Landau, spoke with a charming accent that she thought would add to a presentation she had planned. She asked him to come on her show and read a story, *Winnie the Pooh and the Boa Constrictor,* to her television students. To her delight, he agreed. Then she tried to figure out a way to make the story even better. She contacted LaMar Farnsworth, the director of the zoo in Salt Lake City, asking if it would be possible for him to bring a boa constrictor to the studio for Dr. Landau to use as a visual aid. Mr. Farnsworth agreed to bring a snake that he said was dormant and would be safe to use for the program. When advised of the plan,

Dr. Landau hesitantly agreed. The day arrived and everything was set.

At the studio, the zoo director took the sleeping snake out of its cage and carefully wrapped it around the professor's neck and chest. The show's director called, "Hit the lights!" The cameras rolled, and Dr. Landau began reading. Slowly, as if on cue, the visual aid, warmed by the bright lights, began to come to life. With the snake slithering around his neck, Dr. Landau either forgot or didn't care that the cameras were on. He jumped from his chair as Mr. Farnsworth ran to his aid. Together they returned the snake to its cage for a trip back to the zoo. Filming was stopped and rescheduled for a later time—without the help of the visual aid. After that incident, Ardeth wondered if perhaps there were times when she got too carried away with her planning!

At the end of her one-year contract with the television network, she decided that the glamour of having her own TV show, where she was both the writer and narrator, was nothing in comparison to the joy of being in the classroom with the children. Although she had gained some wonderful friends and created unforgettable memories, she decided that teaching into a television camera was not for her. In her journal she wrote, "It appears that I'll be back in the classroom with those darling children again."

CORRELATION

In 1967, while serving on the YWMIA board of her stake, Ardeth was called by Elder Richard L. Evans, a member of the Quorum of the Twelve Apostles, to serve on the Youth Correlation Committee of the Church. She had been recommended by a former member of her stake presidency who knew her skills in working with young people. Her assignment was to read lesson materials that were being prepared for teachers of youth in Sunday School and MIA meetings. The material was then discussed in Youth Correlation Committee meetings held every Sunday morning. Occasionally, the committee also met with the Adult and Children's Correlation Committees.

Most of the people on the committee were older than Ardeth and had many years of experience in working at the general level of the Church. They were people Ardeth had read about and for whom she had great admiration, men and women of wisdom, experience, breadth, and depth. She often felt so consumed with her own sense of inadequacy that she was not able to listen or think clearly. She felt she was not contributing.

After frequent pleadings with the Lord that she would be able to fulfill her assignments, she gained new insight as welcome counsel from the Lord came into her mind. She recorded it in her journal: "You have a perspective that others don't. It may be very minor, but it is part of the whole. As long as you are consumed with thinking about your own inadequacies, I can't use you for the benefit that you've been called."

Ardeth felt that she had received a bit of a reprimand but knew it was important that she quit thinking about herself and her inadequacies. She felt it was as if the Lord was saying, "If you'll pay attention and do the best you can, I'll tell you what to say and do." Ardeth also gained a new understanding that Satan can cause people to focus on their own inadequacies. The adversary knows people's weaknesses and will try to distract them, often when they have an opportunity to make a great contribution.

In addition to teaching junior high school, Heber was occupied with his calling as bishop. Chief among his many responsibilities was the assignment to build a new meetinghouse and have it paid for within three years. In addition to her work on the correlation committee, Ardeth began to receive numerous requests to speak to Church groups in the area. Of this time she wrote: "Heber and I seem to be totally consumed with school and Church. Even in the middle of the night, I'll lie awake and finally whisper, 'Heber.' He'll say, 'What? Are you awake correlating?' and I'll say, 'Yes. Are you bishoping?'"

Ardeth was back at Oak Hills School in her fourth-grade classroom, happy in her work with the children. She was now in her fourth year of teaching, and some of her first students were in Heber's classes at the junior high school. The Kapps' love of children included those in their neighborhood, many of whom felt free to come and go in their home at will. On one occasion, Ardeth was downstairs when the door opened and she heard the footsteps of a four-year-old neighbor boy. She called, "I'm down here." A little voice responded, "I just wanted to get something." Then a moment later, "Mrs. Kapp, how do ya' open the marshmallows?" She told him to bring them downstairs, where she could help him. Satisfied, the child left, but within the hour he returned with a friend. She heard the sound of many footsteps and the opening and closing of drawers. This time he didn't call for help. Evidently, he could handle the situation himself!

BYU—Teacher and Student

As the 1967–68 school year came to a close, Ardeth agreed to begin the summer helping to organize the curriculum for a new program for elementary students at a nearby school. She planned to return to her regular classroom in the fall. However, other forces were at work that would change her course.

While serving on the Youth Correlation Committee, she became acquainted with Dr. Max Berryessa, chairman of the Children's Correlation Committee. Dr. Berryessa supervised student teachers in the College of Education at BYU. Some of his students had trained in her classroom at Oak Hills Elementary. Not only was he pleased with her work on correlation, he was also impressed with the teaching skills she had passed on to these new teachers. Consequently, he spoke of her remarkable teaching abilities to the dean of the College of Education. Just prior to the time for her to sign a contract for the coming school year at Oak Hills, she received a telephone call from Dean Alley. He offered her a position on the faculty where she would be assigned to supervise student teachers. The offer was conditioned upon her working toward a master's degree at the same time. Surprised but pleased for the opportunity of a new challenge, she accepted.

She began her work at BYU in the fall of 1968. This shift in focus began a change of direction for Ardeth, as she became both student and teacher. After careful consideration, she decided to pursue a master's degree in counseling and guidance. It was extremely interesting for her to both observe and participate in the teaching and learning process from many different perspectives. While working toward the advanced degree, she was a student. In another setting, she became the teacher, striving to help her students learn how to become great teachers. At times she sat in the back of a classroom in an elementary school watching children respond to the teaching style of one who was learning to be a teacher. As she watched the students and the teachers, at the

Ardeth received her Masters of Education degree from BYU, August 20, 1971. Left to right: Tammie Quick, Kevin Fronk, Jeffery Duke, Carolyn Rasmus, Ardeth, Sally Barlow.

same time being both student and teacher in her various situations, she came to realize even more strongly the sacred trust that a teacher must accept as she seeks to mold the thinking process and instill in each student a love for learning.

As a supervisor of student teachers, one incident made her more keenly aware than ever before of the teacher's responsibility toward her students. She worked diligently, maintaining a friendship with her students, encouraging and helping them in every way she knew how. Most of them fulfilled her expectations. One student taught her a lesson she has not forgotten. She was a delightful young woman, fun to be around, and one who seemed to be enjoying her school experiences. With a strong desire to attend BYU, she had spent years doing the hard labor of a farm worker in order to save enough money to reach her goal. Once she arrived on campus, however, it was as though she had reached the goal and there was no need for further work.

Ardeth was concerned with the young woman's lack of diligence in her studies and her preparation for classroom teaching. Ardeth continued to encourage her and tried to maintain a positive attitude with the student. However, at the end of her student teaching experience, the young woman had failed to meet the requirements. Ardeth had no option but to call her in to explain the results of her failure to prepare and her lack of commitment. Bursting into tears, the young woman responded: "If you had talked to me in the beginning like you're talking to me now, I could have made it." From then on, Ardeth realized her responsibility to be not only fair and friendly, but to be firm about her expectations as well.

Ardeth also recalled lighter moments that came as she was supervising student teachers. "The students were located in schools throughout Davis County, where I would go to observe them. Just because I had been to a school once didn't mean I could find my way again, nor did having a map ensure direction. I relied on a full tank of gas, and left early for my appointment to allow for getting lost. I also spent time in earnest prayer and sang, 'Lead Me, Guide Me' as I drove. I kept track of my mileage, for which I was reimbursed. That used to worry me because I realized that someone else was paying for my excessive use of gas while I found my way. Then I came to the conclusion that since they had hired me to do the job, they had to take my weaknesses along with my strengths!"

As she continued in her master's program, she felt impressed to change her course of study to that of curriculum development. Uncertain as to the reason but never hesitating when she felt the guidance of the Spirit, she made the change.

On August 20, 1971, she reached a milestone she had never even contemplated during her challenges in the Glenwood Elementary School many years earlier. At commencement exercises, she marched in line with her fellow graduates toward receipt of her master's degree. A thought flashed through her mind: "Not too bad for someone who 'was not college material anyway'!"

CHAPTER ELEVEN

The Times That Bind

VACATIONS

One of the advantages of teaching school was the opportunity for summer travel. Through the years, Ardeth and Heber have enjoyed vacation trips with Ralph and Sharon. Even though the Larsens lived away while Ralph attended dental school, they returned to Utah for the summer. Both couples enjoyed not only the travel, but also spending time together. In 1967, the foursome traveled through the northwestern part of the United States with a camper attached to the back of Heber and Ardeth's truck. Ardeth recorded the following about their first night's accommodations somewhere in Idaho: "Spent the night in a corn patch. Didn't seem to matter at midnight!"

As they drove, the travelers enjoyed the beauties of nature they viewed at every turn. They stopped at various locations to hike, play on the beach, swim, or dig for sand crabs. In Oregon they visited a lumber mill, as well as the famous rose gardens. Heading for Seattle, Washington, they drove along the Columbia

Heber and Ardeth on vacation riding in the sand dunes along the Oregon Coast, 1998

River, enjoying its spectacular beauty from various lookout points. As they traveled along the coastline, Ardeth became unintentionally responsible for "cheering the gang. One look at my hair brought fits of laughter—or was it tears. I learned not to have a new permanent before going to the coast with all of its humidity. As Heber said, 'my hair was lovely, my genealogy uncertain.'" As they got further inland her hair "tamed down." "Sharon said I wasn't as entertaining, but very lovely."

Finally, they arrived at Vernon, British Columbia, where they spent several days with Ardeth and Sharon's sister, Shirley, and her husband Ron Burnham. They particularly enjoyed spending time with the Burnham's children, including their seven-month-old daughter, whom they were seeing for the first time. The three sisters stayed up until the wee hours to catch up on all of their visiting. Their vacation trip lasted for just over two weeks, but they built family memories to last a lifetime.

During parts of July and August, 1968, the Kapps packed

their camper for another trip, this time to the eastern part of the United States. They stopped in St. Louis to pick up the Larsens, then headed for London, Ontario, Canada, to visit their brother, Gordon, and his family. As part of their travels, they also visited eastern United States landmarks. Their stops included the nation's capitol, where they soaked up the history that had significance in the building of a nation. In addition, they traveled to upstate New York, where they visited the Sacred Grove and other sites of importance in Church history. They attended the Hill Cumorah Pageant and were inspired by the beauty and majesty of the production. They returned home having gained a greater appreciation of the sacrifices of their forefathers.

As often as time and circumstances permitted, Ardeth and Heber visited Ron and Shirley and their family, as well as Gordon and his family. They sought opportunities to become well acquainted with their nieces and nephews. Rather than being viewed simply as relatives who lived far away, they desired to have a close relationship with these children.

Ardeth loved living close to Sharon, who had also settled in Bountiful after her marriage. She missed their regular association while Ralph and Sharon were away, but was happy that after graduation from dental school in 1971, Ralph planned to return to Bountiful to open his practice. In the meantime, the Larsens announced the expected arrival of their first baby in the summer of 1969, which added to Ardeth's anticipation of their return home.

SHELLY

Early in the morning of June 3, 1969, Ardeth and Heber were on their way to a much-anticipated vacation in Hawaii. As

Shelly and Ardeth dressed up to play "old lady"—a frequent and fun request from Shelly

they drove to the airport, Ardeth remembered something she had forgotten. Heber quickly turned the car around and headed for home. As she dashed into the house, the phone was ringing. Since they were in a hurry, she hesitated, almost not answering, but was so happy that she did pick it up. Calling from St. Louis, Sharon shared the news of her little daughter's unexpectedly early birth. Although premature, she was perfect. They planned to name her Shelly. Sharing the news of her birth was only the beginning of the love shared by the two sisters for this new little life sent from heaven. Despite her excitement to record the details of the Hawaiian trip, Ardeth's first journal entry for that day began with two words: "Shelly born!"

After they returned from their trip, a package came in the mail. Inside was a tape recording entitled, "Sounds of Shelly." In addition, Ardeth unfolded a brown piece of paper, cut in Shelly's exact shape so she could imagine her size! When Shelly was a month old, Ralph and Sharon returned to Utah for the summer. Sharon dressed little five-pound Shelly in her most adorable outfit, laid her in a basket, and set it on Ardeth's front porch. By the baby's side was a note which read, "Hi Mommy Ardie. I am Shelly. Can I spend the summer with you?" Attached to the note was a "User's Guide," created by Sharon for Ardeth's use in how to care for her! Ralph and Sharon rang the doorbell, then hid and watched. Sharon said, "It was love at first sight! We have joked ever since about Shelly having two sets of parents."

From that time on, Ardeth's activities, interesting as they were, paled in comparison to the time she and Heber spent with Shelly. She plainly expressed her feelings in her journal: "July 20, 1971. Hurray! Yesterday I took my orals for a Master's degree and evidently passed with flying colors, according to the comments. But more importantly, Sharon and Shelly returned from St. Louis to stay with us for a few weeks until Ralph finishes his teaching assignment there and returns to Bountiful to begin his practice. It is impossible to express what a wonderful, enriching experience it has been to have little Shelly's spirit in our home. Somehow it helps put things in proper perspective as one thinks of things of importance. Each maneuver she makes just warms your entire being. What a joy, what a blessing, and they're here to stay! So great to have a sister so close to share things so important."

A few weeks later, she wrote: "Ralph and Sharon are in their apartment now. It is so great to drop in and have that little Shelly come running full speed ahead with her arms outreached in a great hug. She is a gift for all of us. She lightens our souls, brightens our lives, and gives us a close touch with things spiritually pure."

Shelly quickly became an integral part of Ardeth and Heber's lives. Family bonds, already strong, were more deeply cemented than ever before, due in large part to Ralph and Sharon's willingness to share their daughter. Ardeth sprinkled the pages of her journal with the joy she felt at being part of Shelly's life:

April 4, 1972: "Little Shelly is the joy of our lives. I talk with her each day. Each Sunday . . . she comes over for our 'golden hour.' We play, read, have supper. . . . It's the precious hour of the week. It is such a refining spiritual lift to be around her. Sharon and Ralph are unbelievable in the way they share her with us. We are so grateful. I hope they somehow understand our appreciation for this wonderful gift of sharing."

July 1, 1972: "How many moms and dads with just one little girl, . . . would teach her to call us Mommy Ardie and Papa Heber. . . . Little Shelly is a light and a life to each of us."

October 11, 1972: "On my way home I stopped to see Shelly. I lose my sense of well-being if too many days lapse without contact with that precious little soul."

January 20, 1974: "Shelly is a radiant, happy, lovable little angel. She just lifts your whole soul. I couldn't love one of my own any more. . . . We all love her so much. What chance has she got as an only child of four parents and grandparents so close! She is a gift straight from heaven for all of us."

February 20, 1977: "I stopped by to tuck Shelly in bed and she said she wished we were the same age so I wouldn't die first. We talked about the possible age of our spirits and she was happy to know that it was just my body that's getting older. That gave me great insight that made me happy too. She is a precious little soul."

For her part, Shelly grew up thinking that it was normal to have two sets of parents. Sharon remembers that Shelly used to say, "There is only one Shelly, so you will all have to share!" And share is just what they did. Years later as an adult, Shelly said, "Ardeth has always been part of my life. I didn't realize what a wonderful privilege it was to have two incredible moms."

A favorite game for Shelly was to dress up and play "Old Lady." "That means we dress up in shawls and long dresses and drink grape juice out on the patio in crystal goblets that are very fancy like at a fancy restaurant." She also remembers sleeping outside. "We'd have sleep-overs on her balcony. We'd get out our sleeping bags and eat old Halloween candy! Now that I'm older, I think, 'She slept outside with me instead of in her nice warm bed with her husband!' I just thought she wanted to be sleeping out on the balcony with me! She was always into the whole experience of helping children explore and imagine. She still does that with my cousin's daughters."

From Sharon's perspective, "You can never have too many people loving your children! During Shelly's teenage years, when we had the difficulties that are normal for teenagers, when they don't think their parents know anything, she would talk to Ardeth. She would tell Shelly the same things I would have, but it was more credible coming from her. I have been so grateful to have another voice saying the same things I would say to my precious daughter."

After sharing many precious times with Shelly during her growing up years, the day came when Shelly received a mission call. She went to the temple for the first time on December 21, 1991, accompanied by her parents, and Ardeth and Heber. Ardeth was then the Young Women general president. Sharon and Shelly were escorted into a room where Shelly would receive temple instruction. Ardeth was told that only one escort was permitted, and she was left to wait outside. Ardeth attempted to briefly explain the situation to the temple worker and inquired if it might be possible for her to also accompany Shelly. The worker, who didn't recognize Ardeth, would not make an exception. Ardeth would not use her position to gain admittance. By this time, she was near tears. She thought, "Shelly is the closest I'll ever come in this life to having a child, and I can't go with her." Even though she was the leader of 450,000 young women, she had never had this opportunity. In the meantime, Shelly and her mother were waiting and wondering what had happened to her. Ardeth offered up a quiet prayer. Just then, the temple matron walked by, recognized her, and asked her why she was sitting there. Ardeth explained, "My niece is going through for the first time. Her mom is her escort, so I'm just kind of waiting. The matron responded, "We'll have to do something about that. You're welcome to come in if you would like." As she entered the room, Ardeth caught Shelly's happy glance and the threesome joined together. It was a testimony to her that Heavenly Father hears every prayer, even those offered in the silent recesses of the heart.

Ardeth has never forgotten that experience. She had many occasions to recall it in the years she served as matron of the Cardston, Alberta Temple. She was more sensitive to the needs of those who came to the temple than she might otherwise have been. Wanting always to be in tune with the needs of the temple patrons, she never forgot the spiritual sensitivity of the matron in the Salt Lake Temple.

Near the end of Shelly's mission, Heber received a call to preside over the Canada Vancouver Mission. Ardeth would be released as the Young Women general president to accompany her husband into the mission field. Their service was to begin on July 1, 1992. Sitting across the desk from President Thomas S. Monson as he issued the call, a thought popped into Ardeth's mind. What if Shelly were to marry before their return? President Monson explained that while a mission president was never to leave the mission area, there were some things for which the president's wife could return home. Immediately she asked, "What about the wedding of a niece, who is the closest to a daughter that I have?" President Monson reflected on an aunt of his who had no children and had been like a second mother to him. He said, "I believe those relationships can be as close as your own children. I think that would be most appropriate for you to come home." She wrote, "Five years of not seeing Shelly! Oh, I don't know if I can do this. Well, okay, but if she gets married, I have to come home."

As Ardeth had foreseen, Shelly did marry while she and Heber were in the mission field. Having President Monson's approval, Ardeth returned home for the wedding. On August 11, 1993, Shelly Larsen was married to Steve Colvin in the Salt Lake Temple. Ardeth, who arrived a few days prior to the wedding, wrote, "Meeting Steve was a joy—a remarkable young man—talented, sensitive, and just right for Shelly. It seems as though they are the perfect match."

Ardeth, Shelly, and Sharon on Shelly's wedding day. Ardeth received permission to leave the mission field for this important occasion.

As for Shelly, she could not picture her wedding without Ardeth being there. "I don't know what I would have done if she hadn't been there. We might have gone up to Canada to be married because she had to be there as far as I was concerned. I'm close to Heber too. Recently, I saw him perform a sealing, and I said, 'Oh Heber, I should have waited for you to come home and you could have married us.' He said, 'No. You shouldn't have waited. It would have been two more years! No, you were wise.'"

The love between Ardeth and Shelly has only deepened with the passing of time. And now that love has been extended to include Shelly's husband, Steve, and their four young boys. Steve and Shelly have appreciated the example Ardeth and Heber have been to them. Shelly said, "I think they are what we're supposed to strive to be like. "Other than my parents, if I could pick out anyone in this world that I would try to pattern my life after, it is them. They're the closest to perfection I have ever met. They're always serving, they're always humble, they're non-judgmental. Steve loves the relationship because they are the most doting grandparents. Our children have three sets of grandparents! Ardeth and Heber call on birthdays, and they send presents. When they can, they come to our home in Arizona. Heber is wonderful. He wrestles with the kids and gives them horsey rides."

When one of Shelly's children was born, Sharon was away on a Church assignment, so Ardeth traveled to Arizona to help out in her absence. She arrived before the baby was born, and Shelly, knowing that Ardeth had never had that opportunity, asked her to come into the delivery room. "She was right there when the baby was born," Shelly said. Ardeth added, "I've never seen a spirit come in like that—to see him take his first breath and cry. We know the spirit's there, but to see that rush of life! It was a very special time."

KENT

On Saturday, December 16, 1978, a new little son was born and adopted into Ralph and Sharon's family. Ardeth wrote, "If they can get Shelly's approval, his name will be Charles Kent Greene Larsen. He is wonderful!" They brought him home a few days before Christmas. It was late in the evening before Heber and Ardeth got to see him. "As we walked into their home it was a sight I shall never forget," Ardeth wrote. "In one of their loveseats by the Christmas tree, Ralph sat on one side, Sharon on the other, and Shelly was in the middle holding that precious baby boy. It was an inspiring sight. An eternal family. Shelly was so excited to show us all of the baby's things. She skipped down the hall saying, 'I'm a big sister, I'm a big sister.' The baby is very beautiful. As soon as I held him I felt he really did belong to our family. Everything else seems of little consequence now. Plans for Christmas have changed, and Shelly doesn't care anything about gifts. Neither do any of the rest of us."

On June 21, 1979, Ardeth wrote, "On this special day, we went into the sealing room and Kent and Shelly were brought in. It was a precious, beautiful moment. They both looked so beautiful. The look on Shelly's face was one of ecstasy and excitement. She was so thrilled after Kent was sealed to their parents. We all knew that baby belongs in our family. Little Kent is in our heart like Shelly. I know that Sharon and Ralph will share him like they share Shelly, and he'll bring much joy into our lives."

Shelly and Kent were not the only niece and nephew in the lives of Ardeth and Heber, but they were the ones who lived close by. Consequently, they have had more opportunities for shared experiences. However, just as dear to them are the children of Ardeth's sister Shirley and her husband. Ardeth desired to be involved in the lives of all of her nieces and nephews as much as she possibly could. She took advantage of every opportunity to strengthen her family relationships. For instance, in August 1979, Ardeth took ten-year-old Shelly with her to Vernon, British Columbia, to help take care of Shirley's children after the birth of a new baby. Shelly bottled fruit with the older girls, cleaned and cooked and enjoyed the association of these precious children. She was ecstatic at having so many cousins to play with and was reluctant to leave when the time came.

FAMILY TRIBUTES

In 1986, Ardeth was presented with Lambda Delta Sigma's "Elect Lady" award. Among the many written tributes she received at that time, none were of more importance to her than those by her family, almost all of whom were in attendance.

A niece, Jennifer Burnham, wrote, "I recall being at Temple Square with you and seeing a woman approach you with her retarded daughter. The mother expressed her child's desire to meet you and as the handicapped girl stumbled forward, face beaming and arms wide open, I felt uncomfortable and wondered what you'd do. You stepped forward with a smile to match hers and put your arms around her—and I understood a new dimension of love."

A nephew, Matt, expressed: "You have always said that one never gets to choose his relatives, but I couldn't have a more special aunt than you."

Her sister Shirley wrote: "You have a tremendous power to enrich people. . . . You have been and continue to be my ideal woman."

Her brother-in-law Ron Burnham noted his enjoyment at witnessing "the ongoing miracle of a bond of mutual regard between you three sisters that is so sacred and uplifting and delightful that your husbands sit by in awe when you, Sharon, and Shirley get together. . . . I love you like a sister."

When "Ardie" was young, her cousin Colleen wrote, a young boy lived next door. "Because of illness, [he] was often confined to his bed for weeks at a time. Ardeth would stand outside his bedroom window, which overlooked her yard, and bring him up to date on the happenings at school. True friendship based on the pure love of Christ developed between them."

Shelly wrote, "You have always been special to me. You have been my other mom. . . . I love you so much and I want you to know that I will still love you even if you are old and gray and bent."

Sharon's creative tribute took the form of a poem, which included these lines:

She's my anchor, my light, my P.R. man
She's just what I'd like to be.
She's real and honest, uncluttered and fun.
And she has always loved me.

Another tribute in the form of a poem came from her brother, Gordon, quoted in these excerpts:

The prairie cold, the dust, the wind
Are now the social pains;
But giving, loving, caring have
The same sustaining claims.
You know that and you're giving,
You know and share your love,
You care and offer sustenance
With help from God above.
But you fought inferiority;
You struggled to be hardy.
What does it mean to be elect?
It's a lady name of Ardie.

FAMILY TIES

Following a mission to Australia, Gordon Kay, the oldest of the Greene siblings, attended the University of Alberta, where he graduated with a music degree. During that time, he married Lucy Seneshen. Following graduation, he and his family then moved to Bloomington, Indiana, where he pursued a doctoral degree in musicology. Upon receipt of the doctorate, he moved his family, to which six children had been added, to London, Ontario, where he taught at the university. He later moved to Waterloo, Ontario, where he became dean of the College of Music at Wilford Laurier University.

A gifted musician, Gordon plays several instruments, has led many choirs, and has a beautiful singing voice. According to his sisters, he is "absolutely brilliant." Sharon says that he is not only a musician and an artist, but a historian as well. "He connects happenings in history together better than any college professor I ever had. He can connect what was happening with world history, Church history, music, and poetry and art all together in a fun, palatable way. He is a master teacher and is in demand to teach music courses from jazz to Gregorian chants to symphonies. He is retired, but teaches extension courses for several universities in Ontario and in Florida during the winter."

Although Gordon has not been active in the Church for many years, the ties with his siblings remain strong. He attends family reunions and enjoys visits with his sisters on special occasions. He said, "I have three remarkable sisters whose accomplishments continue to amaze me and whose love continues to sustain me. Thinking about my sister, Ardeth, the mind fills with wonderful images, the heart with joy. Many times I have been filled with admiration to observe her speaking at general conference and have wished that we lived close enough that I could partake of her remarkable spirit daily."

Shirley met and married Ron Burnham, a native of British Columbia, where they lived and reared their eleven children.

Three sisters raised on the prairie stand atop the Empire State Building while Sharon and Ralph were on a public affairs mission in New York.

After the children were on their own, and following Ron's retirement from his dental practice, they accepted a call to serve in the Seattle Temple. Ron became a counselor in the temple presidency, and Shirley served as an assistant matron. Coincidentally, their service corresponded with Heber and Ardeth's service as president and matron of the Cardston Temple.

Ralph and Sharon looked forward to continuing their close association with Ardeth and Heber upon the Kapps' return from their temple assignment in the fall of 2003. However, Ralph retired from his dental practice, and a mission call came sooner than they had anticipated. One week after the Kapps returned from Cardston, Elder and Sister Larsen began their service as public affairs missionaries in Manhattan, New York. They returned to their home in Bountiful in May 2005.

Sharon and Shirley have followed in the footsteps of their older sister. Sharon served on the general board of the Young

Women from 1974–1978 and as a counselor in the Young Women general presidency from 1997–2001. In addition, she has served in the Relief Society and Young Women's organizations in her ward and stake and served as an Institute teacher. Shirley, likewise, has held both ward and stake assignments. She has been a ward and district Young Women president, a ward and stake Relief Society president, and was a seminary teacher for more than twenty years—while being a mother of eleven children. She has also served as assistant matron of the Seattle Temple while her husband served as a counselor in the temple presidency.

For the three "Greene girls," consistent service to both Church and family comes as a natural outgrowth of their heritage and their faith. They, along with their husbands, continue to contribute to a legacy that is felt not only by their family, but throughout the Church.

Left to right: Shirley Burnham, Sharon Larsen, Ardeth, Gordon Greene

CHAPTER TWELVE

Heartprints

Connections

Ardeth prizes a collection of Heber's letters, written over the years, reflecting love, humor, encouragement, and cherished memories accumulated over a period of more than fifty-five years. In her words, "Letters are important. Written love notes, even those hurriedly penned during busy times, become more precious as the years go by. E-mail letters that are usually brief and are not distinguished by the handwriting, or that are read quickly and then deleted, are never a substitute."

The first exchange of letters between Ardeth and Heber began with a letter of thanks from Heber, who, as a young missionary, had spent the night as a guest in the Greene home. This was followed by a letter from Ardeth, thanking Heber for the thank-you letter! These letters of friendship continued and, after they were engaged, became increasingly frequent and romantic. With Ardeth in Glenwood and Heber in Ogden, their courtship was continued by correspondence. Telephone calls were

Surprise! Early morning at Ardeth's home, with a plate of heart-shaped cookies and with hearts pasted all over. The note reads, "You're having a heart attack. We love you.—YW Orchard Ward."

expensive and infrequent. The mail was delivered to Glenwood's small post office each Monday, Wednesday, and Friday. Those days found Ardeth anxiously waiting for it to be sorted, which seemed to take forever.

When a letter would come addressed to her from Heber, Sharon and Shirley, almost as excited as Ardeth, would coax her to let them see and read the very last line of the letter, which always ended with, "Oceans of love with a kiss on every wave." An "X" rode the peak of every wave that traveled across the bottom of the page, supporting the message of love. When she reported to Heber the excitement of her little sisters in reading that last romantic line, he never disappointed them as they continued to examine the bottom of every letter. That tradition still continues, even extending to the next generation.

Ardeth's later travels on assignment took her to various parts of the world, sometimes for weeks at a time. To ease their separation, Heber typically wrote several letters, sealed them in envelopes, inscribed on each envelope the date on which it should be opened, and secretly tucked them into her suitcase. At the first opportunity on a trip, she anxiously checked to see if the letters were there. They always were. Sometimes it was hard to refrain from opening and reading them all at once, but she never disregarded the date.

While serving as a counselor in the Young Women general presidency, she traveled to New Zealand for an extended period. After one long day, she was looking forward to a letter that would help her feel closer to Heber. It came with a message still vivid: "While you are in that beautiful land of New Zealand, be sure to pay attention to all of God's beautiful creations so you will have some good ideas for when we create our world." That gave her much to think about, both then and since. Heber's letters have continued over the years, both at times when she was away and when she is home, for an occasional happy surprise.

HIS LETTERS

While Ardeth was away on one assignment, he wrote:

February 3, 1990
Ardie Pal,

Tonight as I sat at my messy desk and thought about a lot of things, you were in my thoughts as I reviewed some of your many great contributions to this world. I thought about you being gone and us being separated. Except for a cause greater in our separateness than the selfish possession of our togetherness, the price would be too great a disadvantage. I

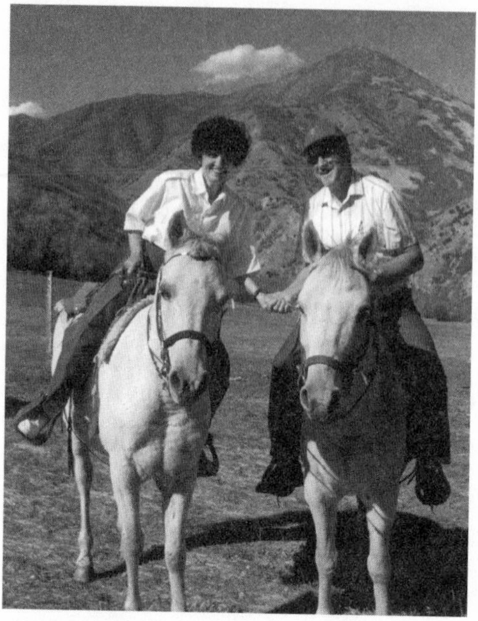

Ardeth and Heber in the mountains just prior to leaving to preside over the Canada Vancouver Mission

thrill with how we have grown in so many ways. And I am grateful to our eternal Father for the vistas He has allowed us to see, for the understandings He has given our contemplations. I think I grow more understanding and appreciative each day as the experiences of that day present themselves to me for the lessons they possess for my learning. I'm grateful!

Your travels have taken you often and far. The panoramas of those experiences are as different as the varied location and different settings are. Yet the sameness of every one of them is that there are people there to be fed the spirit and the hope and confidence that you bring to them. They hunger, not for the potatoes and bread that nourish the body, but for the hope, the laughter, the joy, the confidence, the sweetness, the humor, the nourishment of the soul that breathes into them the breath of life to carry on and keep trying to do and become better. And so, when you've slogged through the rain of doubt and the fatigue of having tried so many times before, the loneliness, the doubts of whether or not it can really be worth it, does it really make a difference, [you can find] the answer in the words of Stan Cottrell, "One person can make a difference." Absolutely! You can—for "*Many people are anxiously awaiting your arrival in the next village. Your passing through will bring endless joy.*" And in your case, where you cannot go, your books and writings will go for you. I pray for your protection, your energy of body and strength of spirit, that you can continue to nourish people's souls.

I love you so————o MUCH!
HBK
XXXXXXXXXXXXXXX!

On one occasion, as if he knew her thoughts, Heber made copies of a message for Ardeth and scattered them throughout the house, even in drawers and cupboards. Although he was unaware of her discouraged feelings, she felt he must have been inspired to help lift her when she was down.

June 29, 1990
ARDIE DARLING

YOU ARE A
MARVELOUS
MARVELOUS
MARVELOUS
MARVELOUS
MARVELOUS

MARVELOUS MARVELOUS MARVELOUS MARVELOUS MARVELOUS SOUL!

After Heber was called as a mission president, their days were crowded, and attention to the missionaries seemed to claim most of his time. She missed the letters that had come at random intervals throughout the years. One day she came upon a letter he had written her years before. It was a wonderful letter, filled with expressions of his love. While grateful for those past expressions, they had now become infrequent. Smiling to herself, she thought of a plan. Mischievously, she laid the old letter on his desk in the mission office, tucked among a pile of weekly letters from the missionaries. Attached to it she wrote: "Could you update this?" She hoped for another of his detailed letters, which always made her feel so good. She had not received one since arriving in the mission field.

The next morning the same letter was on her desk. It had been stamped with the current date and a bold notation in the corner that read, "Reconfirmed!" She reported to him that while it was efficient, it was not quite the response for which she had hoped. From then on, Heber rearranged his agenda to include an occasional letter to her, even during the busiest times.

MESSAGES FROM HER

Feeling that letters are important and that even a note expressing love becomes of increasing importance as the years go by, Ardeth has likewise responded with her own messages of love, appreciation, and encouragement. As she and Heber were ending their missionary service and preparing to return home, she wrote:

January 28, 1995

Dearest Heber,

As I reflect on our journey together the past forty-five years, I marvel at the goodness of our Father in Heaven, as he has blessed us, guided us, heard our prayers, and provided opportunities that we could never have dreamed possible.

Yes, we have built beautiful homes, churches, a mission office that stand as symbols of your ingenuity, ambition, and faith. But as you so frequently speak of the spiritual and the physical, it is in your influence in the lives of people over many, many years that stands in an eternal perspective of a labor that cannot be measured—except to remember the words of the Savior, "The worth of a soul is great . . ." Together we have walked a path that has touched many souls over forty-five years. What could be of greater worth?

The eternal nature of life has always been so real to you, (perhaps because of your experience with the death of loved ones at an early age). You have a vision that never dims.

You are a builder, a teacher, a servant of the Lord, but most of all, you are my husband, my friend, my eternal companion.

I'm impressed with your generosity, always saying "we

can afford it," if it involves someone else, but not so if it is something for you. I've watched the young missionaries as they feast on your wisdom, your inspiration, your humor, and your guidance and direction.

As we leave the Canada Vancouver Mission and reflect on the wonderful memories, we can see some mighty growth rings for us individually and together. You have carried the load in a most remarkable way and are well deserving of all of the accolades of members and missionaries.

We came, we served, we have been blessed, and now we go home better prepared for our next opportunities, which in an eternal perspective may be more significant and far more reaching than anything we've done thus far. As Churchill said, "This is perhaps the end of the beginning." You are so blessed. And so am I!

Oceans of love and a kiss on every wave.

Ardie

Four years after returning from their mission, Heber received the following letter:

To My Wonderful Heber on Our 49th Wedding Anniversary
June 28, 1999

A giant in our home is the message I proclaim
I'm blessed and honored to carry his name
From a humble beginning he struggled along
Mid poverty and illness and a mother's song
To his country and church he devoted his attention
And lived by the Spirit and received revelation
As I look back on how our love has grown
Each year sweeter far than we have ever known

The future if it's half as good as the past has come
to be
Eternity will be only half enough to share my love with
thee
When life is spent without note of worldly fame
The Savior will then proclaim "He honored my name"
I love you sooooooooooooooooooooooooooo much

Lucky Me,
Ardie

LETTERS TO FAMILY

Ardeth has not confined her letter-writing expressions to Heber alone. At designated milestones along life's path, she has felt to capture and then to send her feelings to other loved family members. Following the pattern set by her father long years ago, she penned her thoughts to Shelly on the day of her wedding. It was written with all the feelings of a tender parent.

August 11, 1993

Sunrise, sunset, swiftly fly the years. I remember so well, Shelly, when your mom and dad left you in a basket on our doorstep with a detailed "Owners Manual," tied with a pink satin ribbon to your tiny wrist. Papa Heber and I carefully read the detailed instructions and carried them out exactly as requested, except for the time you were to be tucked safely into bed!

Maybe that was the very beginning of your challenge in getting to bed on time. Perhaps we're responsible. But you were in your jolly jumper and your little toes in white satin slippers would not be stilled. Those little toes were born to dance and that night they made their first debut with a very small audience, but never a more appreciative one.

We soon began to realize there was only one Shelly, and we would have to share. It must have been rather challenging for you at times to be the only child for so long to be shared between two sets of parents. That is, until Kent came to the rescue. Ever so often as you would sense even in your tender years how much we all loved you, you would try to explain, when it was time to take you home, "Mommie Ardie, there is only one Shelly and you have to learn to share."

Over the years when you danced right through the toes of your pink ballet slippers, your mom and dad would keep one of the little slippers and we would keep the other. We also have tucked away for safekeeping a collection of colorful scarves used to wave over our heads as you and I would dance around the coffee table in the living room. You would call to see if you could come over and play "old lady," as you called it. Together we wore hats and scarves and bracelets and beads and we danced to the music until it was time for "tea." The new carpet would be all frizzed up, leaving little footprints that I resisted vacuuming until I knew you would be coming again. As we ate tiny jelly sandwiches and talked about important things, I remember the day when you promised to love me when I was old and gray and "bint."

It was our annual trip to the Nutcracker at Christmastime that opened your eyes to new possibilities in the field of dance. You were only six, or maybe seven, when you tried to get your daddy to catch you as you jumped into his arms like the ballerina you had seen on stage, but somehow, something was amiss. Your daddy just didn't quite do it right, you explained. But then, he hadn't seen the ballet either.

Only a sunset or maybe two, it seemed. . . . It was homecoming at Davis High and you were the Homecoming Queen. [Then] at BYU there were many lessons to learn about determination, dedication, commitment, endurance, hope, prayers and faith, and all else that's required for an eager young coed to join the BYU ballroom dancers and still carry on an active social life and, by the way, maintain a very respectable GPA.

Your admiring audience was increasing. While the crowd in the Marriott Center applauded the first-place winners as you and your partner executed the Latin dance with such a flair, in my mind I saw our little Shelly in her "jolly jumper" wearing little white slippers.

At the airport in Salt Lake City we bid you farewell, not in dancing slippers but in tracting shoes, off on your way to New Zealand as an ambassador of the Lord Jesus Christ. . . . We were anxious for your letters from the mission. Would your heart and soul be in your mission like it was in your dance? You wrote home, "I ride my bicycle in the rain and sing, 'Called to serve Him, Heavenly King of Glory.' I have never been so happy in all of my life. I love our investigators so much, I try to be exactly obedient so that when I pray for them, it will work." And it did work. Many lives were blessed as we shared our Shelly with an ever-increasing circle of contacts, investigators, and converts.

Another sunrise and back to BYU. You were chosen once

again to join the BYU Ballroom Dancers. And now those toes, once in tracting shoes, were trained and prepared to dance on the magnificent stages in far-flung places of the world. We rejoiced in the opportunity to share our Shelly with the world.

Another sunset and we were to face a new challenge. We had learned to share you with the world, Shelly, but could we share you with "the one"? Yes, you taught us years ago. "There is only one Shelly and we would have to share." And in answer to your prayers, a kind Father who knows how important making right choices can be has spoken to your mind and to your heart in answer to prayer, guiding you in choosing the right partner in preparation for a grand performance, . . . for time and all eternity. Yes, Shelly, we're prepared and excited about sharing you with *the one. Your chosen one. Your Steve.* And now, our Steve. . . .

There will yet be hours of practice, maybe even times of sore toes and aching muscles, discouragement, and endurance, all a part of the preparation for the grand and final performance. There will be angels round about you to bear you up and your love for each other and for the Lord will carry you through. God bless you, Shelly and Steve, as you learn the steps, execute the movements, attend all the rehearsals and know that we will be cheering you on to that final grand and command performance of the only dance that really matters.

Love you forever,
Ardie

A heartfelt letter of reflection, remembrance, and congratulation was written to Shelly's mother at a significant milestone in her life.

September 30, 2002

To My Dearly Beloved Sister Sharon,

At this historic time in the history of the Church and in the world, I pause for a moment this morning just a few days prior to your release, after serving five years as a member of the general Young Women presidency. Words cannot express the deep sense of joy I have felt as you, with the Lord's guidance and direction, have magnified your calling in such a remarkable way. In many ways it has almost seemed like a parent/child relationship, with magnified joy beyond my own experience for your calling. I guess that is because I have felt an inside connection, knowing something of what it requires. With that thought, I must comment on the tremendous support you have had from your darling, faithful, wonderful, generous Ralph. What a team you two make and will continue to make.

Sharon, your talks have been classic, quoted and referenced and repeated over and over. The many comments I have received concerning your ability cause me to fight two sins, one of envy and the other of pride. As the door closes on this grand experience, I am reminded of the words of Winston Churchill. "This is not the end. It is not even the beginning of the end. It is, perhaps, the end of the beginning." I believe this for you and Ralph.

As you think about your moment in time, I am sure you remember your travels to far off places where you met with the Saints. Also your meetings with the leaders at Church headquarters, living at Eagle Gate, the home of the prophets, your first meeting in the grand Conference Center, and the world Olympics. Should your name be Esther, for you to have been where you have been for such a time as this? You might ask, "Why me, why now, why here?" As the answers unfold year by year, you will come to see that it was planned long ago.

With more years than you, and still feeling a motherly sensitivity for you, if you have any growing pains, I just want to counsel you to enjoy this short pause in time. If you could walk away from this calling without any feelings of loss, it would mean you hadn't put your whole heart and soul into it. I know you have. Whenever there is a change, there is a sense of loss. As I heard mentioned to one at the time of release, "Don't feel bad about the release, just be grateful that it happened at all." I know you feel that with your whole heart.

I'm looking forward to our days together with Shelly and those precious little boys. What a perfect transition, to focus on all that really matters. And thank you for so generously sharing those treasures with Heber and me.

I wish I could express all that I feel in my heart about how you have blessed so many and earned the respect of all with whom you have worked. You continue to nurture all with your forever radiant, happy, enthusiastic party spirit, while nurturing a deep sense of spirituality and gospel knowledge. How did I get to be your sister? Some day we will see the big picture. In the meantime, we will watch with interest as the pages of life are gradually opened, and one day the veil will be drawn. Then we will better understand the significance of Elder Featherstone's setting-apart blessing for you when you were told that we were dear friends in the pre-existence. I believe that, and we will continue to be dear friends in the eternities.

Love you forever,
Ardie

CHAPTER THIRTEEN

Expanding Responsibilities

Changes

In January 1971, Ardeth recorded in her journal, "I write not as 'the bishop's wife,' but as the wife of President Kapp of the Bountiful Center Stake of Zion. Today was truly a beautiful meeting—to see Church government in action—the Lord's way." Knowing of a pending change in their stake presidency, Ardeth had a feeling that the change would involve Heber. Her feelings were confirmed when, on January 13, 1971, he was sustained as first counselor during the stake reorganization.

Elder Marion G. Romney, who presided at the conference, pronounced a blessing upon Heber while setting him apart for his new calling. Following the conference Ardeth wrote, "Elder Romney talked with us about not having a family. In the blessing, he mentioned that the Lord had heard our prayers and was blessing us in His wisdom. He acknowledged our patience, reminding us that any things we may feel deprived of by way of blessings would be compensated for many fold. He told Heber that he would be a great counselor, the people will love him, . . . and that he will have a bit of heaven in his home and will be blessed in his work. . . . We both felt to rededicate our lives and time to the callings which have been entrusted to us. Truly we have witnessed the scripture: 'Trust in the Lord with all thine heart and lean not unto thine own understanding.'"

Several changes had also taken place with Ardeth's correlation committee assignment. The committee's work was expanded to include lessons for young adults; its name was changed to Youth and Young Adult to reflect the change. Elder Thomas S. Monson was appointed chairman, and several new members were added, including Ruth Funk, who previously served on the Adult Correlation Committee. As Ardeth and her colleagues visited following a meeting a few weeks later, they each expressed a feeling of urgency about their work. They all felt they were on the verge of something significant and very meaningful in the development of curriculum for the youth and young adults of the Church.

Her optimistic spirit was in evidence on her birthday, March 19, 1971, when she wrote: "And a Happy Birthday to me. I got up at 6:00 A.M. to see what forty was going to be like, and found it to be quite alright. It's a beautiful day, the world looks promising, and the future bright!"

In addition to her work on the correlation committee, Ardeth was working to complete her master's program at BYU. She also continued with her teaching duties and other faculty assignments in the education department. Occasionally, her schedule called for her to be in two places at once, and she wrote,

"Oh such conflicts. They really tear me, wondering where I should be."

Ardeth received her master's degree in summer commencement exercises at BYU. She had no plans to pursue a Ph.D., preferring instead to focus on "being a better wife, homemaker, and neighbor." She loved her job in the education department and would continue her work there.

The summer was made even more exciting by the news that her parents planned to sell their property in Glenwood and move to Bountiful. She looked forward to having them nearby. In August, following a family reunion, she and Heber helped them move. "The folks have been here with us for three weeks now, and they seem to be making a very good adjustment," she recorded. "It's delightful to have them with us. They are a great help in keeping things caught up both inside and outside."

A PRIVILEGE AND A BLESSING

In December, Elder Thomas S. Monson hosted a Christmas party for members of the correlation committee. Still hardly believing that she belonged among such a distinguished group, she wrote, "I never get used to being in the presence of these great leaders. It is truly a privilege."

At the dawning of the new year, 1972, she wrote, "A fresh new beautiful year. The past has been wonderful, the present is glorious, and so we look with eager anticipation to the future and all that it might hold." As she was to learn, the year would hold plenty in the way of change, challenge, and opportunity. Her parents, who had accepted a call to serve in the England Leeds Mission, entered the mission home on January 7, departing for their field of labor one week later.

In the spring, the Kapps began work on another home. In April she had the opportunity of attending the Regional Representatives seminar, presided over by President Joseph Fielding Smith. In attendance were all of the Quorum of the Twelve Apostles, the Assistants to the Twelve, the First Council of the Seventy, and the Presiding Bishopric. About that experience she wrote, "Such a spiritual feast. What a blessing to be in the presence of those inspired leaders. . . . Today I listened to conference and between sessions I read correlation material, but with renewed dedication and determination, and with gratitude for being part of such a program."

In May all of the correlation committees came together for a meeting. They noted that they had accomplished more in five months than they had in the previous year. "We all participated in a testimony meeting and certainly the Spirit of the Lord was felt in rich abundance. It seems that the direction of the wind has changed and the sail is set. For the first time in five years, I believe I see things fitting together, moving ahead and fulfilling the purpose of correlation as it is intended."

A Move and a New Assignment

In the spring of that year, Ardeth and Heber were once again faced with the necessity of finding a place to live. One day Joyce Eggington, who had been house-hunting, knocked on the door. She explained to Ardeth that her husband was in the military and would be going overseas in two weeks. They needed to purchase a home and be settled before he left. Joyce added that, after much earnest prayer and after looking extensively, she drove by Ardeth's home and felt impressed that she should look at it.

When Joyce indicated she had been led by the Spirit, Ardeth

agreed to let her walk through the house. After seeing it, Joyce was positive that it was to be hers. Ardeth said that when she thought of Mr. Eggington defending their country, it helped her to see the situation the same way. She called Heber at work to tell him she had sold their house and they had to be out in two weeks. His response was, "Really? Then you'd better be out finding an apartment. Now!"

On the last day of the two weeks, one family moved out, another moved in, and a prayer was answered. The Kapps not only had to move their own household, but her parents' belongings as well, which they had been storing while they were on their mission. It was the busy end of the school year for Heber, and Ardeth was likewise busy correcting reports and getting out semester grades for her students. In addition, they each had numerous Church commitments, including several speaking and teaching assignments. Somehow, with the help of Sharon, who researched topics for talks, and friends who assisted in the move, they met the deadline with only one brief "incident."

The new owners of the home called while Ardeth was away and asked Heber if they could come in two days early to paint a room. Heber agreed, but when Ardeth got home late in the evening and he told her that painters would be there early the next morning, she responded, "You've pushed me too far. I just can't have anyone here until I get out." Heber told her she shouldn't be that way, but unwilling to back down, she replied, "That's too bad. I am." He then suggested that she take the day off, take Shelly to the zoo, and he would do the painting. Still miffed, she said, "Okay, Little Red Hen!" After a few moments of silence, the storm clouds blew over, and all was well. However, thinking perhaps that wisdom was the better part of valor, Heber called the new owners and asked them to postpone the painting.

After five years, Ardeth had begun to feel more comfortable with her correlation assignment, later saying she should have recognized that as a danger sign. In May 1972, she was asked to serve on the newly organized Curriculum Development Committee. New manuals were to be developed for each of three age groups: Beehives, Mia Maids, and Laurels. Dean Larsen, who became a member of the Quorum of the Seventy, was called as committee chairman. As co-chairs, he called Ruth Funk to represent the youth; Hortense Child, the adults; and Ardeth, the children. Ardeth felt it fortunate that the school year had ended and that, since they were still in an apartment, she did not have a yard to keep up.

Feeling a reluctance to leave her work with the youth and young adult committee, Ardeth nevertheless began to read the new material she had been given. As she pondered her reading, a warm, powerful feeling began to well up within her. Tears fell as the rightness of the call was made known to her. She again recalled the promise of her patriarchal blessing that she would know the Lord's will concerning her and that she would become acquainted with the voice of the Spirit. She knew that voice had spoken to her mind.

She recorded, "I'm sure I couldn't have had quite the personal interest in the children's program without being so closely associated with our precious little Shelly. When I look at her, I feel a complete and total dedication to any effort that might assist her and all other little children to come to know better the purpose of life and their personal relationship to their Father in

Heaven in a way that will affect their every thought, action, and decision as they meet the joys and challenges of this mortal life."

In a letter to her parents, Ardeth told of her increasing testimony of the Book of Mormon. "As you know, I have read it many times before, but when I decided to write a paragraph concerning my testimony of it for the front of the book, I decided I wanted an even more 'sure knowledge.' What a blessing this has been to me. My Tuesday fasts and my regular study have been something which will remain with me forever. Those Book of Mormon prophets have come alive for me in a way it is impossible to express. The messages have been as though they were written personally to me. . . . I always knew that the Book of Mormon was true, but somehow it is different to *know that you know.*"

In June, Ardeth and Sharon took Shelly and traveled to Vernon, British Columbia, to help Shirley after the birth of her fifth child. It was a wonderful opportunity for the three sisters to be together, as well as for little Shelly to become reacquainted with her cousins. Never idle, in addition to the regular housework, Ardeth and Sharon bottled fruit, sewed curtains, and organized the kitchen. They spoke in sacrament meeting and at a fireside, prepared food for a missionary conference, defrosted the freezer, and cut Shirley's daughters' hair. Along with reminiscing and visiting, they even wrote a road show, a ward assignment of Sharon's.

On July 2, Ardeth learned of the passing of President Joseph Fielding Smith and noted "the powerful example he has been." Then, with a positive look forward, she said, "President Lee has always seemed very special to me. I have no adjustment in seeing him as the Lord's chosen prophet. With his special background in correlation, it is evident that he is the man for the hour."

SECOND COUNSELOR

With the approach of fall, Ardeth and Heber were still working to complete their home. Ardeth returned from school in the afternoon of November 7 to the sound of the telephone ringing. A voice said, "Could you and your husband meet with President Harold B. Lee tomorrow morning in his office at 11:35?" She took a deep breath and replied, "We'll be there." Together they wondered what a call from President Lee could mean. Could it be a mission call? Would they be asked to move away from home? What about their home under construction? How could they sell a half-completed home? They spent a restless night, but by morning were mentally prepared to respond to the call, "whatever it might be," Ardeth wrote, "and whatever adjustment it might require."

They were visibly nervous the next morning as they entered the Church Administration Building. President Lee was warm and friendly in his greeting. He asked them to try to relax, but then offered, "I'm sure you know this is not just a casual visit." His remarks were directed to Heber, as he explained the need for constant organizational changes to accommodate the ever-growing Church, making particular reference to the youth program. Ardeth sat by Heber thinking, "Whatever he wants him for, I'm sure he'll do a good job, and I'll be willing to support him." It wasn't until he had spent a considerable amount of time that he said to Heber, "We're reorganizing the youth organization and I would like your permission to call your wife to serve."

Young Women Presidency, 1972. Left to right: President Ruth Funk, Hortense Child (Smith), Ardeth.

She wrote, "Only then did President Lee approach me. Such order, such rightness, such beauty in the Lord's plan."

It was a great lesson to Ardeth that even the prophet would follow established procedure. "I think it was such a relief to Heber that he was willing to say yes to almost anything because we realized that we could stay at home. Given our financial situation, with a home under construction, that was important right then." The shock, however, was almost overwhelming to her.

Ardeth was to serve as second counselor in a newly envisioned young women's program. As President Lee explained, it was to be called the Aaronic Priesthood MIA. Ruth Funk had been called as the president. Hortense Child, a long-time friend to Sister Funk, was the first counselor. Speaking of that experience, Sister Funk recalled, "I asked President Lee who should be considered for the counselors. He said, 'Ruth, the Lord told me I was to call you. In like measure, He will tell you whom you are to call.' I prayed night after night for some time that I would be so guided." President Funk received an immediate confirmation that Sister Child should serve as a counselor. Knowing the Lord's will concerning the other counselor took considerably longer.

Sister Funk had known Ardeth briefly because of their service on their respective correlation committees. They became somewhat better acquainted during the year they served together on the new curriculum committee, but she had not thought of her as a counselor. As she explained, "After about ten days, praying fervently, one night I had a dream. In the dream, I saw Ardeth, and I was told, 'This is your counselor.' I went to sleep again and I had the dream twice more that night. That morning, I got up and called President Lee. When I told him about the dream, he said, 'You've been told.' There's no question, she truly was called by the Lord." When Sister Funk shared with Ardeth the experience of how she was called, Ardeth was convinced that it was right.

President Funk later expressed her thoughts regarding Ardeth: "I loved the way she thought and enjoyed her immensely. Her maturity was amazingly unusual. She had confidence and vision. She's a woman of courage. If there is something that needs to be done, she'll find a way to do it. She loves to be given an assignment, with the results that are expected, then to be left alone to do it. She has wonderful people skills. Those are all the makings of a great administrator. She is a marvelous speaker, as well as a writer. She reaches the hearts of people because they can relate to the marvelous analogies she uses."

With the organizational change came new leadership for the young men as well. Robert Backman was called as president, with Jack Goaslind and LeGrand Curtis as counselors. The two presidencies were to serve under the direction of the Presiding Bishopric—Bishop Victor L. Brown and his counselors, Vaughn J. Featherstone and H. Burke Peterson. The new presidencies were set apart on November 17, 1972. Ardeth described the experience as one of the most spiritual times of her life.

The setting-apart blessing, given by President Marion G. Romney, was one Ardeth would always remember. In addition to giving her direction concerning her new responsibilities, the blessing was specific to Ardeth's and Heber's personal circumstances. They were told that the blessing of children which they had desired had been withheld for a righteous purpose. When Ardeth heard this, she felt a peace come to her heart. She wrote in her journal, "If I had had this knowledge and feeling twenty years ago it would have been so much easier. I would have anguished less, but I would have been deprived of the spiritual growth which has come. This blessing was a confirmation to me that the Lord hears our prayers, and according to His wisdom and timing, tends to the welfare of His children." For Ardeth this blessing was a fulfillment of the scripture, "Dispute not because ye see not, for ye receive no witness until after the trial of your faith" (Ether 12:6).

The young men's and young women's organizations would be working more closely together than had hitherto been the case. As Ardeth explained, "I felt that President Lee was saying that building on the foundation that has been established, we now need to take another step forward, but perhaps with a different focus." President Lee emphasized that it was time for the youth to assume greater leadership roles than in the past. He said that they needed to have more responsibility and more accountability, with more local leadership involvement. There was much seeking, searching, studying, and praying as the new presidencies worked together to know the will of the Lord concerning the program for the youth of the Church. As they counseled together, they identified some specific guidelines. While greater emphasis was to be placed on youth leadership, adult leadership must always be close at hand. The need to identify the place of the youth in the family as well as to honor and help strengthen families was to be given increased emphasis.

Ardeth found that with the demands of her new calling, she could not continue her teaching assignment at BYU. She made plans to leave in April. Giving up her salary would create an uncertain financial future, and both she and Heber knew that some adjustments would be necessary. Completing their home and then selling it was one possibility they considered. Then, not long after her call, Heber was approached by a developer in the building industry asking if he would consider leaving the teaching profession and join him in his construction business. The offer represented an increase more than large enough to compensate for their diminished income, and Heber made the change. To them, it was a testimony that the witness comes *after* the trial of your faith.

OFFICIAL ASSIGNMENT

Ardeth and Heber moved into their new home on the Monday before Thanksgiving. Two days later, she left for her first official assignment—regional conferences in Great Britain. She enjoyed a Thanksgiving dinner on the plane and anticipated a reunion with her parents who would be in Leeds, England, to attend the conference. Not even stopping to sleep, she read all of the material to be presented in the meetings during the flight. She knew that she must be directed by the Spirit in her teaching and training.

As Ardeth and her traveling companions got off the plane, they were met by a group of sisters who obviously had not heard of the change in presidencies. With disappointment showing clearly on their faces, they asked: "Isn't Sister Jacobsen coming?" referring to the recently released president. Ardeth's response lightened the mood: "If you feel bad about it, how do you think I must feel?"

She called her mom and dad as soon as she got to her hotel room. Speaking with her parents made her feel more secure, but she still remained both nervous and excited about her participation in the conference. She wrote, "Oh dear, I'm feeling the need of so much help. I'm so thankful for the prayers that I know are being offered in my behalf and strengthened by the memory of the marvelous blessing I received through President Romney. Somehow I'll make it. Oh my, I'm going to need a lot of help. I must get on my knees, then review all my material and pray for strength beyond my natural ability. Tomorrow night I'm sure I'll feel much better."

The conferences went well and she was buoyed by the enthusiastic response of the area leaders with whom they met. In addition, she was happy to have time to spend with her parents. Her dad was appreciative of the opportunity to give her a father's blessing, which they both felt was particularly significant at this time.

A June Conference Theme

In January the new presidencies began work on plans for their first June conference. MIA June conferences had been held each year since the early days of the Church in Utah. Although MIA workers across the Church were invited, the bulk of Church membership at that time resided in the United States and Canada. The conference took place over several days and included lesson displays and workshops held in chapels all over the Salt Lake Valley. Workshops were held in all of the areas relating to Mutual activities, including music, dance, speech and drama, sports, and camp. They were prepared and executed by the MIA general boards, who wrote plays and music in addition to the lessons for the various age groups. Everything presented during the June conference was made available to units throughout the Church. The conference usually concluded with a dance festival held in the stadium at the University of Utah and a music festival in the Tabernacle on Temple Square.

The new presidencies were told that the guidelines for the conference needed to be finalized by April, in time to be presented at the Regional Representatives seminar. The responsibility was almost overwhelming to Ardeth, and she wondered what contribution she could possibly make. They knew they needed to have an MIA theme that would fit the new program. During one of their Thursday meetings, they were told that the theme presentation had to be submitted to Correlation by the following Monday. It seemed impossible to have something ready in so short a time. As the presidencies met together, Ardeth said she felt that they could come up with something. They said,

"Well, fine. We're meeting again Sunday. See if you can come up with something."

As she pondered a possible theme, a scripture came into her mind: "This is my work and my glory—to bring to pass the immortality and eternal life of man" (Moses 1:39). She talked her thoughts through with Sharon, then went home to bed and got up at 4:00 A.M. to begin working on the best way to present that theme. She later recalled that experience. "I had heard about these things happening before, when you just write as fast as you can. . . . I experienced that! About 5:00 A.M. I needed a response. I had shared previous spiritual experiences with my sister, Shirley, who lived in Canada. I called her and told her what I felt. She gave insights that enhanced what had unfolded. I wrote as fast as I could."

Ardeth made the presentation the next day. When she finished, President Backman said, "That just sends chills down my back." Ardeth wrote later, "When it was presented in the Tabernacle, I'm sure no one else knew where it got its start. That didn't matter. But [having the presentation accepted] was the little testimony that I needed that said, 'Yes, we can use you, and if you do your best, it can happen.' It was important to me to know that in this new calling."

ON HOLY GROUND

The two presidencies worked long hours, often late into the night, preparing for June conference. They met with the Presiding Bishopric, receiving inspiration, encouragement, and confirmation when things were right and continuing their work when it wasn't right. After their work had been reviewed and approved at various steps along the way, principles of the new program were finally ready for formal presentation to the First Presidency and Quorum of the Twelve Apostles in their weekly meeting in the temple. At that time, they received a telephone call from President Lee saying that he thought the meeting was of such importance that the two presidencies of the new Aaronic Priesthood MIA should be invited to attend.

As Ardeth later recounted, "We could hardly believe it, especially when we learned that President Lee said that according to his knowledge this was the first time in the history of the Church when any woman was permitted to be in attendance. We had gone into the room where there were portraits of all of the General Authorities. As we waited, I remember wondering if this was how Moses felt when he heard a voice tell him to take off his shoes for he was on holy ground. About 10:00 we were told we were to go in. Such an experience is impossible to relate. The formality, the order, the spirit, the tremendous feeling of power and the sacredness of the entire setting was almost overwhelming. . . .

"Following the presentation, which was made by Bishop Brown, a vote was called for and we were asked to participate in the vote. There was some discussion on some points, but with very minor changes the entire presentation was accepted. . . .

"As we left, we rejoiced in the approval we each felt and felt an extreme urgency now to develop the structure that had been approved."

Several years later, Elder Jack Goaslind, a counselor to President Backman at the time of their presentation in the temple, recalled that event as a highlight of their shared experiences. Following their presentation, before leaving the temple, the two presidencies assembled together in the stairwell, where

Young Men and Young Women general presidencies, 1972. Left to right: Ardeth, Hortense Child, and Ruth Funk; Robert Backman, LeGrand Curtis, and Jack Goaslind (all three later became General Authorities).

they knelt in prayer to express their gratitude for such an experience.

Following the meeting in the temple, they worked diligently to have leadership materials prepared for their first June conference. The conference was of historical significance in several ways. For the first time, it was a priesthood, rather than an auxiliary, conference. President Lee conducted and gave the keynote address. The new program was introduced.

There were more than thirteen thousand leaders and officers in attendance at this historic conference. Sitting in the Tabernacle in the red chairs, with the General Authorities behind her, was more than Ardeth could comprehend. As she stood at the pulpit, addressing an overflow audience, she felt that her responsibility was too great and her ability too lacking. That night she wrote, "I hear a familiar whispering that reminds me that the Lord has guided my steps thus far 'for a wise and glorious purpose,' and he will not abandon me in my hour of greatest need in his service."

A Growing Year

In July 1973, Ardeth's parents returned from their mission in England. Her mother had broken her hip during the last few months of their service and used a cane to help her get around. Ardeth was happy to have them upstairs in their new home while Heber finished an apartment for them downstairs. She was grateful to Heber for his concern for the welfare, comfort, and happiness of her mom and dad, particularly during this busy and challenging season of her own life.

Ardeth is no stranger to hard work, but she can't think of a time when she worked harder than during this calling. Most days were spent in lengthy meetings with the presidency addressing concerns and making plans. Then followed the work of carrying out the plans. There were also numerous training and speaking assignments, which often involved lengthy travel. Once when she returned home feeling the weight of her calling, Heber asked her, "Do you think when you're released from this calling, there will be anything of Ardeth left?"

During this period she experienced absolute fatigue for the first time in her life and often went home with her chest aching. She wrote in her journal in October 1973, "My frustration and challenge right now . . . is feeling that I am being pulled through life to meet deadlines without my own choice of managing, planning, and organizing myself to meet what needs to be done. I must somehow get hold of the reins and be in the driver's seat for my own life. . . . There must be a way to accomplish the work, yet manage one's own life." Several weeks later, she wrote of the changes in her life since her call to the presidency just one year earlier: "The weeks slip by into months and months into years. It hardly seems possible that just a year ago my lifestyle was completely [different]. It has been a growing year, and in the words of Michelangelo, it has provided both the agony and the ecstasy."

In December 1973, Ardeth was approached by the editor of the *New Era* to write a response for the Question and Answer section. As she later wrote, "I struggled with that, and once again, it seems as though I just think it through, then pick up a pen and somehow it seems to go together. When I turned it in, I received a call from the editor commenting on the 'excellent article.' He said the whole staff was impressed. That is encouragement for someone desirous of writing and just barely breaking through. Who knows, if enough eons go by, I may even yet one day author a book—a secret desire, never seriously expressed aloud."

Because Ardeth had been called by President Lee and had shared several special experiences with him, his unexpected death on December 26, 1973, came as a great shock to her. She recorded: "Our hearts are heavy, and we must 'Trust in the Lord with all thy heart and lean not unto thine own understanding.' Our Beloved Prophet, Harold Bingham Lee was called home at 8:55 P.M. We are heartbroken and shocked. Oh, such a loss. But no righteous man is taken before his time, and so the security comes in having faith in the Lord Jesus Christ. I feel the loss of a personal friend and a prophet that I have had the privilege of knowing. Tonight, Heber offered a beautiful prayer and I feel close to the Lord. Sometime we'll understand."

On December 30, 1973, Spencer W. Kimball was ordained and set apart as the twelfth President of the Church. His counselors were N. Eldon Tanner and Marion G. Romney. Ardeth said, "I am sure everyone feels very much at peace and comfortable in the knowledge that he is a prophet and the one whom the Lord would have serve at this time."

FARAWAY PLACES

Although future Church assignments would take her to nearly every corner of the globe, there are none that she remembers with more gratitude or emotion than her first visit to some of the islands in the South Pacific. In March 1974, she and three traveling companions flew to Samoa for regional conferences, where they were to teach and train local leaders in the new Aaronic Priesthood MIA program. She had always appreciated the beauties of nature, but was at a loss for words with which to describe that island paradise. "This has to be the design for the Garden of Eden," she wrote, "absolutely beyond expression."

Attending the conference meetings, she was struck by the friendliness of the people and impressed with the spirit she felt among them. After what she felt was an effective and tremendous meeting of the Apia Samoa Stake, she was taken on a tour of parts of the island. She later wrote about that time: "The next few hours [after the meeting] were indescribable—like trying to explain a testimony. You can't describe it, you have to experience it. . . . We drove to the center of a big volcano. President McKay visited this area and said it was the most beautiful spot on earth. He blessed the area, saying the inhabitants would never lack for food or have wars. It seems like a hallowed spot, a Garden of Eden."

After the tour, they were to return to the church house for a dance and a feast. Because of a flat tire, they arrived late, hot, and sweaty, with no time to bathe or change clothes. She said that they arrived at the church "in sad shape." After a delicious banquet, the visitors were showered with gifts of woven place mats, shells, and leis. The stake president spoke of his appreciation for their visit and prayed for their protection as they traveled. Then everyone began to sing. "As I shook hands with each one there and looked into their eyes and felt their genuine love, . . . I saw their beauty and I wept. They seemed touched by my visible emotion and responded with childlike trust. I could hardly control my feelings and am weeping now as I write. . . . Many kept coming back and shaking hands two or three times. *I have never*

Ardeth wrote: "Saints are so kind, generous, appreciative in all parts of the world. Spirit speaks to spirit if you don't know the language."

looked so bad or felt so good. I don't know why, but the whole experience seemed to be so special to me. I hardly wanted to talk, it was such a treasured moment to cherish."

Leaving Samoa, they traveled to Fiji, then to Tonga where they were met by the Regional Representative, Elder John Groberg, and his wife, Jean, who accompanied them for the next week.

The morning after their arrival in Tonga, she wrote, "When it rains here, the heavens open up like a fire hose. It is just unbelievable. It poured down all night. I can imagine how Noah felt with the flood."

Ardeth and her companions met with and taught the new program to the stake Aaronic Priesthood MIA advisors. She said, "We taught them the program and tonight they stood up and taught the people. . . . It was very effective for them to teach their own." Toward the end of the meeting, the power went off and the rain continued to pour down. With only the light from three flashlights, the meeting came to a quick conclusion with the members singing "We Thank Thee, O God, for a Prophet." It was a marvelous experience that she would never forget.

Following another meeting, she wrote, "The Tongan members seem to have a singleness of purpose. They are intent and beautiful."

Ardeth experienced similar feelings for the people in every area they visited. Whether Fijian, Tongan, Samoan, or Indian, she felt "they are beautiful and you have a feeling of excited urgency about this whole area, like a newborn baby, growing visibly each day."

Years later, Elder and Sister Groberg expressed their

admiration and appreciation for Ardeth's visit. "It was obvious to those people that she really loved them, and . . . they loved her in return."

Ardeth felt the same about the Grobergs. She wrote, "The Grobergs are very impressive people. He understands the needs of the people and has a great love for them."

After a one-day stop in Tahiti, they left for home, having been gone for nearly three weeks. Ardeth recorded, "We've traveled 16,500 miles, been on sixteen different planes, and participated in nineteen different meetings." That never-to-be-forgotten experience left an indelible impression upon her mind and upon her heart. She wrote, "I'll never be quite the same person as I was before. I can work an eternity in the Lord's service and will be indebted forever for this experience."

Her Majesty Halaevalu Mata'aho, Queen of Tonga, December 1991, with Ardeth and Jayne B. Malan

CHAPTER FOURTEEN

Carry On

NEW LEADERSHIP

During the opening session of the April 1974 general conference, President Spencer W. Kimball was sustained as prophet, seer, and revelator and as President of the Church. A great outpouring of the Spirit bore witness of his calling. The Young Women general presidency were uncertain as to whether or not President Kimball would see the program for the young women in quite the same way as President Lee. But as Ardeth said, "If he didn't, it was important for us to be in line with the present prophet."

Following conference, Ardeth was hospitalized to undergo serious surgery. The morning that she entered the hospital, Heber and her father administered to her. Heber pronounced a blessing that gave her a very secure, comfortable assurance that all would be well. She wrote, "It was a very meaningful, beautiful blessing and indicated that the Lord accepted my life and I was forgiven of all sins, and that although some organs of my body will be removed, the time will come when our promise of a family will be fulfilled. What a blessing it is to have confidence in the Lord's timeline." After a week in the hospital, she returned home with instructions for a month's convalescence.

In the meantime, June Conference plans were being finalized. Although she was still recovering from the surgery, Ardeth met with the members of both the Young Men and Young Women presidencies as often as she could to help with the planning. The Young Women leaders knew that the Young Men's presidency would be released soon and wondered if they themselves might be released. Ardeth wrote, "I really don't know whether I will be involved after June or not. But this I know for sure, more and more each day. The ways of God are not the ways of man, and He will reveal His will to the Prophet, and President Kimball is surely a prophet. There will always be an opportunity to serve in the Church somewhere."

At a special meeting on Sunday morning, prior to the June conference sessions, all of the Young Women board members were notified that they were to be released in the general session, as were the Young Men presidency. There were now to be two organizations: the Aaronic Priesthood and Young Women. They would work together under the direction of the Presiding Bishopric, who would also serve as the presidency of the young men. The Young Women general presidency was released and then sustained to continue serving under the new organization.

Along with several former board members who were called back, seven new ones were called, including Ardeth's sister, Sharon. Ardeth had the opportunity to be in attendance at Sharon's setting apart. Ardeth recorded, "Bishop Vaughn J.

Featherstone gave her a beautiful blessing, saying we were precious friends in the pre-existence. Maybe that explains my deep feelings for her and for Shirley—ever since they were tiny."

PROMISED BLESSINGS

In August the members of the Young Women presidency were set apart by the First Presidency. The day before, Ardeth fasted in preparation for the blessing she would receive. She also prayed to her Heavenly Father regarding the concerns of her heart. Following the blessing she wrote, "President Romney pronounced the blessing, and his words were a testimony to me that God lives and he has heard my prayers. Answers to specific concerns were given through him. . . . As though he was reading my mind, President Romney spoke of each concern, and I literally felt my burden lifted, a physical experience that I'll never forget. . . . Now I must go forward confidently, with peace of mind, in good health, with all of the gifts and blessings needed to carry out my responsibility."

Despite such blessings, as long as she could remember Ardeth had had difficulty in maintaining her own self-confidence. That did not deter her, however, from a constant seeking and striving to reach self-imposed goals to become the person she wanted to be. "I struggle with a need for self-confidence, . . . but as it begins to grow, it is so foreign to me. I worry about lack of humility. As I think about all of the blessings requested by Bible characters, . . . I believe my wish might be *'To become pure in heart.'* Every thought, every motive, and every desire would be to be pure in heart."

A FAST-MOVING CURRENT

More quickly than seemed possible, it was time for June Conference, 1975. The theme for the conference, "Lengthening Our Stride," was an echo of President Kimball's clarion call.

Just prior to the beginning of the conference, Ardeth felt like she was "at the very top of a roller coaster, ready to begin the rapid descent into the final stretch. It will be a historic conference, especially since President Kimball is going to announce that it is to be the last June conference. No time for the luxury of nostalgia. The Church can no longer be reached in the traditional methods of the past." Regional meetings were to be the successors to June conference. President Kimball said, "We will take the program to the people, rather than having the people come in."

Although principles and guidelines would continue to be

Ardeth and Heber, June Conference reception line, 1973 or 1974

provided from Church headquarters, leaders in local units would now have the responsibility for creating their own materials relating to youth activities. Ardeth relates, "This was a difficult time. Because people were used to receiving materials, it was almost like saying there would be no drinking water. People couldn't imagine they could survive without a June Conference. We were asking people to create materials that would be best for their own people. It was like weaning a baby." The result, however, was that "people began to become more self-reliant and less dependent for specific information from Church headquarters."

In 1976, the Young Women's presidency was told that another change was in the offing. During the previous four years there had been numerous sequential organizational developments in the program. In October 1976, they were told that they would no longer work under the direction of the Presiding Bishopric, and in December, Elder Marion D. Hanks was announced as the advisor to the Young Women's program.

Development of any new program is sometimes long, and implementation can be fraught with frustration. The goals and objectives as developed under the leadership of President Lee did not change. However, with several changes in leadership, the implementation of the new program proved to be challenging.

Finally, by 1977, everything seemed to be falling into place. Along with the change in the organizational structure, there was also a change of terminology. The term "activity night," which had been used to denote the weeknight meeting, really hadn't been accepted by the members of the Church, and Church leaders decided to go back to "Mutual." Ardeth was grateful that as she continued to travel on speaking assignments, many priesthood leaders mentioned that the youth were starting to assume responsibilities and that the program was finally beginning to take hold.

The work progressed. New age-group manuals were developed under the responsibility of the Curriculum Development Committee, of which Ardeth had earlier been a part, and came out in the fall of 1977. The manuals were scripturally oriented, and each lesson was based on a scriptural reference. An activity book also was formulated; it contained scores of ideas for all sorts of activities.

YOU SHOULD BE A WRITER

In the meantime, in addition to numerous speaking opportunities, she was also beginning to be asked to write short articles for Church publications. One of her articles printed in the October 1975 *Ensign* was titled, "You're Like a Mother." The response to that article was overwhelming, and she said, "It had to be the result of inspiration. I could not otherwise have possibly achieved such positive results. I have had letters and calls and notes from everywhere. . . . As many men have commented as have sisters. It has been a thrill to think of the lives this small effort has touched. Oh, the joys and rewards of service."

Later that year, she confided in her journal that the editor of the *New Era,* Brian Kelly, had complimented her on an article and said "that I should be a writer. I didn't tell him that my professor at the 'U' asked me how I got through freshman English!"

Finally, Heber, who constantly encouraged Ardeth in her desires to write, issued her a challenge. He said that he was "going to build a house for sale, and that he would get it built and sold before I would get a book written and published,"

Ardeth wrote. "Well, I got up my courage and called Eleanor Knowles, one of the top editors for Deseret Book Company. . . . I told her that I felt we needed a book for girls." The editor was immediately interested in her idea, saying that she had read some of her published articles and stories and liked them very much. After some discussion, Ardeth agreed to have a manuscript ready in six months.

Meanwhile, Heber continued to work on the house he was building. He finished the construction about the same time Ardeth completed writing her first book. But he slightly delayed selling the home so her book could be published first.

Miracles: Not Only in Pinafores and Blue Jeans

The culmination of all of her preparations came on April 1, 1977. She received her first, newly printed copy of *Miracles in Pinafores and Blue Jeans* at the Deseret Book Store. Ardeth was invited to sign copies of her book at an autograph party during the Saturday evening priesthood session of general conference that week. She recorded, "The books arrived in the store at noon on Friday, and by noon on Saturday they were selling so fast that they were afraid they would run out, so they took them all off the shelf until the time of the autograph party. . . .

"The big evening started at 7:00 P.M. When I went in, people were lined up at the table waiting. . . . It was a delightful evening. They gave me a beautiful large white orchid corsage, and I sat at a table with my books piled high."

In the four months following its publication *Miracles in Pinafores and Blue Jeans* sold nearly six thousand copies. She wrote, "I can hardly believe it. I really know that that book was the result of much help beyond my natural ability."

That first book was followed the next year by *The Gentle Touch,* chronicling some of her classroom experiences with elementary school children. Students preparing for teaching careers, as well as experienced teachers, gained insights into how to better become a positive influence in a child's life. The book became a best-seller, selling 8,000 copies in a single month. It was also on the required reading list in an education class at BYU.

At the request of Deseret Book, she wrote a booklet called *All Kinds of Mothers* for Mother's Day in 1978. It dealt with the responsibility that all women have in the role of mothering, whether or not they have children. It was a nontraditional approach to motherhood, and the response was overwhelming. The first printing of one-hundred and fifty thousand copies sold out, and more were printed later.

She began work on her next book, *Echoes from My Prairie,* with her father. Designed to provide life lessons from their experiences as a father and a daughter, it recounted pivotal events from her life as a young girl growing up in a small Canadian prairie town. It became an immediate best-seller.

Now the author of more than a dozen books, Ardeth has also penned numerous articles which have been published in a variety of books and magazines.

In 1990, she was honored with the Deseret Book "Excellence in Writing" award. Part of the tribute paid at that time read, "Few writers in the history of Deseret Book have had as great an impact on the lives of readers as has Ardeth Greene Kapp."

AN HONORABLE RELEASE

Ardeth's mother never completely enjoyed good health after they returned from their mission to England. Since their return home, she had sustained a broken hip in a fall, severely limiting her ability to move about, and a general decline in health followed. Her dad still remained healthy and active, doing seventy-five push-ups to celebrate his seventy-fifth birthday on October 3, 1977. In February 1978, however, he experienced difficulty swallowing, and his doctor hospitalized him for some testing. It was the first time he had ever been in a hospital, and he insisted that he was fine. But the tests revealed he had stomach cancer.

By April, Ardeth struggled to balance her need to help her parents and the simultaneous need to be in the office. At that same time, she had a strong impression that Heber would be called as a stake president. She began to feel a great urgency to be at home, and yet the demands of her calling were great, requiring significant time and energy. On Mother's Day, May 14, she met with Sister Funk and learned that President Kimball was planning to release the Young Women general presidency. Ardeth returned home that day and told her dad, "We're going to receive an honorable release." With tears in his eyes, he said, "That's all you can ask for. And that's all I ask for. An honorable release." News of their impending release would not be made public for nearly two months.

Ardeth's dad confided in Ardeth that he didn't believe he had much time left in this life. He told her that his greatest concern was for her mother. Ardeth assured him that they would take good care of her. She told him that on an eternal time scale, it wouldn't be long before all of his family would follow him. "I put my hand on his knee and he put his hand on mine and said, 'Your hand looks like Grandma Greene's.' I said, 'I hope my spirit looks like hers also.'"

In the Sunday morning session of their stake conference on May 20, Heber was sustained as the new stake president. Although Ardeth was fully supportive, she wondered how much help she could be to him in his new calling, while at the same time caring for her mom and dad.

Although he maintained an optimistic attitude, Ardeth's dad's health was in a definite decline. "Dad has had a difficult day," she wrote at the end of May. And "Mom seems to be slipping in her memory, and she becomes nervous if Dad leaves for even a few minutes."

Rumors began swirling that she would be called as the new Young Women's president, even though no formal announcement regarding their release had been made. Finally, a few weeks prior to their official release, she was told the name of the new president. It was not her. She called to tell Heber, and his response was one of real excitement. He said, "I can think of a hundred ways you can help me." Ardeth was grateful that she would now have an opportunity to assist him.

Ardeth often reflected on the rich and rewarding opportunity it had been to be mentored by such experienced and dedicated leaders as Ruth Funk and Hortense Child. Ruth was a patient tutor who taught Ardeth about optimism, endurance, and total commitment.

Pondering her release, Ardeth wrote, "As I reflect on the glorious, unbelievable experiences and also the struggles of the past five and a half years, I marvel at the blessings and opportunities the Lord has provided for me. . . . It has been a choice and sacred privilege. . . . My patriarchal blessing tells me that I will be surprised in the days to come at the blessings the Lord has in store for me. And I certainly have been surprised. But at forty-seven years of age, I don't believe I'm all through. I believe there will yet be many wonderful experiences as I strive to assist Heber in whatever way he sees fit."

A Release and a Calling

Ardeth's upcoming release was not the only noteworthy event she recorded in her journal in June 1978. On June 8, Ardeth heard the news of the revelation that had come to President Spencer W. Kimball in the Salt Lake Temple. She wrote, "Every worthy male member of the Church may receive the priesthood, without regard to race or color. I could hardly believe my ears. To think that it should occur in my day! As I consider all of the ramifications and the expansion of the missionary program, but especially the impact on individual soul. A black man in the mail room of the Church Office Building just sat down and wept all day—so much joy! Surely a history-making day of the greatest magnitude. How blessed we are, how thankful for a prophet to guide us in these latter days!"

As the date for her release drew near, Ardeth penned her thoughts in her journal. "When I think of my release, I have a warm excited feeling. The other evening, I just couldn't go to bed. The evening was too beautiful to leave, so I sat on the balcony watching the lights twinkle and listened to the night sounds. I guess it's much like a missionary returning home. The time has gone so fast. The acquaintances and the friends, the brothers and sisters, have been so dear, like family. The memories are precious, the spiritual growth almost unbelievable. Now I have a great coming-home feeling—back to my stake, my ward, my neighborhood, and my family."

Ardeth had a high regard for Elaine Cannon, who was called as the new Young Women general president. Ardeth said that long before she ever dared to talk to Sister Cannon, she admired her. "I once attended BYU Education Week, where I heard Sister Cannon speak. During her lecture, I knew she knew the Savior, and I know He knows Elaine. I'm thankful it is so comfortable to sustain and support her."

After her release on July 12, 1978, she wrote, "My words are enemies to my thoughts, so ineptly expressing what I feel. Such joy, such gratitude and thanksgiving, and much, much more. I crossed the finish line, maybe not the winner, but I ran the full race, never letting up, having won the reward of feeling that I had done my best. I honestly feel that with all my weaknesses and failings, which I openly acknowledge, that the Lord accepts my effort and I am in His favor. I feel a great anticipation and exhilaration about the future."

At church the day following her release, many fellow ward members approached Ardeth and said, "Welcome home." That same day, she was called to be the ward Laurel advisor. She was excited about this new calling, saying that with the Lord's help, she knew she could reach each one. "This church is so great, and I want them to know their Savior."

A Return to Their Prairie

Returning home in the afternoon on the day of her release, she and her dad sat outside in their lawn chairs while she told him the details of the day. She thanked him for the part he had played from the beginning of her life in her preparation for that calling. They spoke of their struggles and their victories and the experiences they had had together. He told her that he knew he was losing ground, then asked her how she thought it would end. She said she thought, that because of his righteousness, when he was ready to transfer, that would be the time. He expressed to her his frustration at being unable to do the many things he would yet like to do. She responded that if he didn't experience this frustration, he would never be ready to let go, saying that this, too, is a preparation. He agreed. "We spoke of all we are learning and how very real and close the other side becomes as you approach the infield. Those relatives and friends who have gone before become alive again as you anticipate that reunion."

Ardeth and her dad prepared an outline for *Echoes from My Prairie,* the book they were planning to write together. She savored every moment she spent together with him. One evening at dusk they went to the garden to water. "We stood with our arms around each other, listening to the creek, the birds, and smelling the night air, with the full moon coming over the mountain. As we started up the garden path, almost grown over with oak, he said, 'I'm going to miss you when I have to go away.' I said, 'You'll never be far away,' and he said, 'Don't forget me.' Up at the house we sat on the lawn chairs under the balcony. We embraced and shed tears together, then reminisced about how he had disciplined me as a youth and how strong-willed I was, but what a sweet relationship we have had."

Her dad expressed his desire to return to his Canadian prairie home one more time. He told her that they must finish their book. They planned to go to Canada in July to recapture the details of the stories they planned. She told him that she would finish the book no matter what. He said that he knew she would finish it, but that he would like to be able to see it. Although he did not live to see the completion and publication of the book, his influence is felt throughout its pages. Ardeth told him that "the things that make up this book will last forever."

Before they left on their trip, her dad was beginning to feel sick all of the time. Heber took him to the doctor to see if there was something he could be given to relieve his distress. The doctor told them that the cancer had gone into his liver, and that he probably had about three months left, at best. On July 16th, all of the family gathered for the first Greene family reunion. Although everyone enjoyed it, they were touched with sadness, knowing that it would likely be the last time they would all be together. In the evening, after everyone had gone to bed, Ardeth went downstairs. Her dad was sitting quietly at his desk. She asked him what he was thinking and he said, "When I think of all the money spent on my illness, I think I should have bought some horses and a chariot and gone up like Elijah!"

The following Wednesday, Ardeth and Sharon, with Shelly in tow, left with their mom and dad to drive him home to Glenwood for one last time. They spent several days visiting with family members and friends. They returned to many of their familiar places, including the short trip to Aetna, the small town where he was born. They also gathered a lot of information for their book. The country had never seemed more beautiful to them. Ardeth remembers that her dad kept saying how beautiful it was. He said that he was seeing it at its best for the last time. They had never seen so many beautiful wildflowers. It was an unbelievable display of glory.

After a week, they prepared to return home. Her dad's sister, her Aunt Alice, put her arms around him and said, "We'll meet again, don't know where, don't know when." There was a sweet spirit, with no tears but with deep emotion and understanding. Her dad experienced no sickness while in Canada, but upon their return, he became very ill and had no energy at all.

A Good Life

Ardeth continued to receive calls asking her to speak to various groups, but because she didn't want to neglect her responsibilities to Heber, her mom and dad, and her new Laurel class, she was only able to accept a few of the requests. Her dad told her that while he didn't want to be a coward and get out before he was supposed to, he was ready to go. Ardeth told him that she didn't think that was being a coward, but that it was evidence of his testimony, his faith, and his belief in the future. He replied that he was full of anticipation of walking through the door. He also began to speak frequently of his daughter, Ardeth's sister, who had died as an infant. He was happy at the thought of being reunited with her.

As her dad's body continued to weaken, his spirit seemed to increase in strength. In August he gave each of his daughters a father's blessing. Ardeth wept as she received her blessing. She told him that one day she would give a stewardship accounting to him on his instructions and blessings. The next day, he gave blessings to each of his grandchildren. There was a sweet spirit, and a feeling of peace filled not only the room, but also their hearts.

August 17, 1978: "The other morning while Dad and I were walking, he said, 'It's been a good year.' I responded, 'How can you say that, Dad?' He said, 'Aw, you can't look at one little part. You have to look at the whole picture. It's been a good year.' I asked him how he had learned to always be optimistic and look at the bright side. He said, 'Well, I had to learn not to let things bother me and determine how I would feel. . . . I learned that I must be happy with the way things are for me. It's been a good life.'"

Ardeth continued to enjoy spending more time in her home and with her family. She began to notice details of things for which she had not had time during the past few years. She said, "I love the smell of the laundry soap when I do my wash—the sounds, the smells, new recipes—an entire day spent out-of-doors, like yesterday. I worked alongside Heber finishing the water system down by the creek, fitting pipes and parts. Last evening we turned it on—a glorious sight—water spraying over the entire area. I trimmed all the roses, used the edger for the first time, did all the lawns, pulled all the weeds from the cracks in the drive strip. I worked hard all day and didn't get tired at all. Heber and I enjoy working together and he seems to be so happy to have me "back."

October 12, 1978: "The time with Dad and Mom is of greatest importance right now. Dad needs support when he goes for his brief walks. I support him with my arm around his waist and carry a lawn chair with us so he can rest at intervals. He's very weak."

October 18, 1978: "Yesterday was Dad's worst day. It was the first day we haven't taken a walk. He looks so very thin. It is so hard to see him suffer so. Each night, I tell them good night and tuck them into bed. Tonight after tucking them in, I came upstairs and shed a few tears. Life is a cycle. I think of all the years they tucked me in."

October 19, 1978: "Today was a significant day, leading to Dad's graduation. I went down this morning and he was almost too weak to get up. He isn't able to eat anymore. He got up for a drink, then went back to bed. Later he got up, took a bath, shaved, and came out and collapsed on the couch. In the afternoon, we walked out in the backyard and sat on a couple of chairs for awhile. Then he wanted to drive down by the garden and the creek. We walked around to the car and I drove him down. He returned exhausted. Tonight I got him settled in bed and put a couple of fresh roses by his bed. He is so appreciative of everything we do. Dad is so anxious to go. I would hope it could be tonight, but we'll see. I'll go down during the night and check on them. I believe we have a few nights left, but we shall await the "due time of the Lord."

October 25, 1978: "Last Friday, October 20, was Dad's graduation. I wish there were words to express the sweet sacredness of the experience. But, like a testimony, it has to be felt."

Ardeth wrote of her experience a few days later at the mortuary. "As I looked with my eyes at Dad's body, I could see it, but I could feel Dad was not there. He was there in the room with us. It was real. What I felt was more powerful and real than what I saw."

The funeral services were beautiful—calm, sweet, and

peaceful. Comments from many indicated that it was like a panorama of eternity and an assurance of the eternal relationship. One person said, "That service removed all doubt regarding the eternal nature of man." In the late afternoon, the children and grandchildren returned to the cemetery. Ardeth and the others joined hands in a circle around the grave and, according to her dad's wishes, they sang, "Don't Fence Me In."

The next morning, Ardeth, who, three months earlier, had accepted an invitation to speak at a Ricks College devotional, flew to Rexburg, Idaho, to fill that assignment. Although she was concerned because of her hasty preparation, she felt the comfort and sustaining power of her Heavenly Father. She later wrote, "Well, it's true again and again. When you have gone as far as you can go, the Lord will make up the difference. The students were most responsive, gathering around until I had to rush to meet the plane." She returned home in time to teach her Mutual class, and it wasn't until then that she realized how exhausted she was.

CHAPTER FIFTEEN

A Time of Preparation

Crossroads

In the days following her dad's funeral, Ardeth had a rare opportunity to stop and catch her breath. She enjoyed being at home helping Heber and taking care of her mom. But during quiet hours she wondered if there was more she should be doing. She pondered, "Are there things I should be doing to affect the lives of others? When it's all over, will I have done what I should . . . ? My blessing says I will know the Lord's will concerning me. . . . It's a crossroads time."

The assignment to teach the Laurel class in her ward was short-lived. In late 1978, Ardeth was asked to serve on a curriculum committee that was charged with revising the Teacher Development course. Although she was sad at having to give up her Laurel class, she looked forward to the new opportunity.

On January 16, 1979, Elder Rex Pinegar set Ardeth apart as a member of the Instructional Development Committee. She thought back to when she was impressed to change her college major at BYU to curriculum development. One reason for the change was readily apparent with this new assignment. The knowledge she had gained there would serve her well in her new assignment.

NEW OPPORTUNITIES

As the new year began, Ardeth's life continued at a rapid pace. In early January, she received many speaking requests. Regarding those speaking opportunities she wrote, "I see it as an opportunity to teach truth, bear witness, and help build the kingdom. Although I turn down many requests, still I accept all that I can. It is not for my own gratification, nor because it is my duty, but it is because I wish I had the trump of an angel and could shout to youth everywhere, 'It's the truth and it does matter. He is coming again and we must be prepared!'"

Still, she wanted time to care for her mother and to help Heber. She struggled with how to balance the requests for her time with her responsibilities at home. She wrote, "I try to determine the proper use of time, but seem never to be quite at peace as I set my priorities. I'd like to do more and be better in so many ways, beginning at home."

As she helped her mom take care of her dad's things, she felt comforted by the presence of her father's spirit. "I feel close to Dad and our shared memories become more dear. I keep wondering if he knows how I feel and that I'm taking care of his things, and Mom. I hope to be doing an acceptable job for him. I wouldn't want my dad or my Father in Heaven to be disappointed in me."

In the spring of 1979, she completed *Echoes from My Prairie,* the book she and her dad had begun together. On the day a copy of the published book was delivered to Ardeth, she took it to the cemetery and, sitting by her father's grave, read the entire book aloud and recorded, "I felt his approval."

I Should Have Stayed in Bed!

Ardeth occasionally had days so full of mishaps that she thought it would have been better if she had never gotten out of bed. On one such day, she hurriedly made two carrot cakes, one for a ward event, and the other for the staff at Deseret Book. She didn't have time to frost the cakes before she was due at a meeting. She put one of them into the trunk of her car, attended the meeting, then frosted and delivered it to Deseret Book. They invited her to stay and eat it with them, but she didn't have time.

When she returned home to frost the other cake, she discovered that it was nearly rock solid. She checked the oven setting to discover that she had baked the cake at a temperature one hundred degrees hotter than what the recipe called for! She hurriedly prepared and baked a cake from a mix for the ward party, hoping to complete it before her neighbor came to pick it up. She was in such a hurry that she frosted it before it had cooled, and the whole center fell in. She covered it over with more frosting and set it outside on the porch, hoping the cool weather would harden the frosting before a further catastrophe could occur. The neighbor picked up the cake from her porch before she had a chance to explain her misfortunes.

Then she became panicky about the cake she had delivered to Deseret Book. She could just imagine how it must have been when they all gathered around to cut it! She was mortified. The next morning she made another carrot cake. Thankfully, the second attempt produced the desired result. Talking Sharon into delivering it for her, she sent it with an accompanying note: "I'm taking a poll. Do you like cakes baked at 450 degrees as well as 350?" She also offered her brother-in-law's dental services to anyone who had tried to bite into the cake. She ended the message with, "My next book is going to be a cookbook!"

Turning her attention to the kitchen, she loaded the dishwasher and turned it on, only to find that she had enclosed part of the telephone cord inside. After freeing the cord, she started cleaning her hand mixer with a wet cloth. She jumped when a shock went through her hand. She hadn't unplugged the mixer. Then, hurrying to finish up, she reached for a sharp knife to put away and cut her thumb! Later, she started to record the day's events in her journal, but her pen ran out of ink. She ended her recitation with, "I think I'll go back to bed!"

INSPIRATION

In March, Ardeth was given the assignment to write the script for a slide presentation being prepared by the curriculum committee. She later wrote, "I felt the inspiration that gave me vision. I saw a learning center in each home. I saw the clouds of darkness, and the home as the refuge. It unfolded so fast, I could hardly write it down fast enough."

As spring progressed, she continued to miss her father. "When I go [to his room]," she wrote in May, "I feel warm and happy. I can still smell the things in his room like they always were. I saw his old shoes he tramped this earth with and tucked them away in a metal drawer. I took his suit from his closet, hugged it, felt in all the pockets, found his comb, a pencil, a toothpick, and a little package of Tic-Tacs. I wept tears of love and joy for such a great dad. I kneel often by his bed to say my morning prayers. There is such peace in that room."

In August of 1979, Ardeth was invited to join the College of Student Life at Brigham Young University.

Ardeth's initial assignment was to establish a leadership training program for the student body officers. She was assigned a small office in the Abraham Smoot Building and began identifying leadership skills for which she would later write lessons. As with many things, Ardeth's enthusiasm and vision expanded the project, and the dean encouraged her to consider working two days a week. She was hesitant because her mother's physical condition required considerable care.

Her mother's health was declining and she became less and less able to care for herself. After praying about the situation, she and Heber hired a couple to live with and care for her mother in her apartment in their home. The arrangement seemed to work well, and they felt it an answer to their prayers, allowing Ardeth to keep up her teaching and speaking responsibilities. Her mother was also happy with the arrangement, which provided her with constant companionship.

Though her work was well-accepted and her assignments increased, Ardeth continued to be burdened with what she called her "limited mental capacity."

She wrote, "Why, when I have so many wonderful opportunities, do I have such a struggle with feelings of inadequacy, that my mind isn't alert, and my retention not good, and I sometimes feel weary and tired? It worries me a lot." She felt as if she had a good mind to think, but her brain power was not alert and quick. It was a constant concern. Her associates were very capable, and she felt she was running to keep up. "I have wondered if mental capacity and faithfulness in the pre-existence were related, since one's ability to learn [here] gives one so much advantage in the world to come," she observed.

To Touch Lives and Strengthen Testimonies

Ardeth's skills as a teacher, speaker, and writer grew as she continued to share her gospel insights with groups far and wide. Speaking requests continued to come. She studied diligently and prayed that she would be used as an instrument in the Lord's hands to lift and inspire those she taught. She became increasingly recognized throughout the Church. People were drawn to her warmth and her enthusiasm, her genuine concern for others, and her testimony of the restored gospel of Jesus Christ.

Although most of Ardeth's work at BYU took place in an office setting, she and the other advisers participated in a variety of activities with the students. One memorable event was a mud football game. "I didn't really want to get involved but felt I needed to be supportive," she wrote in her journal. "They swamped a large dirt field with water until the mud was about three inches deep." Then Ardeth, the other advisers, and a group of students waded in for a game. "I can't say the football experience was great," she said, "but the relationships it helped to form became lasting."

Her responsibilities also included attendance at graduations. One was significant enough that she wrote of it at length in her journal: "I went to the spot where I thought I was to assemble with the other members of the Student Life faculty. I couldn't see anyone I knew and became so frustrated. I felt like a little kid who didn't know where to go. Finally I took off my cap and gown, tucked it tightly behind my program, put it in the car, and went to my office and listened to the proceedings over the radio. . . .

"After the event, one of my friends asked, 'Where were you sitting?' I responded, 'Oh, I sat where I could hear really well. Didn't you enjoy the president's message?' Then we began talking about his talk. . . . Oh, if they only knew my limitations, they would decide on other candidates for other projects."

There were indeed other projects for which Ardeth's expertise was needed. In addition to her work in Student Life, the president of the university, Jeffrey R. Holland, asked her to chair the Advisory Committee on Women's Concerns. Ardeth accepted this assignment with great reservations. She knew about some of the problems women faced at BYU: some concerns about equality in general, and unequal salaries in particular. But by her own admission, she had felt that women who complained about their personal circumstances were often victims of their own attitude or that they lacked the ability to take control of situations in their own life.

As she began to work with the committee and to study issues related to women, however, she realized that her view was uninformed. There were indeed problems in which women were affected. Ardeth began to see a need for both men and women to become better informed, more sensitive, and to take action where possible and when appropriate. She also realized there were no concerns that related to women that did not affect men and no issues related to men that did not impact women. She was grateful that the committee was composed of both men and women and expressed her feeling that they needed both a male and a female point of view in addressing what she called "human concerns."

Under her direction, the committee focused its attention on issues such as upward mobility for female faculty, increased opportunities for reentry students, and the importance of women obtaining a college education. But perhaps as important as the work the committee accomplished was Ardeth's personal education regarding needs of women and the importance of education in their preparation for life.

HOME AND FAMILY

There were days when she wished for a slower pace. She said, "In my heart, I could enjoy pulling into my [familiar] activities of writing and doing a little teaching, . . . but I know that Heber feels very strongly about our need to keep growing and learning and struggling with new horizons and challenges that push us beyond our comfort zone. . . . I don't want to rest, I'd just like to slow down and take time for some other things."

Though both were leading busy lives, Ardeth and Heber reserved time whenever they could fit it in to enjoy nature, the out-of-doors, and doing things together. Heber came up with an idea that would combine all three of these things—motorcycles! He talked with Ardeth about riding to the top of the hills behind their home, turning off the motor, and enjoying the wonderful view and quietness of the surroundings. Ardeth supported the idea of Heber getting a motorcycle, and she could envision herself riding behind him on a motorcycle, but the idea that she would have her own motorcycle was completely out of her range of interest or desire.

Heber insisted that Ardeth would like it if she just tried it.

Ardeth kept thinking, "I know I won't like it, and I don't want to try it!" However, Heber's persistence finally paid off. Ardeth reasoned that he did so many things for her she ought to at least try it.

The day Heber arrived home with a small Yamaha motorcycle for Ardeth, she took one look at it and wondered where she was going to go to learn to ride it. She didn't think it fit with what she wanted her reputation or image to be. Since it was summertime, Heber suggested they wait until dusk and then practice on the high school parking lot. After learning the basics about motorcycle operations, Ardeth practiced driving around the parking lot. The smile on Heber's face kept her going. Each time she passed him, his smile was bigger than the last.

It was not long before Heber was planning an adventure with another couple who owned a motorcycle. The motorcycles were loaded on a trailer and the two couples headed for Moab in southern Utah. The other couple planned to ride together, but Ardeth and Heber each had their own motorcycles. Early the next morning, they donned their helmets and rode from Moab to Dead Horse Point. It was flat, highway driving and Ardeth negotiated the trip without a problem. When they reached Dead Horse Point, however, they headed down an extremely steep trail to the bottom of the canyon.

Ardeth describes the trip: "The trail was only about three feet wide and as I looked over the edge, [I realized] it was hundreds of feet to the bottom of the canyon. Heber rode behind me and kept yelling, 'Just hug the bank.' I *was* hugging the bank of the trail. My knuckles were white from holding onto the handlebars so tightly, and I wondered if I'd ever be able to straighten my fingers again. I never looked right or left, just straight ahead. Every bump in the trail frightened me because I thought, 'Just one slip and I'll flip over the edge and to the bottom of the canyon.'

"Finally we got to the bottom. I was trembling as I got off the bike. Heber came over to me with a big smile. He was so excited. I couldn't hold it in anymore and said, 'I tried it and I don't like it!'

He put his arm around me and said, 'You gave it an honest try and if you don't like it, you don't ever have to ride it again.'"

They finished the eighty-seven-mile ride, returned to Bountiful, and Ardeth made the boy nextdoor an unbelievable offer on a slightly used motorcycle.

Ardeth was at what she described as an interesting time in her life. In addition to spending more time with Heber, she often wished that she could just take care of her home, have a garden, spend more time with Sharon and Shelly and Kent, and write and study. In her heart, she didn't want to do any more than what she had all ready done. But since the blessings of children had been withheld, she wondered about the purpose of her life. She often pondered her patriarchal blessing's promise that she would know the Lord's will concerning her and questioned if there was more she should be doing to fulfill the "wise purpose" it mentioned. She said, "I often feel that maybe that part of my blessing has been fulfilled and I've reached as far as I can, but more often I feel there are others yet to be reached and touched."

As her mother's health continued to deteriorate, Ardeth began to experience an increase in her concern, love, and understanding toward her mother and her needs. She needed and

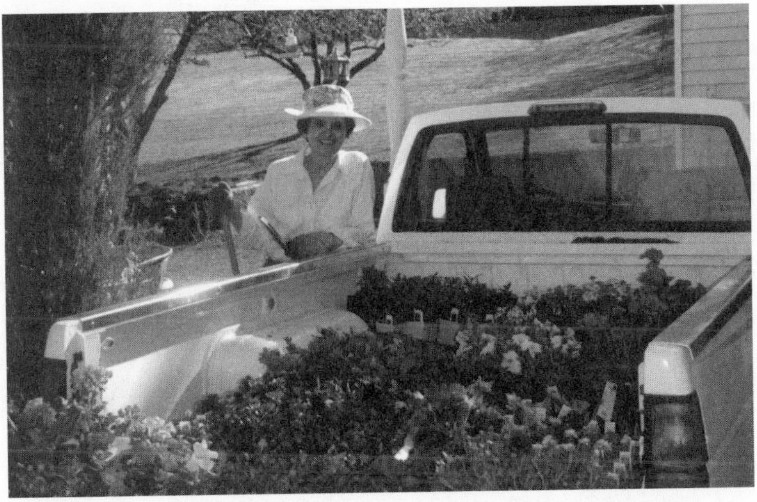

Gardening is an enjoyable luxury. Shown are Heber's truck, Ardeth's flowers.

wanted more time to spend with her. As often as she could, she sat by her bed holding her hand, quietly visiting or reading to her. In the summer of 1982, her mother entered a nursing home, where she could receive needed medical care. She told her children that she was ready to go and asked them to pray for her release. It was hard for Ardeth to see her mother in such distress. She wrote, "I went down to see Mom last night. I felt such tender concern and love for her. I wept as I tucked her in for the night. Today I'm fasting for her release."

After discussing her desires with Heber, she decided to leave her employment with BYU. She felt that her experience there had built her confidence, and she had learned much. Although she found she missed the associations at BYU and was still uncertain as to what lay ahead, she felt right about her decision. "I don't know the future, but I do feel that my prompting to leave BYU and 'come home' has opened a new door to a more important future—perhaps less public, yet more soul filling. . . . I feel as if we are at the close of an era . . . and are on the crest of a new growth cycle. . . . I believe it is a time, at least for me, of less public and more personal and deep-growth experiences."

MORONI'S PROMISE

In August 1982, Ardeth told her bishop, Dallas Bradford, that not only had she ended her employment at BYU, but she had also finished her general Church assignments and could work in the ward. Bishop Bradford told her that Elder M. Russell Ballard had asked him to challenge the youth of their ward to read the Book of Mormon. He asked Ardeth to accept the responsibility to encourage every young person in the ward to read the entire book within the next seven months. While sitting by her mother's bedside, she pondered the bishop's assignment. With her mother's life drawing to a close, she thought about eternity and the importance of this life, and how quickly it passes. She wanted to help the youth of her ward gain testimonies of gospel truths for themselves.

She contemplated a plan that would help the young people get through the Book of Mormon. And just as important, how to get the Book of Mormon through the youth, so they could gain at least the beginning of a testimony of this sacred book. A plan began to formulate in her mind. Following the pattern of Moses in the Old Testament, at Ardeth's suggestion, Bishop Bradford called ten of the young people in the ward to serve as "captains of ten" to direct the program. They called it "The Moroni's Promise Project." Each captain was set apart and given responsibility for ten of his or her peers. Members of the group were to report their progress to the captain. The captains encouraged their team members with a weekly contact, reporting the team's progress back to the ward leaders.

In addition, by way of motivation, the youth and adult leaders decided on what they called "Celebration Stations." These were activities scheduled at intervals along the way to provide continuous encouragement to all of the participants. For example, when they finished reading Alma 32, about planting and nurturing the seed of God's word, they planted a tree on the grounds of their meeting house as a visual reminder.

The program was to be launched at a special meeting on Sunday evening, October 10.

"My Dear, Dear Mom"

On Saturday evening, October 9, the day before the Moroni's Promise Project was to begin, Ardeth was at her mother's bedside. Her condition was worsening. Ardeth and Sharon stayed with her until late in the evening. Early Sunday morning, Heber was at the stake center when he received word that there was a fire in their ward building. Heber hurried to that building. About the same time, Ardeth received a call from the nursing home asking her to "come quick." Just as she entered the doorway of the room, her mother took her last breath. "She was gone!" Ardeth later recorded. "Our prayers had been answered. Her suffering was over and she had gone home. My dear Mom. My dear, dear Mom." She called Sharon, who came immediately. Their dad had "gone home" in that same month four years earlier, and Ardeth and Sharon knew that their parents were having a reunion celebration.

The fire at the church had broken out in the furnace room and was contained before it had spread. However, with the heavy smell of smoke in the building, all meetings were cancelled except sacrament meeting, which was scheduled to be held at the stake center late in the afternoon. Feeling that her mother would not want them to delay their plans, Ardeth decided to go ahead with the program to launch "Moroni's Promise," which also would be held at the stake center.

Even though the captains of ten were not able to rehearse their presentation, "it was beyond my expectations," Ardeth said. She went home from the meeting emotionally and physically exhausted—but still spent the evening with Sharon, planning their mother's funeral.

A POWERFUL, BEAUTIFUL TESTIMONY

The funeral service was held on a beautiful fall day. It was "just as she would have liked it," Ardeth recorded. "In the late afternoon we all went back to the cemetery. We stood around the grave, but instead of singing 'Don't Fence Me In,' like we did at Dad's, we sang, 'In the Garden.'"

The next morning, the family gathered to divide their parents' earthly possessions. Ardeth read their will. About that experience, she wrote, "The first and most important part was Dad's statement that he was leaving for us his testimony, and then went on to bear it. . . . Trust Dad to have the foresight for such a moment." They sorted through their parents' belongings, each selecting items that held special memories for them.

After everyone left, Ardeth surveyed what was left. She knelt by the bed in her mom and dad's nearly empty apartment. She poured out her aching heart to her Heavenly Father. She was grateful for her parents' lives and had full confidence in their continuing relationship, but still her heart was heavy.

At that moment, the doorbell rang. It was someone delivering a small floral bouquet. A card read: "To Sister Kapp from 'The Captains of Ten.'" With tear-filled eyes, she remembered, "There is a future. There are youth and testimonies yet to be strengthened and shared. And with a testimony burning within, there is never emptiness and loneliness." Peace filled her heart. Her life had an essential and urgent purpose: to help each youth in her ward so that of all they would one day share with their families, they would give them the most valuable thing: their testimonies.

At the end of the Moroni's Promise program, 104 of the 120 people (both youth and adults) who began the project finished the entire Book of Mormon on schedule. The remaining participants were determined to read on to completion.

The success of Moroni's Promise caught the attention of members in surrounding wards and stakes, and many used the program to motivate their youth to read the Book of Mormon. Eventually, the *New Era* wrote a story about this plan that Ardeth had initiated in the midst of a personally challenging time in her life.

A TURNING POINT

After her mother's death, Ardeth had a sense of time running out. She and Heber were now the next generation. Friends their own age had passed away. She thought about the time when they would retire. They were moving closer to financial independence and wouldn't have to work unless they wanted to. They both agreed, however, that they would always want to.

One day on a return trip from Hawaii, she met Charles Hobbs in the airport and chatted with him for a few moments.

She had earlier worked with him on a Church assignment. He had established his own company, Insight on Time Management. He noted that more and more women were assuming leadership positions in the big corporations where he was presenting his seminars. He needed a woman on his instructional team, and felt Ardeth would be the perfect fit. He invited her to come to one of his two-day seminars, just a few days away. She agreed to go.

What she learned at that seminar was exciting to her and she wrote, "I consider this week a major turning point in my life. Maybe not turning in the sense of changing direction, but rather a giant step upward to the next rung on the ladder." She was intensely excited about the time management principles that were presented in the seminar. "I learned tools for organizing my time—my life. The insights I got could only have come with the help of the Spirit. The eternal consequences of these tools is electrifying. . . . I thought of Michelangelo. When he caught the vision, his hands couldn't keep up with his mind. The vision released such power."

Ardeth felt confident that she should join the company. "I feel a spiritual prompting," she wrote. "I intend to follow as far as the light takes me."

A few days later she said, "The more I learn, the more my spirit not whispers, but rather shouts, 'This is something you need to be involved with.' I have a wonderful burning, enthusiastic feeling. The company is founded on true principles, and teaches truth to change lives." After a period of intense preparation and one trial run, she was ready to begin presenting seminars.

Not long after joining the company, Ardeth presented a seminar in San Jose, California. After lunch on the second day, she commented to one of her associates that during the next session they needed to cover something exciting in order to hold everyone's attention. At that very moment, the huge overhead chandelier began to sway. She wondered if she was dizzy or going to faint. The local people attending the seminar immediately headed for the door, and she followed.

Outside in the courtyard there was a buzz of discussion regarding the minor earthquake they had just experienced. On the evaluation forms turned in at the end of the seminar, one client observed that the "timing" for the earthquake fit the presentation perfectly. Although Ardeth had once attempted to use a boa constrictor in her television classroom, she had never even thought of an earthquake!

Although Ardeth didn't know it at the time, the things she learned and taught in the seminars provided a tremendous preparation for what was just around the corner.

CHAPTER SIXTEEN

New Beginnings

"What I Knew I Knew"

When Ardeth was released as a counselor in the Young Women general presidency in July of 1978, she cleared the remaining items from her office, closed the door behind her and walked away, not looking back. As she did so, however, she had the distinct impression that at some future time she would return. Never expressing those feelings to anyone, not even recording them in the privacy of her journal, she endeavored to put the thoughts out of her consciousness. Following her release, other events and activities crowded in, and with time she succeeded, at least in part, to relegating her feelings to the further reaches of her mind.

As the years passed, people often made comments to her, saying, "One day, you will be the president." Certainly she was not seeking the calling, but she was unable to dismiss the recurring impressions that came to her mind. She was puzzled not only by those comments, but by her own feelings. She considered her thoughts to be inappropriate and presumptuous.

A month prior to the April 1984 general conference, she once again had an undeniable impression that a major calling loomed on the horizon. When no call had come by the first of April, she became embarrassed and repentant that she had allowed such thoughts to invade the tranquility of her mind. But still, she jumped at every ring of the telephone. On Thursday, two days before the conference was to begin, she received a telephone call. The voice at the other end of the line announced, "This is President Hinckley's office." The message came almost as a relief. She recorded, "I could not deny what I knew I knew." She was invited to be in President Hinckley's office, with her husband, at 10:30 the following morning.

She told Heber about the call and briefly shared her thoughts and impressions with him. At the appointed hour, they entered the office of President Gordon B. Hinckley, second counselor to President Spencer W. Kimball. "He was warm, gracious, and to the point. Without delay he asked me if I would serve as the president of the Young Women. The puzzle came together in my mind. He asked Heber about his feelings and of course, he was supportive all the way and expressed confidence in me and total support."

Young Women General President

The next morning, Saturday, April 7, 1984, Ardeth and Heber entered the Tabernacle just prior to the beginning of the first conference session. They were seated on the front row. She later recalled, "It was an historic conference. Two new apostles were named: Dallin Oaks, my old high school friend, and

Dr. Russell Nelson. Everything about the conference was so spiritual and powerful." When her name was read, she walked across the front of the Tabernacle to take her place with the other general auxiliary leaders. "It was a long walk." Following the session many people gathered to express their confidence and support. Ardeth said, "Oh, the loyalty of the Saints of the Church. A call is made, a title is given, and the members respond in love and loyalty."

During that same session, Barbara Winder was sustained as the general president of the Relief Society and was called upon to speak. Although not given prior notice that she was to address the conference, Ardeth wanted to be ready just in case. Between sessions, she and Heber discussed remarks that might be appropriate. After she put together a few brief notes, they returned to the Tabernacle. When she was called upon to speak in the afternoon session, she was grateful for her preparation.

In her remarks Ardeth reflected on the heritage she had received from her early ancestors and promised that she would keep faith with them. She said, "As leaders of young women, our prayer is to so live that His divine intervention will be felt in our words, our deeds, and in our receptivity to Priesthood power and direction. The forces of evil are real, the subtleties of deceit would strive to divert us from the promises and blessings of the gospel of Jesus Christ. To the young women of the Church in every corner of the world I say, 'we love you, we need you, we believe in you.' I commend the great and noble leaders of youth of the past for the foundation that is in place. With the unified efforts of mothers, fathers, and leaders, we will prepare a generation that will be worthy of His commendation, that He may have a house of worthy members when He returns." She then pledged her heart, mind, and soul to her new calling (*Ensign*, May 1984, 77).

Shortly after her calling she requested a priesthood blessing from her husband, then serving as the stake president. He, along with his counselor, Scott Parker, laid his hands on her head and gave her a blessing that included a promise of "optimism, confidence, courage, with sweetness of spirit, with health and strength physically and spiritually, and with a gift of love for every human being, and especially so for the sisters." Heber also told her he felt impressed that many others on the other side were called to assist her and to be her mentors in this assignment.

One week later she wrote, "This is a glorious experience. It almost seems as though the thickness of the veil is lessened. My prayers are more intense, my desire to do right is stronger, and my faith in spiritual direction is unquestioned. . . . I have literally felt the sustaining power of the multitudes of letters saying they are remembering me in their prayers."

To Gain a Vision

A month went by before her counselors were called. In the meantime, as she listened to the Spirit, impressions and ideas continued to flood her mind, which she recorded as they came. "It is as though my mind has been opened, and ideas never before thought of are coming to me. . . . It almost feels like there is a path of light through the dark, and I just need to take the first steps. As I strive to be in tune, I know I'll know the way. I don't feel uncertain or even overwhelmed. I feel a quiet peace and a sense of excitement. [I] . . . yearn to be a pure vessel through which the will of the Lord will be manifest."

Young Women general presidency, 1984. Left to right: Maureen Turley (second counselor), Ardeth (president), Patricia Holland (first counselor).

A few days before she was set apart she wrote, "I have felt a great sense of peace and optimism and anticipation. I feel happy in my heart. . . . I have been feeling close to Mom lately—reminded almost daily of things about myself that remind me of her." She also found herself pondering the question, "Dad, do you know what I'm doing?" As she thought about it, "Into my mind came his voice in answer to my pondering. 'My dear, you have your privacy, but I know all of the important things.'" Years later she added, "I continue to feel that assurance on many occasions."

On May 11, Ardeth and the counselors she had chosen, Patricia Holland and Maureen Turley, were set apart as the Young Women general presidency. President Hinckley blessed her with "the authority, power, and blessing to do the work concerning the hundreds and thousands of young women who have gifts and abilities that need to be mobilized to move forward in the kingdom." He also gave the *vision* for which she had prayed. He said, "This is a time when we will see the young women of the Church awaken and rise up like a sleeping giant and begin to move across the face of the earth in a mighty force for righteousness."

As Ardeth pondered the great responsibilities inherent with her call, she was aware of her lack of skills and abilities in certain areas. However, she also knew that the Lord would provide others to assist who had the abilities she lacked. Those abilities were found in her counselors and in the dozen women who were called to the Young Women board. They were bright and capable, with abundant skills to contribute to the new organization.

Sister Holland had the wisdom and spiritual insight to be a very inspired and inspiring counselor. Sister Turley had served as a seminary teacher for a number of years and had a very special relationship with youth. She loved them and loved to teach the doctrine with clarity and conviction. In addition to her two counselors, Ardeth requested Carolyn Rasmus, former assistant to BYU presidents Dallin Oaks and Jeffrey Holland, as the administrative assistant. She had complete confidence in Carolyn's organizational skills and would rely heavily on her abilities for the entire length of Ardeth's term of service. While at BYU, Ardeth, in her role as chairman of the Advisory Committee on Women's Concerns, had reported to Carolyn. Carolyn had a dream a few weeks earlier that she would be given this assignment, even before Ardeth spoke with her about it. Totally committed to the work, she played a major role in the work of Young Women, also serving as a member of the general board.

Board and Staff Members

Original board members included Jeannene Barham, Irene Ericksen, Kathleen Lubeck, Maren Mouritsen, Carolyn Rasmus,

Ann Seamons, and Shirley VanWagenen. Additional members called later were Syd Aldous, Joan Clissold, Sandy Eberhard, Camille Fronk, Janet Gough, Marie Hafen, Kathy Luke, and Cheryl Wilcox. There were also capable, dedicated staff members who attended to the many details of the work being done. Geri Mills, Ardeth's faithful secretary, transcribed hundreds of letters that Ardeth dictated, in addition to her many other responsibilities.

Ardeth wasn't afraid to let the board know that she both needed and wanted their help. She expressed her confidence that each one was needed as part of the team and that she valued their contributions. Although previously unacquainted with most of them, she was quick to build a relationship of trust with each one. In that trusting environment, each person felt safe in expressing her opinion even if it differed from that of others. After sometimes lengthy exchanges of ideas, Ardeth had the information she needed to make the necessary decisions, which the board members then supported. This was a pattern that continued throughout her administration.

EXPANDING THE PROGRAM

At the time of Ardeth's call, the world was increasingly discarding time-honored standards of behavior. The sacred role of women was constantly challenged. Long-held rules of integrity, decency, and morality all seemed to be in a downward spiral. The young women of the Church faced an increasingly noisy challenge to exchange their values for the constantly changing fads of modern society. Ardeth and her associates knew that the choices made by young women during their formative years would have great impact upon their future. Declining statistics in Church activity among young women suggested the need for a change. It was in this context that Ardeth and her associates began their work.

They set up what they referred to as the strategic planning room. White butcher paper lined the walls. Here the presidency and board members brainstormed ideas and created blueprints as they began to put together a plan. Some ideas remained, while others were eliminated. As they studied the elements that were written on the sheets of paper, their ideas began to come together. They created a master document they called the five-year plan. They felt they needed to put in place a plan that would be as relevant in ten years as it was then and one that would fit young women all over the world. As they planned, they constantly asked themselves the questions, "Is it universal? Is it timeless? Does it fit the structure of the mission of the Church? Does it address the needs of young women? Is it developmental in the sense of taking them from baptism to exaltation?"

The presidency and board agreed that the first thing they should decide was what they wanted to have happen. When their preparation was complete and the program implemented, what should be the outcome? And more important, what did Heavenly Father want to have happen in the lives of the young women? They also analyzed data to determine where the young women of the Church were in relation to where they needed to be, and they studied the framework already in place, looking for ways to build upon it. They knew that the focus for the plan they were creating must be tied to the ordinances and covenants of the gospel of Jesus Christ.

Over time, the focus for Young Women as it is known in the

Church today began to take shape. As a result of the conflicting messages of the world, the young women needed, first, a clear sense of their true *identity.* It was essential that they know who they are. Second, they should have a sense of *direction,* or what it is they are to do. Once those two questions were answered, it was necessary to answer a third question: *Why* they were here on earth.

The answer to a young women's true identity became the first part of the Young Women theme. *We are daughters of our Heavenly Father who loves us, and we love him.* To the question of direction, the theme continues with reference to the baptismal covenant: *We will stand as witnesses of God at all times and in all things and in all places as we strive to live the Young Women Values.*

The answer to the third question, *why,* comes in the last part of the theme. It clarifies the ultimate objective, which is to prepare each young woman to *"make and keep sacred covenants, receive the ordinances of the temple, and enjoy the blessings of exaltation."* It is in the temple that one's true *identity* is clarified, the *direction for life* is presented, and the *purpose* for life is made clear. Learning the answers to life's questions—*Who am I? What am I to do? Why am I to do it?*—gives meaning, direction, and purpose to life. These three areas of emphasis relate to the three aspects of the mission of the Church: to proclaim the gospel (stand as a witness), to perfect the Saints (live the Young Women values), and to redeem the dead (receive the ordinances of the temple.)

It was important for the young women of the Church to have clearly defined values. A value is different from a goal in that values never change, whereas goals can change with time. Values, like a road map, give direction and provide a basis on which to make important decisions. Individuals may have many values, but the new Young Women's program included seven. The seven values were ordered so that each built upon the next. The selected values were:

1. *Faith.* Faith in Jesus Christ is the first principle of the gospel, the foundation of all that follows (D&C 14:8).

2. *Divine Nature.* This refers to divine qualities that we have all inherited (2 Peter 1:4–7).

3. *Individual Worth.* This value is very personal, referring to one's infinite worth and divine mission (D&C 18:10).

4. *Knowledge.* Gaining knowledge has a divine purpose, helping us to become like God in understanding and guiding our steps in obedience (D&C 88:118).

5. *Choice and Accountability.* After gaining knowledge, one is in a position to make choices and is free to choose and to accept responsibility for her choices (Joshua 24:15).

6. *Good Works.* This value is based on righteous service and a desire to reach out to others (3 Nephi 12:16).

7. *Integrity.* This value serves to activate all of the previous ones, as young women exercise the moral courage to make their actions consistent with their knowledge of right and wrong (Job 27:5).

The Young Women theme is recited each Sunday in every Young Women meeting in the world:

"We are daughters of our Heavenly Father, who loves us, and we love him. We will 'stand as witnesses of God at all times and in all things, and in all places' as we strive to live the Young Women Values, which are: Faith, Divine Nature, Individual Worth, Knowledge, Choice and Accountability, Good Works, and Integrity. We believe as we come to accept and act upon these values, we will be prepared to make and keep sacred covenants, receive the ordinances of the temple, and enjoy the blessings of exaltation."

The Young Women leaders felt a need to provide opportunities for young women to set goals and reach them in preparation for making and keeping sacred covenants. Self-mastery and confidence come through *personal progress.* Personal goals were to be set that would provide *experiences* with each of the values. This would help to build testimonies and contribute to the preparation for making and keeping covenants.

While the desired outcome for each young woman was the same, the focus for each age group was developmental, beginning with prayer, followed by scripture study, all in preparation for the blessings that come through the ordinances and covenants received only in the temple. Colors were identified for each value with thought given to what color would best serve as a reminder of that particular value. For example, the value *knowledge* is green, symbolic of something green and growing. Colored flags representing each value became a part of special occasions, serving as a reminder of these important ideas.

Ardeth asked Janice Kapp Perry to write a song to include all of the values in order, thus capturing in music the message for young women. Sister Perry's initial response was that writing a song to include all seven values, especially in order, would be impossible. However, following a day of fasting and temple attendance, the music came to her, with the words describing the values in the proper sequence. She told Ardeth, "The Lord must want this song." Ardeth said, "I know it is a work that was inspired." The song, "I Walk by Faith," was translated into many languages and became very popular in helping young women learn and better understand the values. The song includes each value in order and concludes with the desired goal of returning to God's presence.

When the *Personal Progress* book was designed, a tissue with the outline of the Salt Lake Temple became the first page, identifying the desired outcome for the Young Women experience. When the reader looked through the tissue, she saw a picture of the Savior. Without a single word, these first two pages provided the focus for the Young Women program: to have their lives centered in Jesus Christ, and to prepare to receive the sacred ordinances of the temple.

Artist Mac Magelby from the BYU art department was commissioned to design a logo for the Young Women. The final work, a stylized torch, was completed after numerous refinements. The symbol of the torch was timeless and universal. It represented light, the light of Christ. It was active, not passive, with the profile of a young woman's face seen on the side of the flame. The symbol of the flame was made into a poster and into a small piece of jewelry designed to be worn as a necklace by young women all over the world. It represented the Young Women motto, "Stand for Truth and Righteousness."

GAINING APPROVAL

While Ardeth felt the quiet peace that the work could and would be done, she nevertheless felt the tremendous weight of the responsibility. The Young Women presidency and general board labored month after month in developing the vision for Young Women into a workable program. Setbacks seemed to be part of the experience. But they felt driven and couldn't turn back.

Ardeth prayed fervently that their work would be acceptable. She also frequently fasted to add greater strength to her prayers. On one occasion, however, a member of the Quorum of the Twelve taught her a great lesson when he said, "Ardeth, quit fasting. The Lord has heard your prayers. Leave it with Him. When the time is right, it will happen."

During those long and tedious days of writing and rewriting proposals and wading through piles of paperwork, Ardeth and Carolyn often worked late into the night on a proposal document that was well prepared, brief, and to the point. She often said, "We are fearless in the face of righteousness, and the cause of young women is righteous." She taught that when a youth is at risk, we "don't give in, we don't give up, we don't give out. We give our all."

Finally, after nearly a year of planning and preparation, the Young Women's presidency were invited to make their first presentation to members of the Church Priesthood Executive Council. Before the meeting, they met and prayed that if their work was acceptable to the Lord, the ears of the Brethren would be opened. They also prayed that approval would not be given for anything that was not right. As Ardeth began the presentation she said boldly, "Brethren, if you want to know about Young Men, you can hear about them at the annual priesthood restoration commemoration. If you want to know about Young Men, you can attend their annual Scouting conference." Then she said, "But if you want to know about Young Women, the satellite screens are dark and the message vague."

She then reviewed statistics showing that the attendance of young women at Church meetings was declining. She spoke about the needs of young women, based on the research that had been done by the Church Research and Evaluation Committee. She explained that young women needed a clear sense of their true identity. They also needed additional recognition, which would help to motivate them and which would reinforce them in righteousness. They should also have a clear purpose and a sense of contributing to the mission of the Church. She then presented the program that she and her counselors and general board had worked on for so long. As she concluded the presentation she asked directly, "In what areas do you share our concerns about young women? Are our plans for meeting the needs acceptable? Do we have your approval to proceed with finalizing these recommendations?"

When she finished the presentation, President Ezra Taft Benson of the Quorum of the Twelve said, "Brethren, I think we should stand in acknowledgment that this is acceptable to the Lord." Then, just as they were preparing to leave, one of the Brethren said, "Sisters, today you have not only opened our ears, but also our hearts." It was a direct answer to their prayer.

Years later, in commenting on their work together, Elder Goaslind, who worked with Ardeth as general Young Men president, remembered, "Almost everything they took forward was approved. That program has been so successful and is still the program for young women in the Church today. I don't think I've ever known a woman with greater gifts and a greater ability to share her gifts than Ardeth Kapp."

Ardeth also had deep regard for Elder Goaslind, saying, "I

had a great respect for his clarity of vision and his confidence in what is needed to take place to move the work forward."

LEADERSHIP PRINCIPLES

During her tenure, Ardeth learned and applied a number of valuable leadership principles. On one occasion, approval for a major, Church-wide satellite broadcast for Young Women was given. The Young Women presidency and board moved forward with great enthusiasm. Their priesthood leader reviewed and approved all of the details. The date was set, though not yet announced to the Church membership.

Then, without warning or explanation, the priesthood leader told Ardeth that the satellite broadcast had been cancelled. Ardeth wrote of the experience, "That just hit me like a bolt. I thought, 'Cancelled? But we have approval.' Inside I wanted to say, 'But you told us we could.' But I didn't say that. I said, 'All right, we will await further counsel.' . . .

"I walked out of his office thinking, well, how do I explain this to the board? He didn't explain it to *me.* As I pondered in my heart, . . . the thought came to me, 'He didn't need to give you an explanation. He was acting out of his calling as an apostle.' I didn't know why except that an apostle had said so."

Ardeth called a special meeting with the board that afternoon, and as the meeting started, she felt a warm feeling and a sense of peace and trust and confidence. She announced that the meeting would begin with singing all the verses of "We Thank Thee, O God, for a Prophet," and then with a prayer. She explained that the broadcast had been cancelled and bore her testimony about what it means to follow priesthood leadership. Each board member responded, and not one negative comment was spoken. Ardeth taught them that an idea might be right, but the timing must be right, too. The satellite broadcast for Young Women was held later, and it was much more timely.

"I believe in who the Brethren are and I don't question the revelation they receive," Ardeth has said. "I also believe that [when] you have a stewardship and a responsibility, . . . you are a resource to the Brethren; you're not asking for something that you want. You're bringing information to them to help them guide and direct what they want for the young women of the Church and what you can help facilitate. Learning to work with the Brethren is to understand that there's only one organizational channel, and it is the priesthood channel.

"They wanted spiritually strong youth. We have the same agenda. My experience has been that in any setting with any of the Church leaders, that even if you have a difference of opinion, if your perception is based on a principle you can identify, then you are listened to and your contribution is considered. We need to understand their vision and the process that is established for us to work through the authorized system of the Church."

Leaders were taught that the auxiliaries are a resource to the priesthood, and the priesthood line is the only organizational channel in the Church. Women leaders should be prepared to make recommendations to their priesthood leaders, Ardeth taught, to give input, and to support priesthood decisions. Ardeth followed these principles in her own stewardship.

Another oft-repeated principle was that "we need to plan with a purpose." Local leaders were encouraged to begin their planning by asking, "What do we want to have happen?" and

Ardeth greets Sister Camilla Kimball at a Young Women celebration

then implementing that purpose, rather than simply asking "What do we want to do?"

The process of conversion, retention, and reactivation—dubbed the "ABCs"—taught them another leadership principle. Church research showed them the keys to conversion and retention were (1) a leader's spiritual preparation, (2) the convert's involvement in meaningful experiences, and (3) leaders developing caring relationships with the convert. A final principle, tying the ABCs together, involved the leader sharing and relating experiences to the gospel.

CALLED HOME

In February 1985, Ardeth was asked to interview Sister Camilla Kimball, wife of President Spencer W. Kimball. The interview was to be produced for distribution on video. Although the Kimballs were living in the Hotel Utah at the time, their daughter, Olive Beth Mack, brought Sister Kimball to the Kimball family home for the interview. Entering the modest dwelling, Ardeth was struck with the fact that it had been the setting for the work of a prophet. The spirit of the home was sweet, humble, beautiful, and inspiring. Ardeth and Sister Kimball sat in chairs facing each other in front of the camera for their three-hour interview. Sister Kimball was open and expressive in her responses to Ardeth's questions. Ardeth recorded, "She laughed and cried and expressed highs and lows, intimacies and public settings, along with her philosophy of life. She is truly a magnificent woman, with deep spiritual roots and a freshness for living that makes you want to stand on tiptoe."

At the time of President Kimball's passing a few months later, Ardeth recalled that interview, gratefully remembering those treasured moments with Sister Kimball, as well as other opportunities she had had to be with President and Sister Kimball. As she remembered, she wrote, "I am sitting at my desk in the Relief Society Building, in the northwest corner. Just outside my window is the tall flagpole, and the flag is hanging at half-mast, blowing in the breeze at eye level. . . . Last night at 10:08 P.M. President Spencer W. Kimball passed away, his mortal life concluded. His great leadership is almost beyond expression."

Almost two years later, after speaking at funeral services for Sister Kimball, Ardeth recorded, "I admired this great and noble woman so very much. She was truly a great example and teacher, and a great inspiration to me personally."

"You Did Look a Far Distance"

On April 18, 1985, a year after she became general president of the Young Women, Ardeth became the first woman to give the baccalaureate address in commencement exercises at Ricks College in Rexburg, Idaho. On that occasion, Heber expressed his thoughts to her in a letter. "As you think of your work today—delivering the commencement talk, and then off for the airport and South America—you'd have to admit that looking out the kitchen window, down the gravel road, you did look a far distance. . . . Your journey has been awesome! . . . How very, very good you should feel about all you've grown to! . . .

"With all the plantings, nurturings, and shapings which you do, could you have ever thought your farm rearing could have had so fruitful a future!"

LAUNCHING THE PROGRAM

On the truly historic evening of November 10, 1985, the Young Women's satellite broadcast drew to a close. The meeting had been electrifying. Those in attendance knew they had witnessed Church history in the making. Three hundred young women dressed in white, carrying flags in the colors of the Young Women Values, marched down the aisles of the historic Tabernacle. Seven young women, each representing a different nationality, came out in native costume and recited one of the values. Then a group of young women stood in the audience, as though spontaneously, and recited each value in the form of a choral reading. As they did their recitation, a huge banner, in the color appropriate to the value, dropped down, showing the value in large lettering, in different languages. It was truly "an historic day."

At the conclusion of the broadcast, each young woman in attendance was presented with a "Young Women Special Edition" of the *New Era,* in which the new Young Women

Values were discussed. This special issue of the magazine was also sent to young women throughout the Church. Young women throughout the world, along with their leaders, began to catch the vision for young women.

The challenge had been issued and the call had gone forth. "Who will stand for truth and righteousness? Who will stand up and lead out in defense of the gospel of Jesus Christ and stand as a witness for Christ at all times and in all places?" And from every corner of the world, the answer would come. "Here am I. Send me." Letters and telephone calls from all over the Church indicated that it was one of the most effective and influential satellite broadcasts ever.

Although the focus for young women had officially been launched, much else would yet be developed. There would be a new *Personal Progress* book for young women. In time there would also be a *Young Women Leadership Handbook* and a Young Women leadership video. And later, a booklet, *For the Strength of Youth,* was written and distributed to both young men and young women throughout the Church.

The years that followed would prove the effectiveness of the Young Women program that was launched at that first satellite broadcast. One letter Ardeth received years later, following her release, suggested that for one young woman, the program had a truly life-changing effect.

"Dear Sister Kapp, Yesterday in general conference it was announced that you were released as general Young Women's president. . . . You were called as president at the time I became a Beehive. Now I am a student at BYU. . . . I will never forget the Young Women's broadcast when the values were introduced and the girls in white marched with their flags. I remember you speaking of a growing wave of righteousness that would cover the earth. That broadcast changed my life. The spirit I felt that night planted in me a fire to live virtuously and righteously and to spread the gospel to those around me. . . . I don't know how I would be able to live independently, as I do now in this world and environment, if I hadn't had the training and the lessons of the Young Women's organization and the values behind me" (Nettie Hunsaker, Provo, Utah, April 5, 1992).

That letter is typical of hundreds of letters received in the Young Women office.

As the Young Women's program was implemented throughout the Church, its effects were noticed by the General Authorities as they met with members around the world. Elder Joseph B. Wirthlin of the Quorum of the Twelve said, "What we have for Young Women is changing their lives. I've heard down at the MTC [Missionary Training Center] that the young women who are going on missions seem to have more of a sense of commitment and interest, and more young women are going on missions. I wonder if their saying every week, 'We'll stand as a witness for Christ' is planting those seeds in their hearts."

It was not only the young women who benefited from the values, as the following letter Ardeth received from a bishop in England testifies:

"Some time ago, I sat in counsel into the early hours of the morning with a grandmother who wanted to die. Her family has endured trial after trial with faith and good heart, but finally, she just felt worn out and unable to cope. After several hours, she became convinced that I was as stubborn as she was and accepted a priesthood blessing. She was uplifted by the Lord's counsel to her.

"A few days later, as I prayed about my ward members, my thoughts were directed to the then new Young Women's handbook. I had been particularly impressed with the Young Women values. I wrote a letter to that sister and copied the Values and associated scripture references for her. I posted the letter and forgot about it.

"The sister in question had not borne her testimony in fast and testimony meeting for many years, but suddenly she was the first to her feet! She told of the inspiring letter she had received, of how she had looked up each reference and how it had changed her life. How indeed! This former agoraphobia sufferer was crossing main roads alone, riding on buses, going shopping, climbing stairs, visiting the hairdresser alone—all things that days before were considered impossible for her.

"She pondered the letter daily, tagged on to her scripture study. To her, it was scripture. Her whole life and her outlook on it has changed. That family *still* has trial after trial to contend with, but she faces those challenges with strength and resolution. . . .

"I . . . felt that perhaps you may enjoy hearing of a senior 'young woman' who has benefited from such an inspired set of values" (Bishop Terry of Newport Qwent Ward, January 6, 1990).

CHAPTER SEVENTEEN

Increasing the Pace

From the Spirit

Prior to Ardeth's first general conference as the Young Women general president, the Young Women presidency and board prepared for the Young Women open house. Open houses were traditionally held the two days prior to the beginning of conference for ward and stake leaders, many from outside of Utah and some from out of the country.

As the first workshop drew near, Ardeth found that unexpected responsibilities to assist in the physical arrangements had crowded in, and despite her best intentions to prepare a message, time had run out. She said, "I went into the room filled with leaders and without notes, spoke to them from the heart. Come to find out, it was not from the heart at all, but rather from the Spirit. One of the brethren came up after and wanted a copy of [my remarks]. I actually did not remember what I had said. He came into the office and reviewed his notes with me. . . . I used the outline from his notes for the other two sessions."

She later recorded, "If there is one thing that I have become more consciously aware of, it is the gentle whisperings and guidance that accompany this assignment. So gentle and so soft that without careful attention, much could go unnoticed, and it makes me ponder how much more I would know and understand if I were better prepared to listen and hear."

Coming Together

Shortly after Ardeth's call, the Brethren determined that the auxiliary presidencies over the Relief Society, Young Women, and Primary should work more closely together, particularly in areas of common interests and concerns. Shortly after the reorganization of the Relief Society and Young Woman general presidencies, the leaders of the three auxiliaries met together. They shared a wonderful feeling of love and unity. They discussed historically significant changes that would be a break with tradition. President Hinckley had suggested the possibility of all three women's organizations being housed together in the Relief Society building. Previously, the women's auxiliaries were housed in separate locations and reported to different priesthood leaders.

On May 30, 1984, Relief Society President Barbara Winder and her counselors, Primary President Dwan Young and her counselors, and Ardeth Kapp and her counselors met together to talk about staffing, organizational structure, and where they should be housed within the Relief Society Building. Ardeth recorded: "A most historic day!!! I believe the heavens are rejoicing. The women leaders of the past must have been privileged to witness the events of yesterday and today."

Ardeth conducted the meeting and read a message on unity,

Left to right: Dwan Young, Primary general president; Ardeth, Young Women general president; Barbara Winder, Relief Society general president, 1985

including two key statements from President George Q. Cannon:

"Suppose that one man has more wisdom than another; it is better to carry out a plan that is not so wise, if you are united on it. Speaking generally, a plan or a policy that may be inferior in some respects is more effective if men are united upon it than a better plan would be upon which they were divided" (George Q. Cannon, *Gospel Truth* [Salt Lake City: Deseret Book, 1987], 163).

"Whenever there is opposition in views concerning points of doctrine or concerning counsel, it may be set down as indisputable that the Spirit of God is not in our midst and that there is something wrong" (*Gospel Truth,* 159).

When the three women's auxiliary presidencies began to work more closely together, they identified four values that they would be committed to—unity, maintaining their identity, establishing better continuity so that they wouldn't lose anyone

Carolyn Rasmus and Ardeth present the readers theater,
Save Me a Place at Forest Lawn.

between the cracks, and equity—meaning that they would share whatever resources they had. "Those became guiding principles in our administrative relationship," Ardeth said.

Along with hard work came an easy laugh and a sense of humor. One Halloween Carolyn Rasmus and Ardeth dressed up as old ladies for a meeting with the general presidents of the Relief Society and Primary. But when the other leaders saw them, Carolyn recalled, they "promptly left the room and decided to call security, not knowing who these strange old crones were." Carolyn and Ardeth had so much fun with it that they continued the tradition of dressing up, and eventually included a readers theater performance of *Save Me a Place at Forest Lawn.*

The permanent move into the Relief Society building took place in April 1988. Sister Winder in particular was essential to making the new arrangement work, Ardeth recalls. "She was supportive in every detail—willing to break with tradition and provide a home for all three organizations in the Relief Society building."

AT THE REQUEST OF THE FIRST PRESIDENCY

In January of 1986, the First Presidency asked Ardeth to go to New York to represent the Church before the U.S. Attorney General's Meese Commission in their final hearing on pornography. She was asked to make a fifteen-minute presentation, which would be included in the final report of the commission. She was surprised that a woman was asked to go and humbled that she was the one selected. She recorded, "It seems incredible. I'll go with faith and confidence that the Lord will provide the way after I've done all I can."

With only one week's notice, Ardeth and Carolyn worked almost around the clock for two days preparing for the presentation. As Ardeth studied, she became even more convinced of the importance of basing one's decisions on values. She decided to focus her remarks on the values needed to keep the moral fiber of America strong.

The commission consisted of twelve people who had been selected by the Attorney General. Ardeth walked into the room at the appointed hour, then waited her turn as those before her spoke passionately against the regulation of pornography, claiming it was a violation of the First Amendment.

When it was her turn, she felt nervous but secure in the message she was to present. She began by saying, "I am a Canadian by birth. More than three decades ago in a solemn ceremony, . . . I raised my hand to the square and took an oath of allegiance which I repeat in part, 'I hereby declare an oath . . . that I will support and defend the Constitution and the laws of the United States of America against all enemies, foreign and domestic.' . . .

"As a citizen of the United States it is with alarm and a great sense of responsibility that I see an enemy invading our great country. I refer . . . to a psychological warfare against the mind of man. I refer to the enemy of pornography, obscenity and indecency."

Throughout the speech, she reinforced the need for society to preserve a climate in which moral values can be taught and cultivated. She focused on the values needed to keep the moral fiber of America strong. "We believe human values are of vital importance. We do not look to government to establish these values, only to preserve a climate in which values may be freely selected and cultivated. . . . This commission has an opportunity to help restore a climate where values can have a chance to survive and thrive." She ended her presentation by saying that "values are not inherited. Values cultivated and nourished for centuries can be lost in one generation. We must earn them anew."

Shortly after returning home, she received a call from President Benson. He said, "Sister Kapp, I'm calling about your assignment to New York. I have read the news releases and heard from our New York people, and I want to commend you on all you said."

Some time after this presentation, Ardeth was asked to represent the Church and serve on the National Coalition Against Pornography. One of the coalition's leaders also asked her to serve on one of its subcommittees, the Women's Task Committee.

COUNSELORS

During the April 1986 general conference, Ezra Taft Benson was sustained as President of the Church. In that same session, Patricia Holland was released as a counselor to Ardeth. With her husband's increasing responsibilities as president of Brigham Young University, she was needed there. Ardeth had known when Pat was called that her service might not be for an extended time. Their acquaintance began years earlier when they lived in the same stake in Bountiful. Prior to his becoming president of BYU, Elder Holland served on the stake high council when Heber was the stake president, and Ardeth and Pat had worked together in the Relief Society. Their mutual love and appreciation had increased during their two-year service together in the Young Women presidency.

Ardeth and Pat Holland were already close friends before they discovered they were related through the Leavitt line.

Ardeth said, "Pat has been a most loyal, noble, and inspirational counselor. Her counsel has been wise, pure, and in tune in all things. She is a pure vessel with her eye single to the glory of God. There seems to be no darkness in her, but a vessel of love and spirituality. I will miss her deeply."

In reflecting on their association together, Patricia Holland said, "The first time I saw Ardeth was at a June conference when she was a counselor to Ruth Funk. She was wearing a bright yellow outfit, and the minute I saw her I felt a divine connection, almost like we had known each other before in a deeply profound way. It was a deeply spiritual moment for me to see her in person." Pat added, "She is an absolutely guileless woman. She has a perfect love for everyone she comes in contact with, always seeing their positive side. She has a god-like love which enables her to see people in their perfect, pre-existent spiritual form. She tries very hard to help people to see that within themselves."

Maurine Turley was released as second counselor and sustained as the first counselor, and Jayne Malan was called as second counselor. Jayne had previously been involved with writing and preparing video programs. She brought valuable skills and experience to her calling.

Jayne felt it an honor to serve as a counselor to Ardeth. She said, "Any of us who have been privileged to work under the inspirational leadership of Ardeth Kapp will no doubt remember her delightful sense of humor, her quick mind, and gift of words. . . . In addition, she was blessed with an unusual power of discernment when it came to anything related to the Young Women program."

During Ardeth's administration, there were two more

"This Is an Historic Day": (left to right) Jayne Malan (first counselor); Ardeth (president); Elaine Jack (second counselor); Carolyn Rasmus (administrative assistant)

changes in counselors. In April 1987, Maurine Turley was released to accompany her husband while he served as mission president in the Little Rock Arkansas Mission. Elaine L. Jack was called as second counselor, and Jayne Malan was moved to first counselor.

Ardeth remembered that both she and Elaine Jack were reared in the same area in Alberta, Canada, Elaine in Cardston and Ardeth in Glenwood. Ardeth said, "To us in Glenwood, Cardston was always the big metropolis, and I had such great reverence for girls from Cardston and looked up to them." During the time of the one-hundred year anniversary of the establishment of the Church in Cardston, Elaine and Ardeth returned to ride in a parade celebrating the event. As they rode together, Ardeth said, "Oh, Elaine, I can't believe that I'm riding in this parade with a Cardston girl."

Elaine laughed and said, "Well, if it wasn't for a Glenwood girl, I probably wouldn't be riding in the parade at all."

Ardeth said, "We were taking such pride in our coming home as celebrities riding in a parade. As we turned the corner on Main Street, that southern Alberta wind came up and just blew the sign right off this lovely carriage that we were riding in. The announcer said, 'These two women must be important for something, but there's no sign on the carriage and we don't know who they are.' We laughed and thought that put us in our place. We thought we were coming home with such importance, and the announcer didn't even know who we were!"

Elaine was called as the general president of the Relief Society in April 1990. Following Elaine's release, Ardeth said, "Elaine always said that she came to work with me to learn how to do it, and I said that she actually came to tutor me and then went on to her own responsibilities. But whatever it was, we learned a lot together and enjoyed working together."

Elaine said, "Ardeth was the best tutor in the whole world. . . . Her skills as a leader are unparalleled, not only her organizational skills, but also the spiritual ones. Each presidency and board meeting was a spiritual feast."

When Sister Jack became the Relief Society president, Janette Hales was called as second counselor in the Young Women. Janette had served in the Utah legislature for a number of years, and she had tremendous respect from men and women in the community. Ardeth said, "Janette Hales is a woman who has incredible judgment, great wisdom, is totally secure within herself, and has a sense of tolerance for youth and a sense of interaction with leaders that's quite remarkable." Subsequent to

Elaine Jack, Relief Society general president, and Ardeth, Young Women general president, celebrate Canada Day (July 1) by singing "Oh Canada."

Ardeth's release, Janette Hales was called as Young Women general president.

In reflecting on their service together, Sister Hales said, "Working with Ardeth Kapp is like taking an advanced course in leadership. . . . Surely Ardeth Kapp will be numbered among the great leaders of the Church in this generation."

The one constant for Ardeth in the changes in the presidency was her administrative assistant, Carolyn Rasmus. Of her service Ardeth wrote, "Carolyn—trusty Carolyn, my special friend, unequaled in capability, support, and loyalty. When Nephi said, 'I will go and do . . . ' a major part of that promise is fulfilled [for me] through Carolyn."

Carolyn remembers, "We worked hard. I don't know that I have ever worked harder in my life. But there was also a sense that we were being moved beyond ourselves by a higher power. I think we knew that the Lord was with us. . . . It was one of the few times in my life when I have felt the spiritual outpouring and manifestation of the Lord's hand in daily kinds of work."

Ardeth was filled with deep gratitude for her counselors, the general board, and the Young Women staff. "These people are not only the people I work with but my best friends. . . . Actually, with the time demands that I have, they are about my only friends! Not seriously, but they do become an integral part of your life."

Reflecting in her journal, she wrote, "I imagine sometimes when praise is flowing and pride is strong, just how long would it last if I tried it alone. We each need the other; we're stronger that way. And so I pray each day for your piece of the whole. . . . Now publicly, we have a call as general board. . . . But in the privacy for just us to share, could our name be changed, would it be fair? Could we, for our own quiet sharing and caring, be from this day forward, not 'Young Women General Board,' but 'Young Women Servants of the Lord'?"

Teaching, Training, and Tributes

In early February 1986, Ardeth, along with some of the Young Women board, participated in leadership training in the Southeast Area of the Church, working with Elder Vaughn J. Featherstone, the area president. They next held training meetings in Atlanta, Nashville, and New Orleans. Ardeth later recalled that about 8,200 people received training, including priesthood leaders. "The spiritual outpouring was monumental, both for the saints and for those of us who took part," she wrote.

Many years later, Elder Featherstone recalled being in a meeting in 1975, when Ardeth was a counselor to Ruth Funk and he was a member of the Presiding Bishopric. "I had the

Young Women general presidency, 1990–92: Jane Maylan (left), Ardeth (center), Janette Hales Beckham (right)

strongest impression come to me. I knew that she would be the Young Women general president and I would be her counterpart."

He has strong memories regarding their service together. "I've never seen her when she was down. . . . She always thought, 'It will come. . . . If it is right, the Lord will bless us and it will come.'"

In further tribute to Ardeth, Elder Featherstone said, "I think her greatest strength is that she has a heart like unto God's own heart (see Acts 13:22). She feels deeply for people, and it doesn't matter what race, what nationality, what color they are. Her feelings are so true and genuine. Anyone who comes under any kind of contact with the aura that surrounds her, just have to be better people because she's so spiritual."

Ardeth notes the "thoughtfulness and consideration and kindness on the part of Elder Featherstone. He is a remarkable man."

Balloons were launched for the first worldwide Young Women celebration.

THE RISING GENERATION

October 11, 1986, marked the first Young Women worldwide celebration. Its purpose was to strengthen testimonies, reinforce the worldwide sisterhood of young women, and to send a message of hope and faith to the world.

In that first celebration, more than 300,000 young women in 128 nations launched helium-filled balloons with messages of testimony and hope attached, creating a rainbow of goodwill throughout the world. Young women included their addresses on their messages, in case the person who found the message wanted to respond.

Ardeth had recorded a message to be played in each location around the world where young women had gathered to launch their balloons:

"Good morning to each of you wonderful young women in all parts of the world. Welcome to this glorious celebration. As we gather today, in many nations all over the earth, we have come to celebrate and remember our commitment to stand for truth and righteousness.

"Almost a year ago, we communicated with most of you, by satellite broadcast, the vision and testimonies of apostles and prophets about the beginning of a glorious new day for young women. . . .

"As we stand together today, in the early hours of this morning, I want you to know that we are seeing the first light of that promised day. . . .

"As Latter-day Saint young women worldwide, we are to move forward and upward. All of this is *not* happening because our challenges are any easier. It is happening because of you. You have begun to answer the call, 'Who will stand for truth and righteousness?' You are beginning to answer, 'I will. Send me.'

"Dear young women, you are a generation known by your Heavenly Father. You are the rising generation and have been reserved and held back until this time. Now you are being called to come forward, to exert your influence, and to become a mighty force for righteousness. You will be able to do this not because you will find yourself suddenly free from temptation, but because you have the moral courage to do what you know to be right. Often, that means being visibly different from the world, and that does take courage. But there is nothing we can't do or accomplish with the help of the Lord and each other. . . .

"Now on this glorious morning, we here in Salt Lake City at the headquarters of the Church join ourselves with each of you in the bonds of sisterhood around the world. At this moment, we trust that your balloons are filled, tugging and anxious, and that we are all ready for that moment we have waited for.

"We pray that the winds and currents will transport your messages beyond your neighborhood and city and out into the world. May your testimonies and wishes of love and hope be an example for righteousness. May they be carried forward and soften hearts. May they bring encouragement to others who want to stand for truth and righteousness and who will follow. May your precious messages be found by those who are seeking truth and will be drawn to it.

"As your balloon rises above the rooftops and the tree tops, may *you* look heavenward as it is finally carried out of sight, and may you continue to look heavenward as you begin each new day.

"We love you. We pray for you and with you. We join our strength with yours this day to keep our premortal promises and 'Arise and inspire the inhabitants of the earth as a mighty force for righteousness.' I promise you that as we do this, we will be blessed."

At the same moment around the world, the young women launched their helium-filled balloons containing messages of hope, faith, and love to those who would find and read them. Carolyn Rasmus wrote, "I have been struck with the fact that, to my knowledge, this is the first time in the history of the Church that all members everywhere were participating in the same thing at the same time. . . . I cannot think of another way in which young women might experience or feel true sisterhood or feel connected to one another."

Some of the Brethren jokingly said, "We read in the Book of

Mormon about the sons of Helaman, but now we know about the daughters of Helium!"

Accounts came back of people who picked up the balloons and found and joined the Church. For instance, a man in France found one of the balloons; he and five of his children came in contact with the missionaries and later joined the Church. The stories were phenomenal.

Because of local circumstances, the young women in Cairo, Egypt, could not launch balloons. Instead, their leader had them write their messages and put them in bottles. They then took them out across the Sinai, swam out over the reef into the Red Sea, and let the messages go. Ardeth said, "Maybe that's the greatest thing to happen there since Moses parted the Red Sea!"

Letters came from members around the world, both before and after the celebration, expressing appreciation for the opportunity to participate in such a momentous event. Typical of many are the following: "Greetings from two small islands in the Indian Ocean, Mauritius and La Reunion. We are few and new, but growing fast in number. We are excited about being a part of this worldwide program. Mauritius has a branch of eighty-one members, with three baptisms as of today. We have a wonderful group of girls, all very new in the Church. There will be nineteen participating from here with messages in bottles into the Indian Ocean" (Letter received from Ruth Ashby, September 14, 1986).

Another, sent to Ardeth at Church headquarters, read: "Sister Kapp, my name is Maria del Consuelo Wong Moreno. I am a Laurel, 17 years old, and I have been a member since I was 11. I would like you to imagine how much I want someone to receive and understand my message and, that as it is read, someone will think about the urgency of everyone knowing the great love our Heavenly Father has for us. I hope that someday all those I know and love will feel the same way we feel. I trust in my Father forever and really desire that our hope may be eternal."

RING THE BELLS

A second worldwide celebration was held three years later, on November 18, 1989. A bell-ringing celebration, held just after dawn with young women all around the world, commemorated the 120th anniversary of the founding of Young Women. On that day more than a century earlier, President Brigham Young took from his shelf the family prayer bell. He rang it loud and clear, calling his daughters together for a special meeting, organizing them into what would later become the Young Women organization of the Church.

Ardeth and Carolyn in the Young Women office. "It Was an Historic Day."

On the day of commemoration in 1989, all across the Church, young women, Young Women leaders, and priesthood leaders gathered together. The priesthood leaders rang bells and called the young women to stand for truth and righteousness and to follow the words of the prophet. In a prerecorded message from Ardeth, distributed to every location, she said: "We have heard the bell ring loud and clear once again. Our great prophet-leader, President Ezra Taft Benson, has issued a call to young women . . . around the world. . . . In behalf of . . . the young women of the Church worldwide, I accept the call for renewed commitment to set aside the things of the world, to unite in strength and power, and to commit to stand for truth and righteousness."

REFLECTIONS ON THE PAST AND HIGH HOPES FOR THE FUTURE

As 1986 drew to a close, Ardeth was feeling introspective. "I walked this morning by the bridge and thought of Dad and Mom. I have felt very close to them lately. Sometimes, for no reason at all, I think of them, and the reality of our reunion one day is so real it brings tears to my eyes."

In early 1987 she received the news that final approval had been given for all of the elements of the Personal Progress program. Ardeth wrote, "I keep thinking my alarm is going to go off and I'll awaken to find it's only a dream." After listing the details of the approval, she wrote, "I came home, fell on my knees, and wept. You don't receive a witness until after the trial of your faith. There is such an opportunity for refining during the process. I am subdued and a more humble, pliable person than ever before."

Ardeth felt such love for the Young Women worldwide that they were, in a sense, her own extended family.

When Elder Goaslind heard that approval had been given, he wrote a letter to Ardeth. "You're a great credit to the Church, and I hope you know what a cherished, sacred experience it is for me to serve with you."

ASSIGNMENTS IN FAR-OFF LANDS

During her time as president, Ardeth traveled to distant parts of the world, teaching and training leaders and meeting with the young women of the Church in many nations. Her travels took her to more than fifty different countries in Europe, Asia, the islands of the Pacific, and North, Central, and South America. One such trip took place in January 1989. Ardeth and Carolyn Rasmus traveled through parts of Australia and New Zealand, teaching and training leaders and meeting in firesides or conferences with both leaders and young women. Elder Glen Rudd and his wife, Marva, traveled with them. Elder Rudd, a member of the Quorums of the Seventy, was then serving in the Pacific Area Presidency.

In speaking of their experiences, Elder Rudd recalled that Ardeth and Carolyn didn't have a lot of bags to carry, only one small suitcase each. He thought, "They're going to be with us for ten days and they can't possibly live out of just those two bags." He was surprised, however, that not only did they manage, but they managed well. He observed that they had obviously traveled before and knew how to do it.

Elder Rudd also noticed that they didn't ask for a lot of favors and were willing to "roll with the punches." He said, "They were willing to accept whatever we did or had planned for them. . . . These two sisters are the two best teachers that I've ever had any experience with."

After attending meetings in Sydney, Australia, the four flew to Auckland, New Zealand, for additional training and teaching.

As Elder Rudd had spent much time in New Zealand, both

Ardeth and a koala bear while on assignment in Australia

as a young missionary and at other times since, he knew the area well. Even though their schedule was tight, they were able to observe the beauties of the New Zealand countryside as they drove. On one occasion, Elder Rudd took them to a beautiful beach near the Tasman Sea. He was somewhat surprised when Ardeth and Carolyn jumped out of the car, kicked off their shoes, and ran out into the surf!

When they reached their destination that night, it was nearly midnight and they were hungry and tired. But they didn't want to eat a big meal and so decided to have a bowl of soup in the hotel dining room before retiring for the night. Not realizing that they had to pay for an entire meal just to get the soup, they were shocked at the bill—$22.00 each for the soup! Elder Rudd remarked that that was surely the highest-priced bowl of soup in the entire southern hemisphere. The story of the soup has become a joke between Ardeth and Carolyn and the Rudds since that time, and they occasionally exchange cans of tomato soup as a reminder of their experience.

CHAPTER EIGHTEEN

To Help Build the Kingdom

Visibly Touched

Although Ardeth has reached the hearts and minds of unknown thousands through her books and speeches, she is also quick to express her love and offer support to individuals.

Early in her administration, she attended a three-day camp that included young men as well as young women. Right away, one young man drew her attention. His manner of dress, including a tank top and headband, set him apart from the others. He was aloof, obviously there because of pressure from others, and seemed to resist any effort to be included with the other youth. Looking for a way to break down his self-imposed barrier, Ardeth tried to draw him into a conversation. Although he was slow to respond, she kept trying.

On an all-night hike, she noticed that he frequently went to the back of the line, carrying his flashlight and making sure that no one was falling behind. His concern for his peers was also evident when he shared his orange, the only food they were given for the hike. The next day, he was attentive to everyone's safety as they each took a turn at rappelling down a mountainside. Noticing all he did to help others made it easy for Ardeth to compliment him. By the last evening at camp, she had observed a change in the young man's countenance. During the camp testimony meeting he said, "I've never felt so hungry inside, or so full of the Spirit. I've never felt so dirty and yet so clean." After returning home, Ardeth wrote him a letter telling him how impressed she had been by his evident concern for the other campers and by his willingness to help them.

Over a year later, the young man's stake president called Ardeth to tell her that the young man had accepted a mission call and asked if he could bring the young man in to see her before he entered the Missionary Training Center. Ardeth didn't recognize him as the same young man she had seen at camp. His mother, who was with him, said that he had kept her letter in his

Ardeth and Gerri Mills, her faithful secretary who transcribed hundreds of letters, in the Young Women office. The similar dress was not planned.

top dresser drawer, and read it often. She explained that he had been visibly touched by the contents, which had helped to greatly increase his testimony.

MINISTRY BY MAIL

Beginning in the early 1970s, Ardeth has kept up an enormous volume of correspondence with young women around the world. Elder Marvin J. Ashton referred to it as her "ministry by mail." During her time as president, many young women wrote seeking her advice and counsel or confessing their weaknesses and asking for help. Others wrote to thank her for a message they had received while hearing her speak, or to tell her how the Spirit that radiated from her had touched their lives. Still others appreciated learning how to lead in their callings, following her example. Some wrote asking her to write to a friend who was experiencing difficulties. Many requested a signed autograph. With the help of Geri Mills, her able secretary who typed the dictated letters, all were answered. The following excerpts are typical of thousands Ardeth received.

"I wanted to write and let you know, as a nonmember, how much I appreciated your talk. I did as you asked and got down on my knees and asked God if He knew I was here! The answer came so quick!! Someday soon I will make the decision to be baptized. I'm very happy I could hear you talk. Thank you again."

"Two years ago I heard you speak at a Young Women's standards night. I don't know why I was there because I 'hated' church. I sat in that meeting pretending half-boredom until something you said caught my attention. You said that if you could reach one girl, you would feel that you had done some

Heber encourages Ardeth just minutes before her first BYU devotional address, "Taking Upon Us His Name," June 1981

good. At that moment, I felt that you were speaking directly to me. I felt the Spirit then and felt remorse for all the rebellion I had displayed toward my Father in Heaven and my parents. I knew that even though I had caused so much hurt that my Heavenly Father loved me. He always had. I had to begin to prove myself worthy of that love. I don't remember what else was said that night, but I do know that the Spirit I felt could only have been there through someone who was in tune and who really cared. Thank you, Sister Kapp, for helping me feel that spirit. When I'm twenty-one, I'd like to go on a mission. Maybe I can help some young girl feel what I felt that night."

Some wrote telling Ardeth that they had succumbed to evil influences and given in to sin. Most were desperately looking for a way out, for hope, and for something to hold on to. To each she wrote a message of love, encouragement, faith, and hope.

After Young Women satellite broadcasts, Ardeth received letters from girls throughout the Church, expressing gratitude for her messages, often thanking her for getting their lives back on track. "I felt a need to write and express my thanks and love for all that you have done for me. When I first wrote you, I was in a bottomless pit. I could see my parents at the top, throwing me ropes, but the taunting voices of my 'friends' kept me from the light at the top of the pit. . . . I could feel Satan's grip holding me tighter and tighter. In the beginning, it was so subtle that I didn't even know it was there. I found myself making mistakes that not only would affect my earth life, but my eternal life as well. I needed help and I needed a friend. . . .

"One night I was in an especially bad mood. My mom wanted me to watch a tape of the Young Women broadcast. I didn't want to, but she said there was a really good talk she wanted me to hear. After a big argument, I agreed to watch just one speaker and that was it. You were the speaker my mom wanted me to listen to. You gave a beautiful talk about friends. Those words you spoke touched me. I knew that you were speaking to me. That night you literally saved my life. Your talk was a miracle to me. As I looked up from the pit I was in, I could see the light again. That was when I wrote you, and you threw me a rope. A rope that extended to me unconditional love and friendship.

"Sister Kapp, you turned my life around. I can never be able to fully express my thanks to you. As you said in one of your stories, this saved many lives. My turnaround insured safety to my children and grandchildren. I made a promise to my Father in Heaven that if He helped me and gave me strength to get through this that I would *never* go back to my wicked ways.

"My brother, Jesus Christ, paid for my sins. He hung on the cross for me so that I could repent of what I've done. Turning back now would be a slap in His face. I can't imagine the pain and suffering He went through, but I do know the pain that I went through. Even though I'm still going through pain and most of my friends have rejected me, I have found *eternal* comfort in the arms of my Father in Heaven."

The Ministry Continues

Over the years, this ministry has expanded to include not only young women, but men and women of all ages. Like ripples in a pond or seeds in an apple, her influence is far reaching, the effects of which cannot be measured. Those needing or seeking reassurance, comfort, counsel, encouragement, or guidance—all come under the umbrella of her concern and caring. To some recipients of her notes and letters, who may or may not be acquainted with her, they come as a surprise.

In her most recent book, published in the spring of 2005, Ardeth writes, "Notes of encouragement, even to strangers, can have a lasting impact on the sender as well as the receiver" (*Better Than You Think You Are* [Salt Lake City: Deseret Book, 2005], 15). In reviewing the book, Jerry Johnston, *Deseret News* writer said, "The comment sent me scuttling to my files. For many years Sister Kapp served on the paper's board of directors. I've kept about a dozen notes she sent me. Each is specific in detail, personal, and sincere. Each, I remember, served as a quiet gust of wind to fill my sails" (*Deseret Morning News,* April 2, 2005).

Others who have likewise been the recipient of written words of encouragement from Ardeth can attest to the benefit of her quiet boost. Her notes and letters are sent indiscriminately to both the well-known and the unknown.

One such letter received by a grieving family coping with the unexpected death of a daughter and sister said, "In this very hour, all that we know concerning our Father's love for all of His children reminds us that His love exceeds anything we can possibly understand in our mortal condition. Your love for your precious daughter is coupled with His love for your precious child, who is also His. Carry in your heart the words of the Lord for these trying times. 'Look unto me in every thought; doubt not, fear not' (D&C 6:36). Close your heart on those things that can intrude on the source of peace when we trust in the Lord. Let your hearts find peace in the sure knowledge of a loving Father in Heaven who understands all the whys and wherefores. We do not."

Read over and over by every family member, the message brings continued peace and comfort.

In late November 1996, Ardeth recorded: "My 'ministry by mail' is enormous. Just this very week, I've mailed out three packets of my writings to childless couples who have written, pouring their hearts out in anguish. Mail from our missionaries and all of the correspondence following each speaking assignment continues to pour in. They are wonderful letters of appreciation that must be answered."

TESTIMONY OF A YOUNG WOMAN

Typical of many young women who have come under the umbrella of Ardeth's care is one who was fortunate enough to be personally tutored by Ardeth. Somewhat rebellious and disengaged from Church activity, she was thirteen when her mother persuaded her to go to her meetinghouse to hear a Young Women satellite broadcast. She went unwillingly and sat through the meeting with arms folded and a scowl on her face—until Ardeth began speaking. Although the young woman has forgotten Ardeth's specific message, she knew it was intended for her. Not long afterwards, her Beehive teacher asked the class to write a letter to someone who had influenced their lives. Although she didn't mail her letter until a year later, the girl told Ardeth how she had been struggling and how she felt that the message had been just for her. When she finally mailed it, she received a quick response. Ardeth told her that she was a beloved daughter of God and that she would be pulling for her.

When the young woman came to Salt Lake City, she called Ardeth's office and was able to meet her. She continued to correspond with Ardeth, never missing an opportunity to hear her speak. When she expressed an uncertain testimony, Ardeth invited her to lean on hers until she developed one of her own. Finally, the day came when she no longer needed to lean on the testimonies of her parents, teachers, or friends. Her own testimony became so strong that she filled a mission, describing it as one of the best experiences of her life.

Some time after her return from the mission, this same young woman took an Institute class Ardeth was teaching at the University of Utah. In a discussion after class one evening, she told Ardeth that since she had not yet married and begun a family, she felt that she was failing in life. Ardeth said, "Plan your life as if you were never going to get married. Do things that will

In the Resource Room in the lower level of the Relief Society building. Ardeth explained the Young Women principles and values to daughters from around the world.

fulfill you. If you do get married, great! If you don't, you will still have a full life."

Ardeth began encouraging her to go to school and complete a college degree. The young woman had not enjoyed school and had not done well in high school. She was afraid to try. She avoided going to school and tried to avoid conversations about it. Ardeth, no stranger to struggles with school, persisted, continually encouraging her. With Ardeth's prodding, she finally began. Ardeth gave her constant encouragement and helped her feel good about what she was doing. She told her, "Remember not only *who* you are, but *whose* you are. You have a divine nature. You really are royal."

After a year and a half of persistence, this young woman had not only learned how to study, but she began to enjoy learning. Whenever she started to feel down, she picked up a letter from Ardeth, which gave her direction and the mental attitude to keep going. Ardeth told her, "Stay strong in your faith and be true to your testimony." Whenever the young woman thought of that advice, she did a mental check to see where she was and where she needed to be. Not only did she graduate, she did so with honors.

She is quick to give credit to supportive parents, family, and friends. Chief among those supporters is Ardeth, of whom she says, "I've never had a friend who wanted more for me than Ardeth. I truly feel that she wants me to make it home. I've never felt like she was too busy for me. She always says that she is there cheering me on. And she is. With all of the great women in the Church, I don't believe there has been anyone who loves the Lord more, and who has been such an influence for good on this earth. She doesn't waver. I believe her every thought is about how to do the Lord's work, how to build the kingdom, and how to be about her Father's business."

Four presidents: President Gordon B. Hinckley presents President George Bush to Ardeth (Young Women president) and Elaine Jack (Relief Society president)

Ardeth and the Young Women general board

CULMINATION

During Ardeth's administration, it became traditional for her to use the first board meeting of the new calendar year as a time for review, update, and articulating the vision of their calling. At a board meeting on January 9, 1991, she quoted from the minutes of January 9, 1985. "There will be three particular guidelines for our work: (1) We are to move orderly and in unity and to keep our eye on the distant horizon, not to be distracted by the things the adversary uses as a ploy to dilute our efforts; (2) We will move with a great sense of urgency during our time of service, and our task must be clear; (3) We must never become discouraged. We may get tired and out of breath; however, discouragement is the adversary's tool."

During the first meeting of 1987 she said, "We need to move fast enough to accomplish the things that need to be done, but slow enough to be in tune with the Spirit as we march together."

At the beginning of 1988 she started her message with the following statements, alluding to the Young Women Values and

Prior to their mission call, Heber served as a Regional Representative and was called as assistant coordinator for the Bountiful Temple project. They participated in the groundbreaking May 2, 1992, before leaving for the Canada Vancouver Mission.

the many other aspects of the program that had been developed: "We have a track; we have the train; we must now be focused on empowering the train through faith." She noted that "over the past five years we sought to be inspired and enlightened, to ask the right questions. As we look back, we have ample evidence that when we asked the right questions, we did receive answers."

As 1991 began, she admonished, "We have given a lot of time, thought, and prayer to the preparation of materials, but they are not the most important things. Our focus must be on the light of Christ which is in every individual. Nothing we have put in place should interfere with the attention leaders must give to the things of the Spirit. All that we are doing must help young women develop faith in the Lord Jesus Christ. The most important thing we can do is to help young women know the Spirit and feel it in their lives."

Toward the end of 1991, Ardeth pondered a possible change in assignment. "During the past several weeks, the Lord has spoken to my heart, my mind, my spirit. I have felt increased peace, faith, patience and purpose, direction and gratitude, inspiration and revelation. In recent months, people have frequently made reference to the length of time I have served as Young Women president. It has been on my mind recently. The idea of being released is not new. Come April, I will have served eight years as president, six years as a counselor, and six years on correlation, plus three or four years on writing committees. I've wondered how I will feel when I'm released. I think I will feel that with Heber's help, we did our very best, not withholding anything we might have done or given. Because of that, I will feel very good.

"I feel like I'm learning more about prayer and communication with my Father in Heaven and how quickly he hears and

Ardeth and Heber in the Young Women office when they opened their mission call to the Canada Vancouver Mission, February 1992

answers. I would like to be like Nephi with so much faith, angels would minister to me daily. Sometimes, I think they do. I know they do."

CALLED TO SERVE

On January 3, 1992, Heber received a call to serve as mission president, and Ardeth was told of her impending release. "It is interesting to me how the Lord prepares people for calls," she said. "But I think the Lord is equally concerned about preparing people for releases."

Though she knew she would be released, she kept working diligently in her Young Women assignment. She remembered what her father had taught her and she said to the Young Women board, "We're not quitting until April. We will plow to the end of the row."

As Ardeth thought of preparing her annual board message, which always included a vision for the coming year, she wrote, "It has been an interesting process because I have not been able to sense a clear direction. It has been like coming to the end of the page on the computer monitor and the screen won't roll up. I couldn't see beyond. I didn't have the anticipation for the future that I'd had in the past."

After receiving their mission call she said, "I had a peace come into my heart. I thought that the reason the inspiration for the coming year hadn't come to me is that it will come to someone else. This was a testimony to me that when we have the responsibility and need to receive direction, it will come. The direction wasn't mine to receive."

Elder M. Russell Ballard attended the first board meeting of 1992 and explained to the members that Heber had been called to serve as a mission president. He added "That will require that he take his companion with him."

When the priesthood leaders left the meeting, one of the board members went to the blackboard and wrote, "An Historic Day!!" They began reminiscing about their shared experiences of the previous eight years, remembering Ardeth's always optimistic outlook that "this will turn to our good." They recalled the planning meetings where the first question was always, "What do we want to have happen?" immediately followed by "Plan with a purpose." And last, they remembered the creed that was not only originated by Ardeth, but which described her: "Never give in, never give up, never give out. Give all!"

"I'LL GO WHERE YOU WANT ME TO GO"

On January 31, 1992, she wrote, "The last day of the first month of the year, and the first day of the rest of my life! What a glorious and exciting time this is." While preparing a talk she titled "In His Steps," she wrote: "It seems to me there are two great pillars that, if followed, allow us to be 'in His steps.' The first comes from the example the Savior gave early in his ministry when He said, 'I come to do the will of the Father, for the Father sent me.' Then at the close of His ministry he said, 'I have finished the work Thou gavest me to do.'

"Those seem to be, for me, the bedrock anchors between which we do all of our work. First, to do the will of the Father, and secondly, we finish the work we are given to do. I have a sense of closure and completion concerning this phase of the work that I have been given to do. Everyone in our office is working diligently to finish up the details that we want to have in place prior to my release."

During a meeting in mid-February, Ardeth received a telephone call from the missionary department advising her of a letter for her and Heber. She dispatched a staff member to pick it up, then awaited the arrival of Heber, who was on his way to the office. When he arrived, the presidency and staff joined in singing "I'll Go Where You Want Me to Go," while someone took pictures. Then they opened the envelope and read, "You have been called to the Canada Vancouver Mission." Ardeth squealed, Heber was excited, and the counselors and office staff said, "An historic day!" Heber and Ardeth made the announcement in their neighborhood by running a Canadian flag up their flagpole.

When their mission call was announced in the *Church News,* more people called the office to offer congratulations. "It's sort of like getting your funeral eulogy without experiencing death!" Ardeth said.

Elder M. Russell Ballard and Elder Mack Lawrence meet with the Young Women general board prior to Ardeth's release

The Young Women general presidency was invited to make their final presentation to the Church Priesthood Executive Council on March 18, 1992. Following the presentation, Elder James E. Faust, speaking for the members of the Council, expressed "appreciation and gratitude for your outstanding leadership and service. We have no forum or words to express appreciation for your incredible devotion and service."

In a special tribute given to Ardeth about that same time, Elder Ballard said, "We all recognize that there are those people who come from the premortal world into mortality with certain gifts and talents. Ardeth, you certainly came from the premortal world with a special gift—the gift of leadership. The girls are going to miss you; we're going to miss you—and Heber's going to love it because he will have you back for three years!"

HONORABLY RELEASED

As she prepared for her release, Ardeth recalled a great lesson her dad had taught her. He said, "To receive a calling is a trust,

Elder David B. Haight said to Ardeth, "You've not only opened our eyes, but also our ears."

but to receive an honorable release is a tremendous blessing." She then added, "I truly feel that I am receiving an honorable release."

On April 3, 1992, following the last workshop session of the Young Women open house, the Young Women general presidency and board met in Ardeth's office. Elders M. Russell Ballard and W. Mack Lawrence were also in attendance. As she spoke, Ardeth said, "Our board members had hoped to teach a principle—that calls and releases are inspired. Our tears were tears of joy. There is not one possible way that our release could have been a more positive experience."

Elder Ballard then spoke to the board: "The Lord doesn't worry about where we serve. What counts is how you serve. You have an opportunity to make a significant contribution whatever your calling." Elder Ballard reminded them, "the most significant service is always one on one—a quiet moment behind a closed door, when [we are] able to give a blessing or a little counsel. It is times like that that we can have an effect on another person's life. When we die the Lord will [want to know about] the lives we've touched and helped change and brought to Him. His arm will be thrust around us and we'll feel His love."

Elder Ballard then invoked a blessing on each person present. He said, "The Lord be with you. May He inspire you and enlighten your mind. May you take all you've learned and use it in your new callings to bless the lives of others. I bless each of you personally that you will experience the peace of the Lord, that the Lord will be your companion, that you will experience peace and love and contentment in your home and on your hearth. May our Heavenly Father smile upon you now and always."

In her final conference address Ardeth said, "At the time of my calling President Hinckley spoke of this as a time when the young women of the Church would become a mighty force for righteousness. We are witnessing this around the world. . . . The young women of the Church have a personal statement which declares their identity: 'I am a daughter of a Heavenly Father who loves me, and I will have faith in his eternal plan, which centers in Jesus Christ, my Savior.' . . . I have heard young women around the world repeat in many languages their commitment: 'We will be prepared to make and keep sacred covenants, receive the ordinances of the temple, and enjoy the blessings of exaltation.' Those blessings can be available to all of us—to all our Father's children. . . . It is through the ordinances and covenants available in the temple that our Father in Heaven has provided the way for us to return to Him rejoicing. To these eternal truths I bear my testimony" (*Ensign,* May 1992, 78–79).

INSTRUCTION AND FAREWELL

Heber and Ardeth prepared for their new calling not only through formal missionary training and personal study and prayer, but also by counsel and instruction from several others who had served as mission presidents.

At that time, Ardeth still had several speaking engagements, and Heber had assignments in his position as regional representative. Some evenings they returned home too exhausted to speak. But as the date of departure for their mission drew closer, their anticipation heightened.

At last the day came. They entered the Missionary Training

Mission photo of Heber and Ardeth

Center in Provo, Utah, on June 2, 1992, where they attended meetings and seminars, met with General Authorities and others to be taught and trained in their new responsibilities as leaders of young men and young women in the mission field.

The assignment was new, but the years of personal preparation, a new vision for the work to be done, and seeking to know the Lord's will would continue.

On June 28, 1992, the forty-second anniversary of their wedding, they left the MTC, headed for Vancouver, British Columbia, and to what would be "the most thrilling, exhilarating, exhausting, frustrating, exciting, loving experience of their whole Church service."

CHAPTER NINETEEN

Mountaintop Missionaries

Only One President

Ardeth sat looking out the car window, musing as Heber drove. Returning from their three years in the Vancouver British Columbia Mission, Ardeth's thoughts were reflective. Their last zone conferences had been tender and beautiful. Not wishing the missionaries to focus on their leaving, she and Heber had carefully selected the theme for the conferences—"A Vision of Our Possibilities"—which had resulted in a great forward-looking feeling.

But the reality of their leaving was inescapable. Each missionary wrote his or her last weekly letter to Heber, their president, which also included their personal farewells and messages of love and appreciation. After each conference, the missionaries stood on the lawn outside the meeting place, waving good-bye. Several wept openly. Expressions of deep affection between the missionaries and their president and mission mother were freely exchanged.

"You go your way and I'll go mine." At the border between the United States and Canada, they decided to go his way. Ardeth became a U.S. citizen soon after their marriage.

Ardeth pondered the past three years. Although filled to capacity with marvelous memories, the times had not always been easy. Her thoughts turned back to the beginning. They had arrived in their new location the evening of June 29, 1992. After an overnight stay in a nearby hotel, they called the retiring mission president, letting him know that they were ready to pick up the torch. After a brief orientation with him and his wife at the mission office, they drove to the mission home, where they were given keys to the home and the office, as well as to a mission car. Following dinner with the outgoing couple, they were in charge!

Ardeth was surprised by one aspect of the mission she had not anticipated. She had felt very comfortable and blessed in the things she had been able to accomplish while serving as a leader in Church organizations. According to President Monson, through whom their mission call had been issued, as well as others with whom she had served, she knew how to get things done. Heber, who had served as a bishop, a stake president, and a regional representative, also had a reputation for great accomplishments. They were excited for the opportunity of new leadership experiences in the mission field. They knew the challenges would be different from those they had already known, but they had not before realized how different their leadership styles were from each other. Previous opportunities for them to work closely together in leadership capacities had been minimal, and this new responsibility would prove to be different.

Since she didn't have office skills, Ardeth was grateful that Heber involved her instead in teaching and helping to plan zone conferences. He was anxious that the missionaries see them as a team, teaching and working together. Their approaches to teaching situations were similar, and strengthened each of them. But when it came to problem-solving skills, their approaches diverged greatly.

They were both anxious to be effective and to have success in their new responsibilities, but they came to learn that men and women do indeed think differently. In their new relationship, they eventually learned that drawing on their separate experiences and being able to see things from different points of view was a strength. But at first, their readily apparent differences were of great concern to Ardeth.

Alone in the car with Heber one evening on their way to a missionary activity, she confided, "I don't understand this. We've each served as presidents over Church organizations. We've both been effective. Why isn't it working now?"

With a smile in his voice, Heber responded, "Maybe that's

the problem." In his delightfully humorous way, he reminded her that they needed only one president.

Immediately she understood. They did need only one president, and it was to be him. He was the one who had been called. Her role was to assist and support. She was determined to do her best.

Ardeth could see that she had been more anxious to fix a concern and Heber more anxious to empower the young missionaries to fix it themselves. She wanted quick action. He stepped back and let them resolve it themselves. She understood that his way was the right one for the mission. As they made the necessary adjustments to increase their effectiveness as mission leaders, they grew to understand that each calling is an apprenticeship not only for this life but for eternal responsibilities. This new experience provided invaluable learning opportunities.

Immersed in the Work

During the first four weeks of their mission, they followed as nearly as possible the schedule already in place for zone conferences. It was a busy schedule, but it did allow them to cover the entire mission and become acquainted with the missionaries now under their supervision. It was a profitable if arduous task.

Ardeth also attended a girls' camp held in a location near to one of their zone conference meetings. Approximately eighty young women attended, and for many it was their first camp experience. Expressing their gratitude for her attendance, they gave her a card that read, "We believe in miracles. We prayed for a miracle, and you came!" For Ardeth, it was a sweet experience.

After meeting the missionaries on their first tour through the mission, Heber and Ardeth gained a great sense of love and

All responsibilities were shared equally in the mission home.

appreciation for each young man and woman. Following each zone meeting, Heber held interviews with every missionary, after which they held a testimony meeting. From these meetings, they gained a sense of what truly marvelous young people were under their care. Ardeth wrote, "We feel, without any question of a doubt, that the right people have been brought together to serve with us at this time. Those who are here and those who are yet to come will participate in a most historic, memorable tenure during this time in the Canada Vancouver Mission. As we come to study the gospel, follow the guidelines, give diligent service, serving with all of our hearts, might, mind, and strength, and calling upon the Lord in faith, we know that he will allow great and marvelous things to occur. Our humble prayer is that we will be inspired in working with the missionaries, and that each one will desire to do their part."

They soon recognized the urgent need for more appropriate

and less costly office space. With Heber's thorough research and insight into building, he found that the money being spent on the current inadequate facility would be enough to pay for a new building, built on existing Church property, in just over three years. Preparing a report with the details of his plan, he submitted his findings to the Missionary Department. After careful study, approval was given to build a new mission office on the grounds of the Richmond stake center, located not far from the mission home. The building was completed prior to their release.

In the meantime, they set about to carry on the work within the existing facilities. Ardeth, whose secretarial skills were minimal, had just left a large, private, well-equipped office with an exceptionally able administrative assistant and four capable and efficient secretaries. Access to any needed resource was immediately available to her. Overnight, she found herself in inadequate rented office space in a more public setting. Although a dedicated senior missionary couple were in the office on a temporary basis, she still had to assume unfamiliar secretarial responsibilities. After working in this situation for a short while, she felt impressed to write to every secretary she had ever had to tell them how much she appreciated their skills! Although she had thanked them before, she felt that she had never really appreciated them the way she did now.

Their first Christmas in the mission field found Ardeth and Heber thoroughly immersed in the work. In a message written for the monthly mission newsletter, the *Mountain Top Messenger,* they expressed, "We pray that each of you may have a White Christmas at the baptismal font, where you open the door to the Celestial Kingdom and Eternal Life for one of your contacts. The gift of Eternal Life to one of our Father's children, made available through your diligence, will be a gift which they will celebrate every Christmas with thanks and gratitude to you throughout eternity. . . . May you know how deeply we love and appreciate you for your dedicated service and loyalty to His work."

As she reflected on their first six months of full-time missionary service, Ardeth wrote, "The test is not only for the young missionaries. This is challenging work! I can feel my own personal growth. Elder Ballard counseled us that it would take six months to really get it together. I thought he was referring to the missionaries. I've decided it was a personal reference. After six months I'm happy and at peace. I'm ready to be a helpmate and do all I can in a spirit of unity to support Heber. His way is the president's way. He is living worthy of inspiration and revelation. His prayers are inspiring and it is working. This has been a new beginning. First learning to crawl, then to walk, and now, hopefully, to run."

In a somewhat tongue-in-cheek letter to family and friends, she wrote, "It is springtime in the Canadian Rockies, and I am happy to report that we are no longer in over our snorkel, nor have we taken up deep sea diving, as at one time we thought we should. Actually, we find our missionaries in water up to their waists more often than before, for which we are most grateful. I must admit, however, that on occasion I have the sensation of being on the inside of a washing machine on spin. Does anyone know where I might enroll in a good time-management seminar? I am glad we didn't wait until we were 'older' to have this rich and wonderful experience. Being associated every day with these remarkable young people will certainly keep us young, if it doesn't kill us. And if it does, what a way to go!"

THE TRAIL TO THE TOP

The mission symbol was *THE MOUNTAIN TOP.* To help their young missionaries reach their full potential, Ardeth and Heber developed a program they called "The Trail to the Top." In helping the missionaries understand the program, Ardeth and Heber wrote, "A mountain has great symbolism. Moses climbed Mount Sinai. There he saw God. God spoke to him and he received the Ten Commandments. There are many mountains for each of us to climb. And when we find our Sinai and climb it, climb it to the top. There we will find God. He will speak to us in our minds and in our hearts, by the spirit of revelation." Each elder and sister was encouraged to become a "Mountain Top Missionary"—and many responded with enthusiasm.

As part of the requirements to become a Mountain Top

Sister Kapp (center) and sister missionaries

Missionary—and to provide a pattern for their lives—each missionary was asked to write a commentary or abridgment on each chapter in the Book of Mormon. Ardeth determined to fill the assignment herself. She began with the heading to 1 Nephi, chapter 1: "Nephi knew of his identity. He recognized his goodly parents. He had seen many afflictions, but still considered himself to be favored of God. Lehi 'got the picture,' or the vision. And when he got the 'picture,' so to speak, he could leave everything behind." As her heading for chapter 2, she wrote, "Lehi was totally obedient. He heard the voice of the Lord. He knew the Lord's will and he would follow. Those who will not follow will not have the Spirit."

Ardeth completed her commentary, as each missionary was asked to do, by adding her personal, final testimony, as did Moroni, for his posterity and others who came after him. "This is my personal testimony of this 'miracle on paper.' It is a fact that we can get nearer to God by reading it. [The Book of Mormon] is the word of God. The Spirit has once again borne witness to my soul that these things are true. This record is a second witness for Jesus Christ. I know of His incredible compassion, His obedience, His self-mastery, His mission, His endurance, His model life, His majesty and power, yet His tenderness and intimate concern for the one, me and you. I realize the need for agency, accountability, the purpose and meaning of life, the glorious plan of happiness. The answers are all there—the pattern, the guidelines, the promises, the hope. There is so much evidence of forgiveness. The atonement is for me daily, and for you. Our greatest heroes are there [in the Book of Mormon]. We will know them and meet them. The Savior did come and bless and heal, and He will come again. He learned by the things he suffered. He knows us and our needs, and we can become even joint heirs with Jesus Christ. To this I testify, and pray that all people everywhere might know as Philip, upon finding Nathaniel, said, 'We have found him.' I have found him again and again, every day in every way. And now I close. I say as Moroni to the Nephites (Moroni 10:34): 'To whoever reads this (in years to come), I shall meet you at the pleasing bar of God. Amen. Ardeth Kapp. Written while serving in the great Canada Vancouver Mission."

The missionaries' admiration for their leaders was obvious. One sister missionary, in referring to Heber, asked Ardeth, "How did you find a man like that?"

Ardeth responded, "I didn't find him like that, and he didn't find me like this. We have been working on each other, with each other, and for each other for years. And we're not through yet!"

One young elder was devastated upon receiving a "Dear John" letter. In her attempt to cheer him up, Ardeth agreed to write him a letter of recommendation, listing all of his outstanding qualities, including the statement that if she had a granddaughter his age, she would have him over for dinner every week. After she had signed the letter, he had it reduced in size and laminated so he could carry it in his wallet for handy reference. When word regarding the letter got out, she was flooded with similar requests from the other missionaries for their use when they returned home. At the wedding reception of this missionary some time later, his bride was anxious to let Ardeth know that it was her signature on the letter of recommendation that helped lead to their marriage!

A MIRACULOUS BLESSING

One of the most personally difficult times for Ardeth and Heber in their mission occurred near the midpoint of their service. Heber became ill in the middle of a Wednesday night and was in excruciating pain. When nothing seemed to relieve his distress, Ardeth called an ambulance. The attendants placed him on a stretcher and carried him from the second floor of the mission home to the waiting ambulance. They began the drive to the hospital, about a mile away. Ardeth quickly got into the car and followed closely behind. She was near panic. It had all happened so quickly, and now it appeared to be life-threatening.

What could be happening, and why? Heber had been so healthy. All at once the attention she had been giving to the mission switched 100 percent to Heber. He became her total focus. In the hospital emergency room, she thought, "What if something happens to him?" She felt suddenly alone and she felt their total dependence on the Lord.

After Heber's examination was complete, they were told that his condition was grave. He had been infected with a virus that was attacking the heart valve. Elder Ted E. Brewerton, a member of the First Quorum of the Seventy, was in the area attending a stake conference. Hearing of Heber's illness the following Sunday, he immediately went to the hospital. Doctors had said that the problem was very serious and that if he lived, Heber would be in the hospital for four or five weeks. Invoking the power of the priesthood, Elder Brewerton gave Heber a blessing.

In that hospital room they witnessed a miracle, wrought

through the priesthood's healing power. Heber was discharged from the hospital on Monday, the very next day. Ardeth had been at his side in the hospital for five days. They left with the doctor's instructions to go immediately home. Heber was to be on bed rest for several weeks, checking regularly with the doctor.

Heber, however, had other ideas. He knew his body had been healed and he was well. Instead of returning home, Heber directed Ardeth, who was driving, to the mission office. Although she protested, he insisted. He returned to his labors with faith, gratitude, enthusiasm, and energy. His miraculous recovery had a great positive impact on the missionaries' testimonies. Ardeth felt that she had known before how to pray fervently and receive answers, but this was one of the most intense experiences she had had with prayer. In her heart and soul, she felt the nearness of the Lord, his personal attention, and his approval of their work. She knew they had been given a blessing to carry on and finish their mission. With the threat of the passing of her eternal companion, she was once again reminded of and grateful for their temple covenants, which would make a separation, when it came, only temporary.

TWO BY TWO

As their second year in the mission field drew to a close, and on their forty-fourth wedding anniversary, Ardeth expressed her thoughts in a letter to Heber:

"Thank you for the perfect wedding anniversary present you gave me this morning. I wondered if you realized the full interpretation and significance of the gift when you selected it. The more I think about it, the more perfect it is at this particular time. The porcelain works of art depicting Noah and his wife

Heber and Ardeth in the mission home

with the ark, and all the animals going two by two is so symbolic.

"Noah was where he was because he had been told by the Lord—just as we are.

"In Noah's case, one of the problems was that it rained all the time for forty days and nights. In our case, it has rained at least half of the time for two years. Wouldn't that be about the same?

"And all those he was trying to care for were going two by two—isn't that like our missionaries? When you think of all those animals out of their natural setting and being confined to an ark for forty days, is it any wonder that Noah had problems—and he had no way of transferring any of them!

"His wife was complaining all of the time, singing, 'I hate the rain.' While I don't see any analogy there, the thought does occur to me that maybe it wasn't the rain at all. Maybe she just missed association with those who could understand her plight.

"Now it would be very easy to continue this comparison in

greater detail, but knowing you only want 'the bottom line,' I fear I may have carried this a little too far as it is. Needless to say, this special and thoughtful gift does seem very significant at this particular time.

"Just one more observation. All of the animals going two by two, I notice, are bound together. I like the elephants best because their trunks are intertwined. Do you have to have a trunk to be that connected? I think not. . . .

"With forty-four years behind us, and eternity to go, there are probably other lessons and analogies we might draw from Noah and his Ark, but rain or shine, I'm yours, and you're mine. HAPPY ANNIVERSARY!"

Meaning of a Mission

As their three years flew by, Ardeth pondered the meaning of a mission:

"What is it about a mission? What is it that kindles a response from members of the Church of every age when the word, 'mission,' or 'missionary' is spoken? A Primary child stands tall with eyes bright and enthusiastically sings, 'I Hope They Call Me on a Mission.' A grandparent sends a birthday card across the miles to a grandson or a granddaughter, with a generous contribution tucked inside with a little note—'for your missionary fund.' An entire neighborhood stands watch each day for at least a week or two until the mailman finally delivers the letter that has been anticipated, in most cases, for nineteen years or more. With unsteady hands, and eager to know the contents of the message, the missionary, with the family gathered around, remembers the nights in family home evenings when everyone learned to sing and to commit to the message of the song: 'I'll go where you want me to go, dear Lord.'

"Missions are about farewells and homecomings, good-byes and tears, prayers and many letters coming and going in between. The days are numbered, and some are long, but the weeks and months seem to fly by ever so quickly. Time is measured for each returning missionary in terms of 'before' and 'after' the mission.

"No written description or explanation can ever adequately convey the power and impact of a mission experience, with its boundless benefits and unnumbered blessings in so many unexpected places, with unlimited opportunities. Parents of young missionaries feast on every word scribbled on an ordinary sheet of paper, stuffed into a standard envelope, and delivered through the regular mail system, carrying with it profound messages, written in common words to perceptive loved ones who can read between the lines and discover the miracle of a mission.

"What can happen to a missionary of any age when, for a season, the entire focus of his life is centered in Jesus Christ, and the sharing of His message is something only a missionary can ever fully realize, can never be adequately explained. These enriching, rewarding, and exhilarating experiences are not reserved for only a fortunate few; rather, they are available to all who choose to 'send in their papers,' and walk by faith."

As the missionaries completed their assignments and prepared to return home, Ardeth and Heber experienced difficulties in letting them go. In remembering the departure of one such missionary, Ardeth said, "When we watch a young man grow spiritually, and in leadership capacity, it's like sending one of your children away for an unlimited period of time. We learned to love and admire him. He has incredible leadership ability, spiritual maturity, and a goodness about him that captured the respect and admiration of all the missionaries. We will miss him very much. When his parents came to pick him up, I almost felt in my heart that this was a setting like when King Solomon was trying to decide what was the best thing to do when there was only one son and both mothers wanted the child!"

AN INSIDE LOOK

Heber's and Ardeth's missionaries loved and respected them both. To their teaching and their usually gentle counsel and training, their charges responded with hard work and determination to be the best missionaries possible. Almost ten years after his return, one former missionary wrote of his feelings concerning President and Sister Kapp:

"Shortly after receiving my call, my father, sensing my disappointment at not being called to a mission of 'my' choosing, said, 'Son, I have had the distinct feeling that you have not been called to Canada to convert hundreds. Rather, you will have the opportunity to learn leadership from and be tutored by the Kapps. Heber and Ardeth are very special people, and if you listen and pay attention, they will teach you much about serving the Lord.'

"How true this proved to be. Aside from my parents, the Kapps are without a doubt the people that have had the most influence in shaping my life and my character. I have spoken with dozens of missionaries that served with them and there are many who echo this sentiment.

"When I arrived in Vancouver on a rainy evening in 1994,

Sister Kapp greeted me with the warm smile and energetic handshake that is her trademark. Expecting simply a brief 'hello,' I was surprised and somewhat taken aback when she grabbed my arm, pulled me close and said, 'We've been waiting for you. There is much work that needs to be done and we are counting on you. I hope you work up to your potential.' This brief exchange characterizes how President and Sister Kapp motivated us. In nearly every interaction with the Kapps, you always came away feeling (1) as though you were the most important person in the world, (2) as though your efforts were appreciated and needed, and (3) like you could always do better.

"A mission can be a lonely place. The one way that missionaries report to the President is through the 'Letters to the President.' Sister Kapp and President Kapp read every letter that was sent into the office every week. Sister Kapp went through every letter (except those of a confidential nature marked 'President Kapp, Personal'), underlining certain items and making notes in the margins for the APs and President. These notes highlighted everything from accomplishments to merely a tone of disappointment or depression. While the President and APs would frequently follow up on issues raised in the letters, Sister Kapp spent hours each week calling missionaries, praising their accomplishments, giving them support and a word of encouragement. Particularly with the sisters of our mission, Sister Kapp provided valuable insight and support. Simply knowing that she read every letter, every week, made many missionaries feel confident that their voices were heard and they were not alone.

"This love for everyone was best manifest in the service they gave to each of us. Two experiences stand out in my mind as particularly fond memories. On one occasion, I walked into the mission office and complimented President Kapp on his tie. He responded, 'Do you like the way this looks?' When I responded that I did, he immediately took it off and handed it to me. I kept that tie for years and I often reflect back on how quick President Kapp was to help others and spread a little cheer.

"P-days are often packed with zone meetings, travel, cleaning, and, of course, laundry. Whenever she was in town, Sister Kapp called my companion and me, telling us to bring our shirts over to the mission home. She spent a good portion of the day washing and ironing our shirts. This allowed us to relax somewhat and write those important letters to loved ones. Sister Kapp pressed every one of our shirts by hand, *with starch,* and acted genuinely appreciative for allowing her the opportunity to serve. She used to say, 'When you are famous one day, and I am sitting in my rocking chair, I want to be able to say "I ironed his shirts!"'

"The Kapps are genuinely cheerful people and this rubbed off on many missionaries. It is easy to become discouraged or depressed as a young missionary, and having President and Sister Kapp always in good spirits helped to uplift and inspire. I don't think I ever saw Sister Kapp in a sour mood. Even when things did not go well, or the weather was poor, or someone did not follow through on an assignment, Sister Kapp always kept her cheerful demeanor. The only time I ever saw a hint of sadness or distress was on those occasions where a missionary had made a serious mistake or was not living up to his/her potential. . . .

"President and Sister Kapp would not only give encouragement and praise, but honest feedback in an effort to help us

Sister Kapp and three APs (left to right): Elder Michael Wolfe, Elder Daniel Bryant, Sister Kapp, Elder Darren Henderson. Sister Kapp says, "I ironed their shirts."

improve. Sister Kapp always had personalized stationery in her bag, on which she would write a brief note to missionaries who spoke in zone conference or in a Church meeting, or after sitting in on a discussion. These coveted notes not only helped boost self-esteem, but provided much-needed specific feedback to help us improve. . . .

"If I had to single out one thing that I learned from the Kapps that affects my life nearly every day, it would not be the many sermons they gave or lessons they taught. Rather, it was my continual, quiet observation of how they treated each other as husband and wife. To this day, I have yet to meet a couple who is so in love as Heber and Ardeth, and show it in so many ways. Their quiet devotion and gentleness, mixed with appropriate humor and cheerfulness, was not lost on me. There were many times when we (the APs) would be meeting with President and Sister Kapp, or spending time at the mission home, when there would be some divergence of opinion on a matter. Yet, in every circumstance, no voices were raised, no arguing would ensue. Rather, there would be thoughtful listening, patient urging, and if an impasse still ensued, one or the other might even recommend that 'we think about this and talk later.' On several occasions, I perceived President or Sister Kapp to be 'technically' correct on a minor issue, but they would acquiesce to save peace. At the time, I was of the mind-set that if you are right, you should make sure everyone knows it. I have come to understand, by observing the Kapps, that the tender bond that exists between husband and wife is far too important, and sometimes fragile, to risk on a trivial disagreement." (Letter from Darren Henderson, June 17, 2005.)

Good Things Do Last Forever

Just as Heber and Ardeth were beginning their last round of zone conferences, a letter came from Elder Jeffrey R. Holland. "However challenging and even frightening it is to enter the mission," he wrote, "it is, as you now know so well, nothing compared to the emotion and affection and memories with which you force yourself to disengage and come home. . . . We have known how much the missionaries and members would weep to let you go. Those tears will be mutual, but, thank heavens in the gospel of Jesus Christ good things *do* last forever. Prepare yourselves now for the barrage of wedding invitations and birth announcements that will be part of your life forever. Missionaries will be camping on your doorstep—it's actually a good thing that you have that downstairs apartment—but even the members, who are somewhat farther away, will find their way to Utah with surprising regularity. If we were natives of that great mission, we would want to get here to see you as well, and we are selfishly awaiting your return."

True to Elder Holland's forecast, invitations did come flooding in—first to homecomings and then to weddings. Birth announcements followed, and the Kapps express joy with each new baby that comes into their mission family. Ardeth says, "We claim every one we can!" Every May brings a march of Mother's Day cards to the Kapps' mailbox. With each one comes a flood of tender memories associated with the giver and his or her mission experiences. Ardeth is grateful for the thoughts expressed. The young men and women with whom they served are truly an extension of their family, and their association will be eternal.

REVIVED, RENEWED, AND HEADED HOME!

The Sunday before they left the mission, Ardeth and Heber both became ill. With an infected throat, Ardeth could hardly talk, but that did not deter her from speaking in a zone conference. Heber had a severe pain in his leg and couldn't walk without holding on to Ardeth. They were sick and they were tired. But in spite of that, they were happy. They felt the mission was in very good condition and they were ready to turn the responsibility over to President and Sister Stirling Colton.

After greeting the incoming president and his wife and showing them through the mission home, Ardeth and Heber took President and Sister Colton to the new mission office. They were very happy with the beautiful new facility and were equally pleased that having their own building brought an enormous savings to the Church.

Bidding the new couple good-bye, Ardeth and Heber were just leaving the office when one of the missionaries, who was also departing, arrived with his family. They were excited to see the new office and to visit with President and Sister Kapp. Summoning the last reserves of their rapidly dwindling energy, the Kapps smilingly greeted them before leaving. Upon arriving at the motel where they were to spend the night, they found themselves too weary and sick to carry their luggage to their room. Heber grabbed his shaving kit, and Ardeth managed to carry her toothbrush and handbag inside. Everything else remained in the car. They fell into bed, exhausted but at peace, having crossed the finish line—mission completed, with not an ounce of energy remaining. They awakened in the morning, revived and renewed, and headed for home!

IT WILL SOUND LIKE A LULLABY

After a two-day journey, they were close to home. Ardeth had been instructed to call Sharon when they were an hour or more away. They didn't call until they reached a convenient exit, only minutes away. When she heard Ardeth's voice, Sharon said, "Oh, no! You must give us at least an hour before you come!" They got off the freeway and wandered slowly through the nearby small towns, waiting for the time to pass.

Finally arriving at their address, they could hardly believe what they were seeing. Such a welcome home! Across the front of the house hung a very large sign: "Welcome home, Ardie and Heber!" with a United States flag on one side and a Canadian flag on the other. Red, white, and blue balloons, attached to the sign, bounced in the breeze, and yellow balloons were tied to trees for a block away. From two loudspeakers on the front porch blared John Phillip Sousa's "Stars and Stripes Forever." And all fifty feet of Sharon's famous "Welcome Home" red carpet was stretched up the walk leading to their front porch. Across the porch was a beautiful Young Women Values garden, with every color represented in hanging baskets of flowers. Hot rolls were in the oven and the refrigerator was stocked with food.

When the excitement had subsided, Ardeth told Sharon that in this earth life she could never hope to give Sharon a homecoming equal to this one. "But," she said, "since the chances are that I will beat you to our heavenly home, I will immediately upon arrival begin to organize a great celebration for you when you return home. Those heavenly choirs will make John Phillip Sousa sound like a lullaby!"

A JEWEL ON THE HILLSIDE

Ardeth and Heber spotted the beautiful Bountiful Temple, barely begun when they had left, from miles away on the freeway. It gleamed like a sparkling jewel on the hillside. They kept their eye on it all the way home. Before they went to bed that

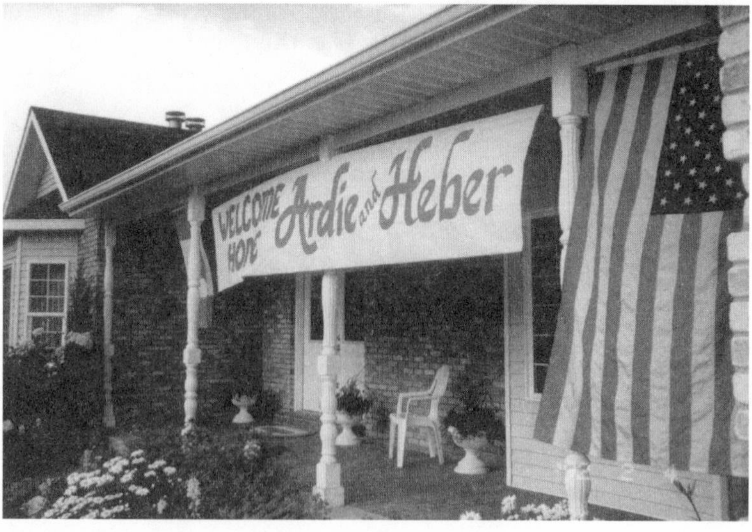

A sweet homecoming, July 1995

night they opened the drapes in their bedroom, and there, perfectly framed in the window, was the temple. It was a thrilling sight. Within days after returning home they attended the Bountiful Temple for the first time. "It was incredibly beautiful, inspiring, and breathtaking," Ardeth wrote. "And in our own backyard. How blessed we are!"

Years earlier, in 1990, Heber had been called as vice president of the Bountiful Utah Temple building project. He was set apart on June 27, 1990, by Elder William H. Bradford, president of the Utah North Area. Mac Christensen, who had been called to serve as Heber's executive secretary for the project, was set apart at the same time.

In blessing Heber, Elder Bradford remarked that Heber had been prepared in every way for this calling and said that he and his companion would share great spiritual experiences during this assignment. In 1992, when they received their mission call, they had a fleeting pang of regret that they would not be there to see the temple through to its completion or be in attendance at the dedication. But with their typical commitment to serve where they were called, they had turned their attention toward the mission.

Just a few weeks after their return, Ardeth and Heber were called to serve two days a week in the Bountiful Temple, an assignment they enjoyed and for which they were grateful. Then on November 21, 1995, Heber was set apart by President Gordon B. Hinckley as a temple sealer.

The opportunity to meet with the prophet had never become commonplace for Heber and Ardeth, and they were full of anticipation for this visit. As they entered the Church

Administration Building, Ardeth remembered walking up those same steps years earlier when Heber was called as a young bishop. Waiting in the foyer of the building, she pondered all that had happened since then. They had both had countless opportunities for service in their callings over the years.

Others waiting to be set apart were waiting with their families. Ardeth recorded, "When families are gathered for these occasions, I am reminded that things are different for us, and I think of the promises of the future. . . . President Hinckley was warm and friendly. He said this calling would be like a benediction on Heber's life. We left the office of the prophet of God, Heber having been given the sealing power that 'whatsoever you bind on earth shall be bound in heaven' (D&C 128:8).

"I wondered briefly if the reference to the benediction on his life referred in any way to the end of his life, but soon put that idea aside, anticipating years and years of service in this great calling. And what a joy that I can serve in the temple, right behind our house, with him. Heber has always spoken with such love and interest in the temple. It is so right for this time in our lives. We have been and are so blessed, and this new opportunity will open understanding to our minds that will give us greater appreciation than ever before for this glorious gospel of Jesus Christ."

CHAPTER TWENTY

The Capstone

At Home

Ardeth was happy to be back in her home. A highlight of the Christmas season was to have Shelly and Steve and their new little son, Jake, visiting from St. Louis, where Steve was in medical school. At the year's end, Ardeth wrote, "Now a bit of the end-of-the-year philosophy and reflection. I am at peace, feel calm—all is well, all is well. Everything precious seems even more wonderful. Heber is so thoughtful, so expressive of his love and gratitude, so fun in his attention to little things, so positive about everything I do. He said, 'I feel so good about our situation. Life is so good. Everything is so perfect. We are so blessed!' I feel the same way. We completed our mission, and home has never been better."

There wasn't much of a time lapse between their arrival home and Ardeth's head-long plunge into speaking, teaching, and writing—activities that had always claimed much of her time and attention. Shortly after their return, Ardeth wrote about an honor she was to receive from BYU: "I am to receive the outstanding alumni recognition at homecoming this fall. Imagine! I can't even spell. . . . And if that isn't enough, I received a request to speak at the BYU devotional, November 7th in the Marriott Center. I spoke there several times as general Young Women president, and also as a member of the board of trustees. I *never* expected that opportunity again."

In addition to their temple callings, Ardeth and Heber accepted an assignment to teach a Gospel Doctrine class in their ward. Ardeth was asked to consider writing a book on leadership and was also preparing a book compiled from interviews and experiences with their young missionaries. At BYU Education Week in August 1995, she gave twelve different one-hour lectures, four in the Marriott Center and eight in the Wilkinson Center Ballroom. Following the BYU lectures, the Education Week staff asked her to speak at their fall retreat at Aspen Grove, the BYU family camp in the Wasatch Mountains.

STITCHING HISTORY

In early 1995, Ardeth received a request to be chairman of a project for the celebration of the centennial of Utah's statehood. Over four hundred authentic pioneer period dresses were needed for docents to wear at This Is the Place Heritage Park by the end of June 1997, in time for the Church's celebration on July 24. Ardeth explained to Steve Studdert, centennial chairman, that she didn't sew, didn't even like to sew, and she definitely was not the right person for this job. Steve asked her to pray about it. She told him that she didn't want to pray about it. He responded that he would call her back.

After mulling it over, Ardeth decided to pray about it, but

"You're not sewing dresses, you're stitching history." 1,775 authentic articles of clothing were made for the project.

with a strong conviction that this was not the project for her. In answer to her prayer, she received an answer, loud and clear: "You are not asked to sew dresses. You are asked to stitch history, to help preserve history, to record history, and to celebrate history." She wrote, "The more I think about it as a means of linking us to the past, and the spiritual growth that can come, I am excited about being part of this great event. It is a combined state and Church project. So exciting!"

Having received a purpose and a plan, Ardeth agreed to the assignment, which became known as the "Stitching History" project. The project was launched at a fashion show held at the Joseph Smith Memorial building on March 12, 1996. Dressed in a period costume, Utah's first lady Jacqueline Leavitt hosted the event. Pioneer dress for men, women, and children were modeled, accompanied by a narrative detailing each piece of clothing and its time and place in Utah history.

In honor of her two grandmothers, Ardeth had two beautiful pioneer dresses made to give to the park. Then she formed a committee, which made appointments to show the dresses to groups statewide from Logan to St. George. At each meeting, women were invited to make dresses in honor of their grandmothers and other pioneer ancestors. Ardeth told them that the history of Utah was written by people of faith, vision, and valor. She invited them to join in an opportunity to help create a legacy that would entertain and educate for years to come. The project gained momentum. People throughout the state began searching the history of their pioneer forebears.

Sewing the dresses was only the vehicle to gain access to countless inspirational stories of sacrifice and courage, gathered by the participants. Each dress was numbered and recorded with the name of the donor, along with a one-page history on file at the park for docents to read and know the history of those whose

Church leaders and wives at This Is the Place *monument during the 1997 sesquicentennial celebration. Ardeth served as vice chair of This Is the Place Heritage Park until she left to serve as matron in the Cardston Alberta Temple.*

clothing they were wearing. When the project was completed, 1,775 authentic articles of pioneer clothing had been received, exceeding even the greatest expectations.

Ardeth was later called as vice chairman of This Is the Place Heritage Park. Elder M. Russell Ballard said, "She has a great sense of history, and she's very creative. Her mind doesn't slow down. It's going 100 miles an hour all the time! She had a vision of what needed to be done there and led a crusade to get those costumes made."

IT NEVER GETS BETTER THAN THIS

On May 8, 1996, she recorded: "This is the best of all seasons. It never gets better than this. Every morning I awaken, roll out of bed, look up at the temple, and kneel and give thanks. Each night at the close of day, I kneel in prayer, look up at the temple in the dark, shining as a beacon, and give thanks for such a blessing. On Friday I bought some flowers to plant in the shade of the crab apple tree. After working part of the day to prepare the ground, it was late afternoon. I was under the apple tree on my knees. . . . My heart filled to overflowing with gratitude—gratitude for the beautiful flowers; gratitude for money to buy them; gratitude for a piece of earth in which to plant them.

"At that moment, the evening breeze from the canyon crept in ever so quietly and the tiny pink blossoms from the branches overhead fell like pink droplets of rain, falling on my head and my hands, covering the ground all around. The birds in the feeders overhead in the apple tree were singing a symphony in the cool of the evening.

"This has been a beautiful day, a gift that God, who gives us all and lends us even our breath in which to absorb the ecstasy

Ardeth loves gardening as time permits.

through all our faculties and drink from the fountain of his goodness. . . . I felt as though I was in His presence, being showered with gifts abundant in the quiet corner of my garden, away from any distraction anywhere. It is a peace that passeth all understanding."

"I KNOW WHERE I WANT TO BE"

In the fall of 1995, Ardeth began teaching an evening Book of Mormon class once a week at the Institute building adjacent to the University of Utah campus. It was a large class of over fifty students, including recently returned missionaries, those preparing to serve missions, and several older adults.

Ardeth enjoyed this teaching opportunity and strove to develop a good relationship with all of the class members. One day an unsigned letter came in the mail, bearing no return address other than a post office box. The writer, one of her students, thanked her for the strength he had received from being in her class. He then told her that his mind had frequently strayed to thoughts of suicide. He said that he was just barely making it from one class to the next, and told of his need for the reinforcement he gained at her class for the rest of the week. Although unable to discern who the class member might be, Ardeth immediately responded. Selecting several favorite scriptures that never failed to bring her peace, hope, and encouragement, she recorded them and mailed the tape to the post office box number. She prayed fervently that it would get to the writer of the letter.

Within two weeks, she received another letter. The class member said that he had played the tape over and over, night and day. The messages contained within the scriptures she had recorded were helping, he said, to heal him of the despair he had felt. Later, long after the semester was over, the person, a middle-aged brother, identified himself, thanking her for what she had done to help him through a very low point in his life.

At the end of the term, class members handed in evaluation sheets with comments for the teacher. One example:

"My testimony has grown and become so much stronger. It hasn't been this strong at any time in my life. The Book of Mormon is now a part of my life. . . . My love for my Heavenly Father, my family, friends, and you is just overwhelming. I know that He lives and I know where I want to be—it's with Him, no matter what it takes."

"I WILL LEARN ABOUT NEWSPAPERS"

In May 1996, President Thomas S. Monson invited Ardeth to meet with him in his office. He told her that the General Authorities would no longer serve on boards of companies, and there would be a change in the *Deseret News* board of directors.

President Monson, who had served as the managing director of the *Deseret News* for over thirty years, then invited Ardeth to become a member of the newspaper's board of directors. She agreed to President Monson's request and served as the only woman on the board at that time.

Following a photo session for the new *Deseret News* board members, Ardeth wrote, "Such a remarkable group of people. How can I be running on that team! President Monson introduced each of us, with a brief biography. He made some very kind and generous comments concerning my gifts and talents. Needless to say, I felt very honored. Still, I feel so inadequate. But, just as I have learned about stitching history and about authentic patterns and fabrics, I will learn about newspapers."

Following an event honoring the outgoing board members and welcoming the new ones, Ardeth wrote, "Oh, I do hope I will rise to the stature of this assignment with the 'News.' I'm concerned. The new board members, and especially the managing director, repeatedly expressed gratitude for my being on the board. I wonder what it is he thinks I can do!"

President Monson felt no such concern. In speaking of her appointment, he said: "I first learned of her outstanding ability as a spokesperson for the telephone company. From the first time I met Ardeth Kapp, I was impressed with her. . . . She has an intriguing way of capturing people's attention. I think it's her radiant smile that clinched it. No one would sleep during any presentation given by Ardeth Kapp!

"She served admirably because she has a good business head, as well as a charming manner."

"WHAT I CAN DO, I WILL DO"

Following a Greene family reunion in Glenwood in June of 1996, Ardeth recorded: "Now for an interesting turn of events. I love my family with all my heart and soul, but when we get together to talk and perform, they all sing and play the piano—so able, so free, so capable. I thrill with their talent. What they take for granted, I yearn for. Not envy, just yearning. When we sit around and talk about music, history, politics, literature, and so on, they discuss names, places, and titles like it was the ABCs.

"I realize how limited I am in all those areas and am reminded of all the seemingly common things I don't know. I am . . . humbled that with my limited natural ability, how many opportunities and blessings come as I respond to the chance to serve."

Then, as if to reassure herself that she does have gifts and talents, she noted that in the six weeks following the release of her newest book, *What Latter-day Stripling Warriors Learn from Their Mothers,* fifteen thousand copies had been sold! One reader said that after reading this book she decided she was a better mother than she had thought she was. Upon hearing that comment, Ardeth wrote, "Mission Accomplished!"

With constant requests to speak, along with lecturing at education weeks and Know Your Religion classes, serving on boards, teaching Institute classes and Gospel Doctrine in Sunday School, and working in the temple, there was little time to slow down. She wrote, "Life is good and rich and wonderful—but busy!" When people asked her what she was doing with all of her time now that their mission was over, she would take a deep breath and try to give a casual response.

Reflecting on all that she was involved in, she wrote, "Maybe it's okay that I don't sing, can't play the piano, and am very limited in so many areas. But what I can do, I will do, to the best of my ability, to help build the kingdom."

"His Promises Are Sure"

Ardeth was reflective one morning near the end of summer. "Oh, what a glorious morning. I am sitting on my favorite white rock at the side of my private retreat in nature. It is magical to observe the seasons by the flow of water that courses over these rock formations, all shapes and sizes, diverting the course of the force of the spring runoff or in the fall, the gentle trickle making music in quiet interludes that escape the ear unless attuned to the subtle sounds of sacred settings. Even the occasional bee is less busy in its pursuit of nature's nectar. The rock supporting my aging body is firm, solid, cool, and comfortable. Hardly a breeze can be felt, the air is refreshing. The sounds of nature are a symphony, and the smells intoxicating.

"Even in this incredibly busy life, I find myself pondering, meditating, and reflecting in ways unfamiliar to the past. Feelings so deep, peaceful, and trusting. I ponder, Is this new dimension an indication that I am approaching the season when I am preparing to die, or is it lifting me to a perspective when I begin to live, even more fully, more meaningfully, more Christlike? In either event, I feel drawn in my thoughts and desires to accept wholeheartedly the invitation, 'Come unto me.' I feel a greater sense of harmony, unity, at oneness in nature, in my marriage, in my associations, and in my soul. In our unbelievable abundance of blessings, I feel to draw away from the excesses of the world that attempt to appeal to the eye and create

Nana Ardie with Shelly's four boys: Trevor, Zack, Jack, and Josh

an insatiable appetite for things that can never satisfy. I'm realizing I'm wanting more and more of less and less—things that money cannot buy.

"I look in the mirror, and where I once felt pleased with my effort to look my best on the exterior, I'm much less concerned with the very obvious and fast-approaching signs of the season. But inside, I feel a beauty that is evolving, even as the exterior is fading. Just as the spring runoff is vibrant, a bit noisy and forceful, the fall is quiet, peaceful, orderly, and subdued. I love this season of my life."

In a desire to express the depth of her feelings, Ardeth wrote a poem "while sitting on a log by the creek in our neighborhood."

There is a place I walk not far from home,
Off the highway where I can be alone.
A quiet place, in solitude.

An invitation for a sacred mood.
The rocks and water make a perfect setting,
The symbols of His life resist the forgetting.
A place for sorting, for sifting, for clearing the vision,
And knowing my weaknesses, He's made restitution.
In my meditation, a form of prayer,
I think and ponder and feel Him near.
When a cleansing is needed, and surely it is,
I remember His love and know I am His.
I've been bought with a price that only He can redeem.
My Savior He is, I carry His name.
In this quiet place like a Heavenly shrine,
I hear in my heart, Daughter, you're mine.

As the year 1998 drew to a close, Ardeth recorded her thoughts and her testimony. "As I bring this brief and personal record to a close, I would hope that through it all there is frequent reference to feelings of gratitude for blessings beyond measure, so customized for my individual need. I know with an assurance beyond question that my Father in Heaven knows me, hears my prayers, watches over me, and provides opportunities far beyond my greatest dreams. I know He knows my thoughts and the earnest desires of my heart. I feel I am loved and accepted with all of my shortcomings. As I strive to do His will, I see my weaknesses. He shows unto us our weaknesses that we may be humble and strong.

"I feel a sense of purpose in my life, and acknowledge the blessed support, companionship, inspiration, and love of my eternal companion. In my daily prayers I pray that we might be wise stewards of our time and our resources and be faithful with all the Lord blesses us with each day. I know God lives, that His Son, Jesus Christ, is our Savior, our Redeemer, King of Kings, and Lord of Lords, the great Messiah. The gospel has been restored through our prophet, Joseph Smith. The ordinances and covenants draw us into the reach of the arms of our Savior. The scriptures, like letters from home, guide us safely home. As Heber and I reread again our patriarchal blessings, we see the hand of the Lord in our lives like we never understood at the time they were given. There is a plan, and when we follow, His promises are sure."

With the passing of another year, Ardeth felt the concerns associated with encroaching age. Early in their marriage when she and Heber had faced the devastation they felt at the realization that they would not have children in this life, her mind had jumped ahead to the time when they would be an older, retired couple with time to be grandparents, and they would have no grandchildren. But even then, a warm assurance had filled her soul as she thought of the scripture, "Trust in the Lord with all thine heart; and lean not unto thine own understanding" (Proverbs 3:5). She had trusted, and now she realized that they, indeed, had grandchildren—the children of their nieces and nephews. She and Heber love these children and, in turn, are loved by them. She rejoiced at the thought. Occasionally, fears crept in, but she chose then, as she does now, to move forward in faith, not fear.

IN HIS HOUSE

Heber was not at home in the afternoon of September 7, 2000, when a phone call came for him from President Gordon B. Hinckley's office. Ardeth waited anxiously until he returned at

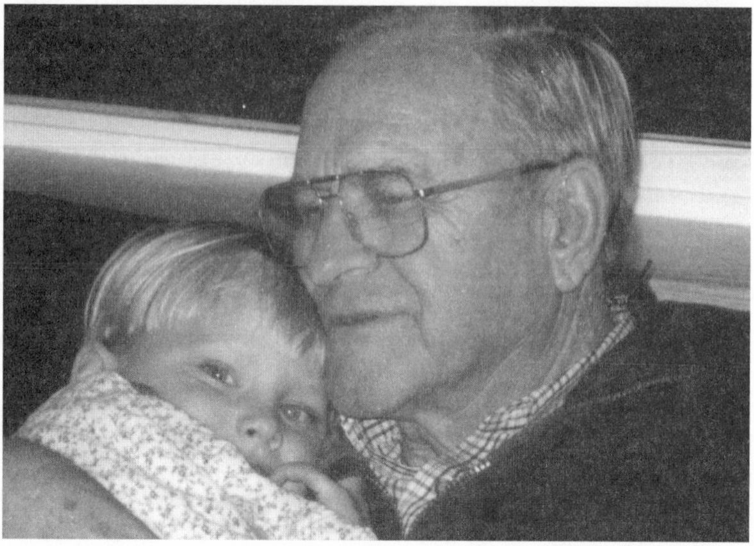

Heber and Trevor, 2005. Heber reminds Ardeth, "The world is filled with people to be loved, guided, taught, lifted, and inspired."

about 5:00 in the afternoon. He immediately called the office, and after a brief moment President Hinckley came on the line. Ardeth listened intently to Heber's side of the conversation, trying to pick up any hint of what the call might be about. Heber became somewhat emotional and said, "President, we would be honored." They were called to serve for the next three years as president and matron of the Cardston Alberta Temple.

President Hinckley inquired about their health. Heber reported that except for a couple of little things related to old age, they were in good health. President Hinckley responded, "You're just a kid!" He then asked Heber to discuss the call with Ardeth. Heber said, "She is absolutely loyal. There is no question about her willingness to go." President Hinckley told Heber that this would be the capstone of his life. Ardeth said, "Oh my, what a life we have shared!"

They would be succeeding Joseph and Elaine Jack as temple president and matron. Ardeth wrote, "What a series of events. When I was counselor in the Young Women's general presidency, Elaine was serving on the Relief Society general board. When I was serving as Young Women president, I requested Elaine as my counselor. We both attended the dedication of the Toronto Temple. Shortly after we left to preside over the Canada Vancouver Mission, they were called to serve as the president and matron of the Cardston Temple. Now they are returning, and we are taking their place."

The Cardston Temple had always been part of her life. Her grandfather had plowed the first furrow during the groundbreaking ceremonies. Her grandmother had served there, as had her parents. It was where she was baptized (the standard practice in Cardston at that time), endowed, and married. Heber had attended mission conferences there. And now they were to serve as that temple's president and matron.

Bride and groom, June 28, 1950, in front of the gates of the Cardston Alberta Temple. President and matron, fifty years later, in front of the same gates.

Then she had another thought. "But, Heber," she said, "I remember the temple president as being an old man."

Heber said, "That's right. As I said in my journal following our first meeting, 'The bishop's daughter is cute and fun, but kind of young.' You're still cute and fun, but not quite so young!" And neither was he!

Training would begin the middle of October, and they were to report at the Cardston Temple on November 1, 2000. They had just six weeks to prepare. But completing the details necessary before they could leave seemed of no concern to Heber. He always looked forward, not backward. When they had been in Cardston earlier in the summer for a family reunion, they had visited with President Jack. He told them that returning home would be a real adjustment because their assignment in the temple had been a bit of heaven.

Ardeth and Heber were set apart for their temple callings on October 16, 2000, by President Gordon B. Hinckley. Then followed several days of training, shared with twenty-three other couples who would serve in the same capacity in temples around the world. Ardeth wrote, "As I come to the close of this chapter of my life, I feel humbled and grateful beyond measure for the remarkable opportunities that have shaped our lives thus far. We look back with awe, and wonder at all that has happened in the last fifty years."

Soon Ardeth and Heber were totally involved and enjoying their new assignment. Two months into their service in the Cardston Temple, Ardeth wrote, "It is relatively easy to record events and happenings, but how do I record with any accuracy,

Temple presidency, matron, and assistant matrons in 2003: Stanley A. and Fay Johnson; Heber and Ardeth Kapp; Brent and Barbara Nielson.

the feelings, insights, emotions, and the lessons that seem to be flooding in."

She mentioned that in addition to their Bountiful Temple assignment, Heber's "retirement time was being consumed with study of maps, campgrounds, and anticipating travel time in our luxurious new motor home. It was wonderful and joyful, but now as we look back, we realize the journey we are now on is more grand even than visiting all of the beautiful places in nature made by the hand of God. Instead of visiting in His garden, we have been invited to spend our days in His holy house."

She also noted, "It has been a wonderful time to return, fifty years later, to the very spot, the very room where we were sealed and began our eternal journey together."

As temple matron, Ardeth was particularly sensitive to the feelings of those who came seeking spiritual direction and the peace to be found in the temple. On one occasion, she noticed a young woman, seemingly burdened, walking toward the door with her head bowed down. Ardeth quickly moved to her side, asking if she could help her in any way. Not slowing her pace, the woman continued her rapid move toward the exit. Ardeth kept speaking, inquiring if she could help. Finally, just as they reached the doorway, the woman stopped, turned to Ardeth and said, "Who are you, anyway?"

Ardeth responded, "I'm Sister Kapp."

After a brief pause, the young woman's countenance brightened, and she said, "When I was a young woman, I wrote you a letter, and you answered!"

Ardeth said, "I would write you another letter if it would help, but couldn't we just talk?" They went to her office, where they shared feelings and expressed love. Ardeth was grateful for being allowed the opportunity to assist, and especially grateful that she had responded to that long-ago letter.

A month prior to their release, Ardeth's knee gave way while going down the stairs in the temple. She gripped the handrail, wincing with pain, but tried not to draw attention to herself. Friends summoned Heber, then helped her into the car. He immediately drove her to the hospital.

Unwilling to give in to the pain, she summoned all her courage, determined to persevere until the last minute of their temple service. Doctors administered what help they could to allow her to continue, and she did persevere even though, much to her chagrin, she needed crutches for a short while. She later remarked, "I wore out my knee in service in the temple, but what a wonderful way to wear out your knee!"

As their release drew near, she recorded: "There is so much to record, and so little time. As we come to the close of this remarkable experience, there are no words to express the growth that has come to me personally, in so many ways. I know my Father in Heaven more surely than I have known him before. I have always had a strong, unwavering testimony. But there is a difference now. I better understand the meaning of the words, 'You don't receive a witness until after the trial of your faith.' I have overcome some weaknesses that have plagued me—not completely, but I am a little less prideful, a little more patient, and so on.

"I have seen the deep love and respect the ordinance workers have for Heber, and their expression of love for all he has taught them about the gospel. I have seen him grow as he has been so focused on everything and anything to do with the temple. He has truly magnified his calling and blessed the lives of many. Even with his severe hearing loss, he has still been able to develop a close relationship with so many. Learning the doctrine related to the temple has been a grand experience for both of us as we have gained a greater insight into this vastly important work."

The last few weeks before they were to return home were full of tender feelings. During the last stake conference they attended, Elder Russell M. Nelson was the visiting authority. They enjoyed a wonderful visit together, and Elder Nelson asked them to speak at both the Saturday evening and Sunday morning sessions. During the conference, he was kind and generous in his comments about their service. Ardeth wrote, "He said, in jest, 'Don't stop in Bountiful on your way home. The growth of the Church in Africa is expanding, and they could use you there!' Then he said that this was not a prophecy, not even a call. Then he paused and said, 'But not a bad idea!' Now people are asking if we think we might be going to Africa!"

MAKING A DIFFERENCE

After their return home in November of 2003, Ardeth and Heber continued to attend the temple. They taught a Sunday School class in their ward and were called to serve on the Council on Youth for the Utah North area, with specific responsibility for Especially for Youth programs.

Ardeth and Carolyn Rasmus have again had opportunity to work together. As members of the Deseret Book board of directors, they were asked by Sheri Dew to present a workshop for some of the Deseret Book employees. Carolyn said, "Little did we know what we agreed to do! It was harder than we thought and required more time than either of us thought we had. But both of us respond to a good challenge, and as Ardeth has always said, 'It couldn't be done, but we did it.' . . .

"The only thing that changed in fourteen years is that we get tired sooner! But when working with a friend, who cares? Work hard, play hard, be honest, and laugh a lot—what a wonderful formula when working with a friend!"

Ardeth continually receives speaking requests, accepting as many of those opportunities as possible. She continues to teach and bear testimony of gospel truths.

FROM APOSTLES AND PROPHETS

The tributes made to Ardeth Kapp could fill a book in itself. Here are a representative three, from Brethren who worked closely with her:

Elder M. Russell Ballard said of Ardeth: "She has a

tremendous insight into people. She's sensitive and has a great desire to know what the Brethren, the leadership of the Church, want, what they see, what their vision is. She is a good thinker on a common-sense level. Those who have good judgment, just common sense, know instinctively what is right, what isn't right, what should be done, what shouldn't be done. Ardeth has that. . . . She has quite a business head. She's bright, a wonderful writer, energetic, has a lot of zest for living. I don't know how Heber keeps up with her. Maybe he doesn't—maybe he just lets her go! She has a good sense of humor. She can laugh at herself.

" . . . Ardeth's name will be numbered among the great women of the Church. I think she's done great things. And she's not through yet!"

Reflecting on his experiences with Ardeth and Heber and their lives of service, President Thomas S. Monson said: "Ardeth Kapp was never meant to occupy a small stage. It takes a large stage to handle Ardeth Kapp at her best. . . . The phrase, 'Doubt not, fear not,' fits Ardeth Kapp. She has never doubted. . . .

"She knew she could make a difference. She made a *big* difference in the lives of the young women of this whole Church, whatever the language, whatever the land. She was a leader for all seasons and for all people.

"I've never seen her admit she was tired, or wanted a rest, or discouraged. Those were words that never entered her head or her spoken vocabulary. She was more of the attitude, 'Come on, let's go do it. Let's get the job done. What an opportunity! Aren't we privileged to be working with these splendid young women of the Church! My errand is the Church's errand!' That is her attitude.

"I'll always remember Ardeth Kapp as one who always left another person happier about living, more pleased with his or her lot in life. It is that spirit of enthusiasm, that looking for tomorrow, trusting in tomorrow, that has exemplified her life. She personifies Proverbs 3:5–6: 'Trust in the Lord with all thine heart; and lean not unto thine own understanding. In all thy ways acknowledge him, and he shall direct thy paths.'"

President Gordon B. Hinckley wrote: "I have known Sister Ardeth Greene Kapp for many years. She is a most able person and a woman of great and noble character. . . . Sister Kapp is a woman of faith. Her life exemplifies the lesson she has taught and the testimony she has borne, and continues to bear, of trust in the Lord and obedience to His words."

Epilogue

Today Ardeth stands at her kitchen window, gazing past the potted flowers on the window sill. She sees the backyard, bordered by flowers and surrounded by huge trees from which golden leaves drift softly down. Secluded in those trees are often ten or more deer who frequent their yard, sometimes making their way onto the patio. The branches of the crab apple trees, with their red autumn leaves, hold bird feeders that attract a variety of birds. They seem to especially like the feeder that Heber made from a bicycle wheel. It is mounted on a tall pole and has eight little cups filled with seed. When the birds light on the cups, it turns like a Ferris wheel. The seed that falls to the ground becomes food for the many quail that come to share in their feast.

Looking beyond the yard, past the trees and bushes, she sees the beautiful Bountiful Temple rising majestically above the city. She ponders the well-traveled road of her life, which has led far beyond the road she once viewed through the windows of her

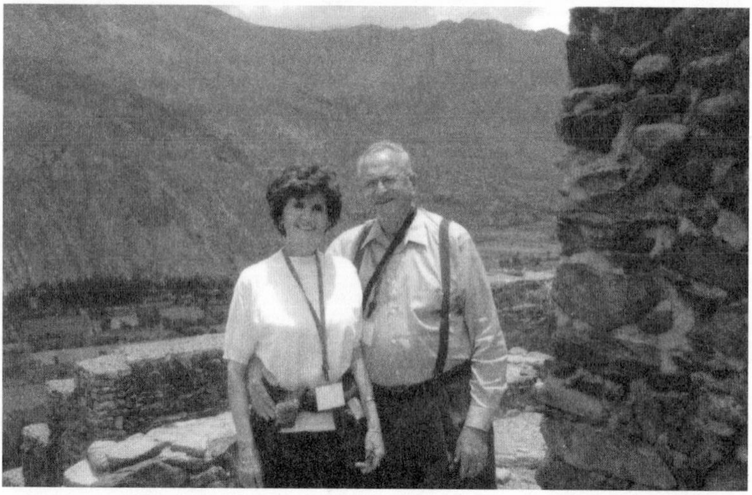

Ardeth and Heber near the top of Machu Picchu, Peru: 2004 and still climbing

Canadian prairie home. Again she remembers the statement from her patriarchal blessing: "You will be surprised in the days to come at the blessings the Lord has in store for you." At the time she couldn't begin to comprehend the meaning of those words. Now, with deep gratitude, she understands.

The road of her life led her to the temple, where she and Heber were sealed for time and all eternity. It led her to Utah, to a home that she and Heber built. The road led to service for the young women of the Church throughout the world. It led to her lifting and inspiring the lives of tens of thousands in audiences both seen and unseen through her writing, speaking, and teaching. The road led her to many corners of the earth, to places of which she had never even dreamed. It led her to palaces and humble dwellings alike.

The road led her back to Canada, where Heber served as mission president. It led her back to the temple where they were married—this time to serve as temple president and matron. It led her to become a mighty force for truth and righteousness around the earth. It led her to an increasingly powerful testimony of the restored gospel of Jesus Christ, for which she has stood as a witness at all times, and in all things, and in all places.

As promised, Ardeth has indeed been surprised at the blessings of the Lord. She feels almost overcome at the evidence of his hand in her life. She has yearned to fill the measure of her creation. She has tried to serve him by serving his children. She has tried to be pure in heart. Long ago, she learned that the only way to be truly happy is to be good. She has always tried to be good. Viewing the beautiful autumn scene outside her window, she catches a glimpse of heaven. She thinks of the road that led from her eternal home to her home in mortality. The passing season reminds her of the road, yet unseen, that will one day take her back to that home she once knew.

Ardeth contemplates the seasons of her life. She and Heber are older now. They have embraced each season in its turn. She thinks about the road yet to be traveled. She has a clearer vision of where it will lead than she had of the road outside the window of her prairie home. She knows that when the time comes for one of them to return home, they will still keep loving each other and will look forward with excitement and anticipation to when they will be together again, "for time and all eternity," through the promise of their temple covenants.

She shifts her gaze from the window and her mind to the present and to the days ahead. Tomorrow, Sunday, she and Heber will teach their regular temple class in their ward. Monday is visiting teaching, and later, family home evening. Tuesday morning they will attend the temple, and in the afternoon a committee meeting with the Council on Youth for the Utah North Area. A member of the Deseret Book board, she will attend a board meeting on the following Wednesday. Thursday morning of that same week, she is scheduled to attend a board meeting of the Utah Youth Village. In the evening she will speak at a women's conference in northern Utah and on Saturday she will address a women's conference in Idaho Falls, Idaho.

Next week she travels to Pasadena, California, to speak at a "Time Out for Women" sponsored by Deseret Book Company. She responds weekly to letters that continue to make their way to her address from people in many parts of the world. She is thankful for the numerous opportunities that are hers to serve. There are still people to be encouraged, taught, lifted, inspired, and loved. Heber and Ardeth continue to work together as a team, always looking forward.

"WHAT DESIREST THOU?"

A worthy summation of who Ardeth Kapp is can be found in a journal entry she made on February 14, 2003, under the heading, "And the Spirit Said unto Me: Behold, What Desirest Thou?" (1 Nephi 11:2):

I desire to keep my covenants to the best of my ability, relying on the grace of God and the Atonement.

I desire to know the Lord's will concerning me and live in such a way as to be guided by the Holy Spirit in carrying it out.

I desire to be a loyal, true, loving helpmeet to lift and build and strengthen and encourage and support my husband as we strive together toward our exaltation.

I desire to develop charity, to see others as Christ would see them, to be nonjudgmental, and to reach out in love and kindness.

I desire to pray with real intent, having faith in Christ so my prayers are truly a communication with my Father.

I desire to feast upon the words of Christ to know what I should do, to find answers, and be worthy and able to teach and write to strengthen others.

I desire to honor my parents and grandparents in gratitude for my noble heritage.

I desire a grateful heart to be mindful every day of the blessings of life as I ponder "why me, why here, why now," and give eternal thanks.

I desire to live worthy of my abundant blessings.

I desire to overcome pride in every aspect that plagues me.

I desire to make wise use of my time and resources, being a wise steward in helping to build the Kingdom.

I desire to take care of my body so I will have health and strength to serve, and when I can no longer serve that I may be taken home without delay.

I desire to submit to all things the Lord seeth fit to inflict upon me, including the aging process.

I desire to fill the measure of my creation, even without children.

I desire a bright mind.

I desire to keep the commandments so that I will be enfolded in the arms of His love and hear Him say, "Well done, thou good and faithful servant."

Ardeth Greene Kapp

Index

Entries for pictures are marked in italics.